Stolen Nation

SOAS Palestine Studies

This book series aims at promoting innovative research in the study of Palestine, Palestinians and the Israel-Palestine conflict as a crucial component of Middle Eastern and world politics. The first ever Western academic series entirely dedicated to this topic, *SOAS Palestine Studies* draws from a variety of disciplinary fields, including history, politics, media, visual arts, social anthropology, and development studies. The series is published under the academic direction of the Centre for Palestine Studies (CPS) at the London Middle East Institute (LMEI) of SOAS, University of London.

Series Editors:

Dina Matar, PhD, Chair, Centre for Palestine Studies, and Reader in Political Communication, Centre for Global Media and Communications, SOAS
Adam Hanieh, PhD, Reader in Development Studies and Advisory Committee Member for Centre for Palestine Studies, SOAS

Board Advisor:

Hassan Hakimian, Director of the London Middle East Institute at SOAS

Current and Forthcoming Titles:

Palestine Ltd.: Neoliberalism and Nationalism in the Occupied Territory,
Toufic Haddad
*Palestinian Literature in Exile: Gender, Aesthetics and Resistance
in the Short Story*, Joseph R. Farag
Palestinian Citizens of Israel: Power, Resistance and the Struggle for Space,
Sharri Plonski
Representing Palestine Media and Journalism in Australia Since World War I,
Peter Manning
Folktales of Palestine: Cultural Identity, Memory and the Politics of Storytelling,
Farah Aboubakr
*Dialogue in Palestine: The People-to-People Diplomacy Programme and
the Israeli-Palestinian Conflict*, Nadia Naser-Najjab
*Palestinian Youth Activism in the Internet Age: Social Media and Networks
after the Arab Spring*, Albana Dwonch

Stolen Nation

The Right to Reparation of Palestinian Refugees

Lena El-Malak

I.B. TAURIS

LONDON • NEW YORK • OXFORD • NEW DELHI • SYDNEY

I.B. TAURIS

Bloomsbury Publishing Plc

50 Bedford Square, London, WC1B 3DP, UK

1385 Broadway, New York, NY 10018, USA

BLOOMSBURY, I.B. TAURIS and the I.B. Tauris logo are trademarks of Bloomsbury Publishing Plc

First published in Great Britain 2025

Cover design: Adriana Brioso
Cover image © Sueddeutsche Zeitung Photo/Alamy Stock Photo

A catalogue record for this book is available from the British Library.

A catalog record for this book is available from the Library of Congress.

ISBN: HB: 978-0-7556-5279-2
ePDF: 978-0-7556-5282-2
eBook: 978-0-7556-5281-5

Typeset by Newgen KnowledgeWorks Pvt. Ltd., Chennai, India

To find out more about our authors and books visit www.bloomsbury.com and sign up for our newsletters.

To my loving parents

Contents

Preface

My interest in the Palestinian refugee issue stemmed from being one myself. My parents are Palestinian refugees and I grew up hearing stories from my grandmothers about Haifa and Akka, the cities they were forced to flee during the Nakba to seek safety in neighbouring Lebanon, not knowing they were destined to a life of permanent exile. When I was a law student, I went on my first trip to Lebanon and to the Palestinian refugee camps of Sabra and Shatila. That trip marked me profoundly; the sight of the mass grave, the open sewage in the narrow allies, the cables and wires hanging overhead and the beaming smiles of children unaware of the opportunities they have been deprived of because of their legal status and identity. Seeing them made me realize the immense privilege I had and how I had to use it to advocate for our rights and amplify our narrative.

The idea for the book was the result of a series of discussions with several experts on the Palestinian refugee issue and/or international law. It started with conversations on the right to compensation with my friend Laila Sahyoun, daughter of a Nakba survivor, while we were studying in law school. After completing my master's in law, during which time I wrote a dissertation on the status of Palestinian refugees in Lebanon, I worked at the United Nations High Commissioner for Refugees (UNHCR) in Amman where I learnt about the peculiarities of the legal status of Palestinian refugees and the 'exceptionalism' that overshadows any discussion of their rights. At one of the coordination meetings between UNHCR and UNRWA (United Nations Relief and Works Agency for Palestine Refugees), I met Dr Lex Takkenberg, author of *The Status of Palestinian Refugees in International Law*. His book was a source of inspiration, and it informed my own research. Its revised second edition, co-authored with Francesca Albanese, is essential reading for anyone interested in this topic. A few months later, at a conference on Palestinian refugees in Damascus, I had a conversation with Professor Michael Fischbach, author of *Records of Dispossession*, a seminal book that details Palestinian refugees' property losses, on the gaps in academic research. He brought to my attention the lack of work on the right to reparations under international law, and I decided to fill that gap. My aim was to answer the basic questions that every Palestinian refugee and their descendants have: How was the theft of a nation given a legal clout? What are my rights? How can I claim them? What will a resolution to these claims look like? It is my hope that this book will provide answers to these questions and empower Palestinian refugees to advocate for their rights. It is also my aim to provide scholars and policymakers with a reference to understand the legal basis for the right to reparation, the mechanisms to resolve mass property claims and the main forms of reparation. It was equally important to highlight the negotiators' failure to adopt a rights-based approach to the Palestinian refugee issue during the 'Oslo peace process' and how centering it in future efforts will be crucial to achieve a just and sustainable peace.

When I initially wrote this book as a doctoral thesis, I thought the Nakba was a moment in history, with a beginning and an end. I discovered over the years that the Nakba is ongoing. This book is now being finalized during the darkest chapter in Palestinian history since 1948, yet perhaps the most important turning point in our struggle for liberation. South Africa has accused Israel of genocide and filed a formal request for preventive measures to the International Court of Justice to halt Israel's military aggression on Palestinians in Gaza, which, at the time of writing, had already claimed more than 23,000 Palestinian lives and displaced 1.9 million people – nearly 85 per cent of Gaza's population. It bears noting that two thirds of the population of the Gaza Strip are refugees and descendants of refugees who were forcibly displaced from their homes during the Nakba. The refugee camps in Jenin, Nablus and various cities of the West Bank are also not spared Israel's brutality. It is the Palestinian people's sacrifice and steadfastness (*sumud*) to remain on their ancestral land that gives me the strength and courage to advocate harder and louder for our rights to freedom, reparation and self-determination. While peace seems to elude us today and the challenges feel insurmountable, I remain hopeful that the truth will shine, the tide will shift and justice will prevail.

Foreword

It is with great pleasure that I accepted Lena El-Malak's invitation to contribute a foreword to her new book *Stolen Nation: The Right to Reparation of Palestinian Refugees*. I have known the author from the time she was working on the doctoral dissertation that formed the basis for the book, and I very much appreciate that she has now taken the step to publish what I believe is a critical contribution to the literature on the Palestinian refugee question.

Al-Nakba was the 'catastrophe' that saw the forced displacement and exile of three quarters of the Palestinian people as Israel was established in 1948. Since then, the rights, situation and future of the Palestinian refugees, and those subsequently displaced, have represented the human dimension at the heart of the unresolved Palestine question. The author zooms in on one particular aspect of the rights of Palestinian refugees: their property rights and in particular the right to reparations resulting from their dispossession in the aftermath of the 1948–9 war.

In a concise and highly readable account, the author discusses rights and law-based approaches regarding reparations for Palestinian refugee property confiscated by Israel during the Nakba. This includes an overview of the laws used to provide legal cover for the dispossession of Palestinians; the legal bases for reparations in international law (including a review of the drafting history of UN General Assembly resolution 194 (III) of 11 December 1948); the forum/fora for mass claims of reparations; the forms of such reparations; and the marginalization of the refugee issue throughout the so-called ME Peace Process.

At a time when more and more Palestinians and their supporters are using the law to pursue justice for Palestine and Palestinians and accountability for the multitude of international crimes perpetrated against them from 1948 onwards, the question of reparation for Palestinian refugees represents a field of mostly untapped potential. The new book will provide both inspiration and the tools to pursue restitution and compensation claims for individual Palestinian refugees as well as for the Palestinian leadership to procure reparations for the Palestinian people at large.

The author makes reference to the UNRWA definition of a 'Palestine refugee' a number of times, in particular its significance in determining the individuals to whom the right to reparation applies. Registration with UNRWA as a Palestinian refugee is primarily for the purpose of eligibility for the services the agency provides, but as demonstrated in the book, it is significant for the refugee's property rights as well.

In this context, UNRWA's registration system has the potential to become the central archive and repository of evidence of the refugees' historic property claims. This would have a huge symbolic and practical impact for the refugees, especially once the registration system gets harmonized and synchronized with the historic UNCCP records. The latter would connect property loss and damages in 1947/1949 to individual refugees and their families and descendants. UNRWA is in the process of integrating its registration system and other historic archives and refugee data maintained by the agency into a Palestine Refugee Data Center, an initiative that deserves strong support, especially by Palestinians in the region and beyond.

The book is timely as it addresses issues that are sadly resurfacing during the genocide in Gaza. Forced displacement has been at the forefront in the current war, with at least 1.7 million Gaza Palestinians internally displaced, many multiple times, and as many as 100,000 displaced into Egypt. The present tragedy is the latest affirmation that the Nakba has been ongoing, as part of a deliberate strategy by Israel to reduce the non-Jewish population of the Jewish state, as well as in the territories it has been occupying since 1967, to the maximum extent possible. The war in Gaza also underscores how Israel continues to benefit from impunity and lack of accountability for its crimes past and present.

The legal analysis in the book will be directly relevant to the massive and unprecedented property losses that Palestinians from Gaza – two thirds of whom are descendents of refugees from the Nakba – have experienced since 7 October 2023. The principal focus at present is to achieve an end to the war and ongoing genocide, but once it is possible for the focus to shift to reconstruction, it is critical that property claims resulting from the war be addressed as soon as possible, inter alia to help fund the massive housing and infrastructure projects that will be required.

The book will fill a gap in the research on Palestinian refugee rights and will serve as a handbook for lawyers and diplomats as well as for academics. It will also turn out to be valuable in providing answers to diaspora Palestinians who are keen to learn about their property rights and the challenges in reclaiming them.

Dr. Lex Takkenberg
June 2024

Acknowledgements

This book was originally drafted as a doctoral thesis under the supervision of Professor Iain Scobbie and Dr Catriona Drew at the School of Oriental and African Studies (SOAS), University of London. I remain deeply indebted to their patient guidance, encouragement and advice. I am also grateful to the generosity of the late Sir Joseph Hotung for setting up the *Sir Joseph Hotung Programme on Law, Human Rights and Peacebuilding in the Middle East*, which awarded me a scholarship to pursue doctoral studies. It is unfortunate that this book was not published during his lifetime.

Throughout my years at SOAS, my research evolved thanks to the work and contributions of Dr Salman AbuSitta, Professor Dawn Chatty, Professor Michael Lynk, Dr Lex Takkenberg, Usama Halabi, Professor Michael Kagan, Dr Anis F. Kassim, Dr Bisher Khasawneh, Professor John Quigley, Terry Rempel and Nadim Shehadi. I am also grateful to the late Ingrid Jaradat Gassner and Karine McAllister and the valuable work of Badil Resource Center for Palestinian Residency and Refugee Rights. I am also indebted to Professor Susan Akram, Leila Hilal and Professor Karma Nabulsi for sharing with me their thoughts and research on the rights-based approach to the refugee issue. I remember with affection and sorrow conversations with my dear friend, the late Dr Shahira Samy, author of a comparative study on reparations for Palestinian refugees. I am grateful for all the discussions we had on this issue during her lifetime. I would also like to thank Dr Victor Kattan for answering some last-minute questions while I was finalizing the manuscript for this book and Professor Natalie Rothman for her help with citations.

To my late grandmothers, survivors of the Nakba, you instilled in me an unwavering attachment to my ancestral home in Palestine. Your stories carried me to Haifa and Akka and I carry these cities and your trauma of displacement in me. I love you and miss you. I am also grateful to the love and support of my brother, relatives and friends who have cheered me on over the years, and I apologize for not mentioning everyone by name.

Finally, no words can express my gratitude to my parents. None of my accomplishments would have been possible without their love, support, prayers, generosity and encouragement. I am also eternally indebted to them for raising me in full awareness of my Palestinian identity and heritage. I honour their struggle and dedicate this book to them and to the people of Palestine.

Selected Abbreviations

CEIRPP	UN Committee on the Exercise of the Inalienable Rights of the Palestinian People
CERD	Convention on the Elimination of Racial Discrimination
CPRR	Council for Palestinian Restitution and Repatriation
CRPC	Commission for Real Property Claims of Displaced Persons and Refugees (Bosnia)
DA	Development Authority (Israel)
DOP	Declaration of Principles on Interim Self-Government Arrangements
ECHR	European Convention on Human Rights
ECtHR	European Court of Human Rights
EU	European Union
GA	General Assembly
GI	Geneva Initiative
HPCC	Housing and Property Claims Commission
HPD	Housing and Property Directorate
ICCPR	International Covenant on Civil and Political Rights
ICJ	International Court of Justice
ICJP	International Center for Justice for Palestinians
ICPR	International Commission for Palestinian Refugees
IDF	Israeli Defense Forces
ILA	Israel Lands Administration
ILC	International Law Commission
IPC	Immovable Property Commission
Iran-US CT	Iran US Claims Tribunal
JA	Jewish Agency
JCC	Jewish Claims Conference (Conference on Jewish Material Claims in Germany)
JISP	Jurisdictional Immunities of States and their Property
JNF	Jewish National Fund
OAS	Organization of American States
OAU	Organization of African Unity

OHR	Office of the High Representative (Bosnia)
OLC	Ottoman Land Code
OPP	Oslo peace process
OPT	Occupied Palestinian Territory
OSCE	Organization for Security and Cooperation in Europe
PA	Palestinian Self-Governing Authority
PCIJ	Permanent Court of International Justice
PLO	Palestine Liberation Organization
PPR	Permanent place of residence
QPCDP	Quadripartite Committee on Displaced Persons
RPA	Rwandan Patriotic Army
RWG	Refugee Working Group
SC	Security Council
TRNC	Turkish Republic of Northern Cyprus
UDHR	Universal Declaration of Human Rights
UNCC	United Nations Compensation Commission
UNCCP	United Nations Conciliation Commission for Palestine
UNGA	United Nations General Assembly
UNHCR	United Nations High Commissioner for Refugees
UNMIK	United Nations Interim Administration Mission in Kosovo
UNRWA	United Nations Relief and Works Agency for Palestine
UNSC	United Nations Security Council

Introduction

0.1 The persistent question of Palestinian refugees

'Where should we go after the last frontiers, where should the birds fly after the last sky?' These were the words of the late Palestinian poet Mahmoud Darwish, written in 1982, the year Israel invaded Lebanon, expelled the Palestinian Liberation Organization (PLO) from its capital and facilitated the Lebanese phalangist militia's massacre of Palestinian refugees in the Sabra and Shatila camps.[1] Today, as Israel commits a genocide of Palestinians in Gaza and displaces 85 per cent of its population amidst calls to expel them all to Sinai and other third countries, the question haunts Palestinians more than ever.[2] The Palestinian story of forced exile began in the late 1940s. On 29 November 1947, the United Nations General Assembly adopted Resolution 181,[3] which called for the partition of the historical land of Palestine into an Arab State and a Jewish State.[4] The adoption of the Partition Plan was followed by sporadic tit-for-tat incidents of violence, which rapidly spiralled out of control. The first Arab-Israeli war erupted on 15 May 1948, the day after the proclamation of the State of Israel.[5] By that time, close to 400,000 Palestinians had already been made refugees.[6] According to the United Nations Economic Survey Mission, the total estimated number of Palestinian refugees reached 726,000 by 1949, when the war had ended.[7] Today, Palestinian refugees are the world's largest and oldest refugee population, with estimates putting the number at over 5.9 million refugees[8] among a global refugee population of 35.3 million.[9] As with all refugee populations, Palestinians fled in fear,[10] leaving behind their homes, their land and their personal belongings. Palestinian materials losses for 1948 property are estimated to be in the tens of billions of dollars.[11] To this day, Palestinian refugees have neither been able to return to their homes inside Israel, nor have they received any compensation for their losses. This book will provide a legal analysis of the Palestinian refugees' right to reparation for property losses they incurred as a result of their displacement and dispossession in the years surrounding the creation of the State of Israel.

0.2 Defining the scope and terminology

For the purposes of this book, the terms 'Palestinian refugees', or '1948 Palestinian refugees' refer to the Palestinians who were displaced in the first and most important Palestinian refugee exodus (also known as the 'Nakba', Arabic for *Catastrophe*), which occurred in the years surrounding the creation of the State of Israel in 1948. We will rely on the United Nations Relief and Works Agency for Palestine Refugees in the Near East (UNRWA)'s definition of a 'Palestine refugee' as a prima facie definition of the individuals whose rights are examined in this book. According to UNRWA, Palestine refugees are 'persons whose normal place of residence was Palestine during the period 1 June 1946 to 15 May 1948, and who lost both home and means of livelihood as a result of the 1948 conflict.' UNRWA services are available to all those living in its area of operations who meet this definition, who are registered with the Agency and who need assistance. The descendants of Palestine refugee males, including adopted children, are also eligible for registration.[12] The rights of 1967 Palestinian refugees and their descendants who were displaced for the first time from the West Bank and Gaza Strip as a result of the second Arab-Israeli conflict in 1967 fall outside the scope of this book.[13] Similarly, this book will not discuss the right to reparation of non-Palestinian Arabs who fled from Mandate Palestine during the Nakba.[14] Nor will it discuss the rights of internally displaced Palestinians, whether they are citizens of Israel who were internally displaced during the 1948 War[15] or Palestinians residing in the Occupied Palestinian Territory (OPT) who were displaced as a result of house demolitions, land confiscations, the construction of the Apartheid Wall or the multiple wars on Gaza.[16]

This book will focus on the right to reparation of Palestinian refugees and the possibility for these refugees, and their legitimate representative, the State of Palestine, to demand reparation from the State of Israel. This book will not discuss the right of neighbouring Arab countries – namely, Jordan,[17] Lebanon and Syria – to demand reparation from the State of Israel for hosting a large number of Palestinian refugees for close to eight decades. Nor will it examine whether these host countries can espouse the claims of Palestinian refugees residing on their territory.

0.3 The refugee issue under international law

In all of the Arab–Israeli peace agreements, minimal reference, if any, has been made to international law in relation to the resolution of the refugee problem.[18] Thus, one of the aims of this book is to draw international law into the realpolitik negotiation framework on the rights of Palestinian refugees, though international law and politics are inevitably intertwined. This is not to argue that international law is the magic formula that will bring about liberation.[19] In fact, there is a lot of scepticism on the role of international law and valid criticism of the way in which it is used as a tool for the oppressor. It is, however, a tool that needs to be deployed more effectively, and it cannot be marginalized in the context of 'peace' negotiations, if and when these resume, under the pretext of political realism. It can also play a strategic role in the Palestinian liberation movement, as more eloquently articulated by Noura Erakat: 'In order to serve an emancipatory function, the law must be wielded in the sophisticated service of a political movement that can both give meaning to the law and also directly challenge the structure of power that has placed Palestinians outside the law'.[20] Chapter 3 will briefly touch upon ways in which legal action before domestic or international courts can serve that purpose.

Besides highlighting the importance of centring Palestinian refugee rights in political negotiations, an analysis of their right to reparation, whether in the form of restitution or compensation, has two additional implications. From the perspective of international law, the assertion that states have an obligation to restitute the refugees' property and pay compensation for the creation of refugees[21] could serve as a deterrent for states that resort to expulsion and population transfers to create or reinforce ethnically homogeneous entities. Thus, calling for reparation within the context of the Israeli–Palestinian conflict could set a significant legal precedent against mass displacements of populations in the Middle East and deter Israel from internally displacing its own Palestinian citizens as well as Palestinians residing in the OPTs. The lack of accountability and total impunity that Israel has enjoyed and benefitted from for the past decades has emboldened it to pursue an ongoing Nakba in slow motion against the Palestinian citizens of Israel as well as in the occupied West Bank and East Jerusalem through house demolitions, settlement expansion and discriminatory laws and policies[22] or through a suffocating siege and an all-out genocidal military aggression aimed at depopulating Gaza and rendering it unliveable.[23] The other implication of studying the right to reparation of Palestinian refugees under international law is the importance of giving refugees agency and providing them with the knowledge to advocate for their rights and understand that they have the right to restitution *and* compensation and that these two are not mutually exclusive.

Besides these legal implications of an analysis of the right to reparation of Palestinian refugees, there was scant academic research on this issue from a strictly legal perspective.[24] With some limited exceptions,[25] the Palestinian refugees' right to restitution has been overshadowed by research on the right of return.[26] As a result, restitution is hardly, if ever, regarded as a separate right, which can be exercised independently of a refugee's choice to repatriate.[27] As for the right to compensation, there is some literature on this issue,[28] although it remains limited. An obstacle to undertaking research on the refugees' right to compensation is the fact that for decades, in the Arab world, advocating any sort of financial solution to the refugee issue was perceived as a negation of their right to return and a form of betrayal, even though most of these governments were never genuine in their advocacy for Palestinian rights. Likewise, Israel's insistence on paying compensation only if it were used to resettle refugees in Arab countries, thus terminating their right to return to their homes inside Israel,[29] has nurtured an erroneous perception that the right to compensation annuls the right to return. Avoiding any discussion of the right to compensation not only reinforces Israel's attempts to present this right as an alternative to the right to return and the right to restitution, but it also betrays the interests of those who genuinely wish to seek compensation for their property, irrespective of whether or not they choose to exercise their right to return and restitution. This book thus aims to clarify the position of international law on the 1948 Palestinian refugees' right to restitution and compensation for their property losses.

0.4 Research questions and outline

In an attempt to fill a gap in legal research on the Palestinian refugees' right to reparation, this book will address the following questions: How did Israel proceed to expropriate property belonging to 1948 Palestinian refugees? What are the legal grounds for the Palestinian refugees' right to reparation for loss of, or damage to, property? Which legal avenues can be used by these refugees, or their legitimate representative, the observer State of Palestine, to invoke the right to reparation? What are the forms of reparation available under international law and what are the legal obstacles to the enforcement of a right to reparation?

How have Israeli–Palestinian negotiations addressed the issue of Palestinian refugee property claims?

The first chapter will provide an overview of the legislation regulating land ownership in Palestine, both before and after the creation of the State of Israel in 1948, with the dual aim of providing a well-rounded source of information for researchers on this issue and demonstrating how these laws were used to dispossess Palestinian refugees. Chapter 2 will examine the legal grounds for the Palestinian refugees' right to reparation. This will include an overview of the law on state responsibility as it applies to the case of Israeli expropriation of refugee property. Chapter 3 will outline the advantages and drawbacks of different legal avenues, which can be used by Palestinian refugees to invoke their right to reparation. Chapter 4 will discuss the two main forms of reparation for property losses: restitution and compensation. It will also identify some of the legal obstacles to the implementation of Palestinian refugee property rights. Finally, the last chapter of this book will provide a critical analysis of the proposed solutions to the Palestinian refugee issue, which resulted from official Israeli–Palestinian talks, two-track negotiations and peace initiatives.

By examining the Palestinian refugees' right to reparation under international law, the author hopes to fill an existing gap in academic research and provide policymakers with a comprehensive legal analysis, which could be used to negotiate and craft a just solution to the Palestinian refugee issue. The author also hopes that refugees themselves will benefit from the findings in this book and make use of them in their individual attempts to reclaim their ancestral homes and demand compensation for their losses and the theft of a nation.

Dispossession in Palestine

1.1 Introduction

The Israeli–Palestinian conflict can be summed up as a conflict over land. Ever since Theodor Herzl, the founder of Zionism, called for the establishment of a Jewish state in Palestine or elsewhere,[1] land has been central to Zionist thinking and policies. In 1901, at the Fifth Zionist Congress in Basel, the World Zionist Organization established the Jewish National Fund (JNF) with the aim of buying and developing land in Palestine exclusively for Jews,[2] thus signalling the beginning of Jewish settlement in Palestine. Since then, several political, economic and legal factors have facilitated the Zionist colonization of Palestine. This chapter will outline the legislation regulating land ownership in Palestine, both before and after the creation of the State of Israel in 1948, with the aim of demonstrating how it may have been used to dispossess Palestinian refugees. Measures taken to expropriate land belonging to internally displaced Palestinian citizens of Israel, or residents of the West Bank and Gaza Strip, fall outside the scope of this chapter.[3] In addition to exploring how pre- and post-1948 land laws and regulations were used to dispossess Palestinian refugees, this chapter will provide researchers and policymakers alike with a rounded source of information on the evolution of land tenure in Palestine in the twentieth century.

The first section will thus provide a brief overview of the various types of land tenures used during the Ottoman Empire.[4] The main aim of this section is to demonstrate that the majority of the land in Palestine was not state owned.[5] This section will also argue that the Ottoman system of land tenure was vulnerable to manipulation and that this vulnerability, in turn, facilitated the dispossession of Palestinians in subsequent years. The second section will discuss the changes to the land regime introduced by the British Mandate. Although the policies adopted during the Mandate represented moves towards a more formal system of regulating possession of land, as this section will demonstrate, they did not halt, and may have even facilitated, at times, the transfer of land ownership to Jews during the Mandate period. Finally, the third section will discuss Israel's use of 'absentee' legislation and other related laws to bring Palestinian refugee property under the control of a Custodian before permanently transferring ownership of it to the State of Israel, the JNF and the Development Authority.

1.2 Land laws in Palestine during the Ottoman period (1858–1917)

Palestine formed an integral part of the Ottoman Empire from 1518 to 1917. As Palestinian land-law expert Raja Shehadeh outlined in his seminal study on land in Palestine, two main principles have dominated the system of land tenure in Palestine during the original Arab and later Ottoman conquests: 'a) The conquerors regarded themselves as the true owners of all the conquered lands, and b) ownership is limited by use'.[6] Hence, in the Ottoman Empire, the sovereign (*Sultan*) was vested with the ownership of all land, with the exception of *waqf* and *mulk* land, which will be discussed below. While the sovereign retained ownership (or *rakaba*) of land, different kinds of tenure regulated its possession and use. In 1858, the Ottomans compiled a Land Code (OLC) to identify the different categories of land in Palestine while the *mejelle* (Ottoman Civil Code), issued in 1869, supplemented some of the provisions on immovable property of the OLC. The OLC classified land into five main categories: *waqf*, *mulk*, *miri*, *mewat* and *metruke*.[7] It is only in the last three categories of land that the State or Sovereign retains some sort of legal interest.

The first category of privately owned land is *waqf* property. *Waqf* is land which has been irrevocably dedicated for pious uses: 'the proprietary right of the grantor is divested and it remains thenceforth in the implied ownership of the Almighty. The usufruct alone is applied for the benefit of human beings and the subject of the dedication becomes inalienable and non-heritable in perpetuity'.[8] *Waqf* is peculiar to Muslim Law although non-Muslim communities were also able to dedicate land to *waqf* according to the ecclesiastical laws of their respective communities.[9]

Mulk is also privately owned land, akin to land held in fee simple absolute in a Common Law system. The owner of *mulk* property could use and dispose of his land freely. The land did not have to be put to a profitable use, nor did the owner have to pay a tithe to the State. *Mulk* land can also be bequeathed by will, according to the religious laws of the community to which the owner belonged.[10] Such land was very rare in Palestine and usually found only at the centre of towns and villages.[11]

Miri was the predominant type of land tenure in Palestine.[12] This category of land derived its name from *Emir* (sovereign), since the sovereign retains ownership (*rakaba*) of the land while granting the right to possession or use (*tessaruf*) of the land to individuals.[13] According to Goadby and Doukhan, the principle underlying the law of *miri* land is that the State would grant a limited interest (*tessaruf*) in the land on the condition that it is kept cultivated.[14] The grantee would then be bound to make the land productive in order to be able to pay a tithe to the State.[15] Hence, the rights of *miri* holders were not absolute. In fact, until the OLC was enacted, *miri* rights were considered personal rights which could not be alienated. The OLC, however, introduced significant changes which allowed for *miri* land to be disposed of, with official permission, and inherited.[16] Even these restrictions on the disposition and use of land were removed through subsequent legislation. As argued by Goadby and Doukhan, Ottoman legislation more recent than the Land Code has amplified the right of the Miri holder (or possessor); and to describe his present position as that of a 'possessor' only is misleading.[17] While formally, the State retained some sort of proprietary rights in *miri* land, in practice, however, the State's right of ownership vanished. According to Granott, the adoption in 1913 of the Law of Disposition removed several restrictions on the use and disposition of *miri* land, thus assimilating the rights of the holder of *miri* land to those of an owner without restrictions.[18] Hence forward, the holder of *miri* land could lease, sell, let and even mortgage the land, without requiring official permission.[19] He could also cultivate it or use it for whichever purpose he desired.[20] As such, Goadby and Doukhan conclude that the most important remaining differences between *miri* and *mulk* are as follows: '1. Miri now cannot be left by will and descends according to a special law of succession. 2. Miri cannot be made waqf. 3. Miri is subject to tithes'.[21] In addition, *miri* land could also become *mahlul* (vacant) and escheat back to the State if left uncultivated for three years or if the *mutassarif* dies heirless. As noted by Palestinian land expert Sami Hadawi, however, 'the restrictive provisions relating to possession were never enforced, and people exercised full unlimited rights of ownership, usage, and disposition whether the land was of the *mulk* or *miri* category; and at no time had ownership of the *miri* category reverted to the state because of neglect of cultivation or for any other cause'.[22] Hence, it can be asserted that the State retained a minimal interest in *miri* land, which diminished with time and was rarely enforced. In other words, *miri*-owned land, which was the predominant type of land tenure in Palestine, is essentially privately owned land.

Under Ottoman land law, the Sovereign also retained legal interest in *mewat* land. According to Article 6 of the OLC, *mewat* land, which literally means dead land, was defined as

> land which is occupied by no one and has not been left for the use of the public. It is such as lies at such a distance from a village or town from which a loud human voice cannot make itself heard at the nearest point where there are inhabited places, that is a mile and a half, or about half an hour's distance from such.[23]

Mewat land consisted mainly of mountainous or rocky areas considered not usable as well as land in the vicinity of a village that had not been cultivated yet.[24] Another category of land defined in the OLC, is land left for the use of the public, or *metruke* land. According to Article 5 of the OLC, *metruke* land is of two kinds: '(i) That which is left for the general use of the public, like a public highway for example; (ii) That which is assigned for the inhabitants generally of a village or town, or of several villages or towns grouped together, as for example pastures (meras)'.[25] Although in principle the *rakaba* (ownership) of *metruke* land is vested in the sovereign rather than in the villagers or community enjoying the right of pasture or use of the land, Hadawi notes that, in practice, the sovereign was not deemed to have actual control over the land: '[t]he control of government over such lands was limited to that necessary to enable the villagers to benefit from them in the way intended'.[26]

To sum up, although in theory the sovereign retained some interest in *miri*, *mewat* and *metruke* lands, these lands were not considered to be public land or state owned. Relying on the definition of 'public lands' introduced by the British Mandatory powers in Article 2 of the Palestine Order-in-Council, 1922,[27] Shehadeh concludes:

> it is apparent from the definition that public lands are restricted to lands which are subject to the control of the government and used in execution of its purposes, such as the erection of government houses, etc. They do not include all land which is not the subject of a grant to the public, and therefore exclude *miri*, *mawat*, and *matrouk* lands whose *rakaba* are in the Sultan, but upon which no actual control is exercised for the public service, by expropriation, for example.[28]

The fact that *miri*, *mewat* and *metruke* lands were not considered public lands and, in the case of *miri* and *metruke*, had a status that was more akin to land that was owned by individuals or a community is significant considering that the expropriation of private property is prohibited under international humanitarian law, as will be discussed in Chapter 2. As Kedar argues, in order to justify the expropriation of private property, settler states typically try to assimilate native land to state land or public land:

> There are several ways in which settlers' legal systems hamper the attempt by natives and other alien populations to claim and protect land in their possession. Often, the settlers' legal systems altogether deny any recognition of native land rights even when the native group has been in possession of the land since time immemorial. This denial is based partly on a 'cultural clash of paradigms' in which the 'modern Western' legal system does not recognize the ways locals organize their spatial relations to land as giving rise to property rights. Typically, settler states regard these native lands as public land, which can be disposed of by governments without the natives' approval or even knowledge. [...] Similarly, Israeli law and British Mandatory law did not recognize land possession by Arabs when this possession did not conform to the exigencies of formal 'Western' law. [29]

As Shehadeh has demonstrated, this tactic was in fact used by the Israeli State to expropriate privately owned property in the Occupied West Bank, where Ottoman land laws still apply.[30] One can therefore conclude that the vague and confusing categorization of land introduced by the Ottomans left the door open for the Israeli government to consider falsely the majority of lands in Palestine (including *miri, mewat* and *metruke* lands) as state owned, in order to expropriate them from their rightful owners.

Another characteristic of the Ottoman land system made it vulnerable to manipulation. As discussed earlier, individual rights acquired over land relied heavily on possession and use of land, instead of formal registration. Registration, however, plays a pivotal role in 'Western' legal systems of land ownership and is an essential proof of ownership. It was, however, rarely enforced by the Ottomans,[31] although it was compulsory in law to register immovable property under the Ottoman land system.[32] According to land expert, Sami Hadawi, 'owing to the failure of the Ottoman land registration machinery, the majority of the lands of Palestine were found on British occupation to be unregistered or under imperfect and obsolete registration'.[33] When property was actually registered, *fellahins* (peasants) were tempted to register their land in the name of larger landowners[34] or to reduce the area of their land in order to pay less tax.[35] Areas registered were thus a fraction of the true land area.[36] In addition to the lack of registration and under-registration of property, the description of lands registered did not include any maps or cadastral surveys to identify the property easily.[37] The Land Registry was, in fact, a Registry of transactions between persons (Registry of Deeds) instead of being a Registry of Title, making specific reference to defined plots of land.[38] All of these factors combined to make the Turkish Land Registers inaccurate, incomplete and subject to manipulation. It also helped concentrate large areas of land in the hands of a few landowners.[39] To complicate matters further and add to the uncertainty surrounding true land ownership in Palestine, Turkish authorities removed many of the registers and records when they left Palestine.[40] As some authors have argued, the vulnerability and imprecision of the Turkish registration system facilitated its subsequent manipulation to the detriment of Palestinian *fellahins* (peasants) and small landowners who, in the absence of an accurate deed and title to the land, had considerable difficulty proving their acquired rights to a specific area of land through use and possession.[41]

In sum, the nature and characteristics of the Ottoman Land System facilitated the subsequent dispossession of the native inhabitants of Palestine through an intricate and confusing categorization of land and an unreliable registration system. As will be discussed in the next section, although the British Mandatory Administration introduced several ordinances to regulate land ownership in Palestine, these ordinances did little or nothing to limit the transfer of land ownership to Jews during the Mandate period, to the detriment of the indigenous population of Palestine.

1.3 Land laws in Palestine during the British Mandate (1920–1948)

The Ottomans' rule over Palestine came to an end following their defeat in World War I. The Ottoman land structure was not, however, terminated with Ottoman rule. Instead of abolishing the land categorization that had prevailed until then, the British Mandate authorities decided to exercise their jurisdiction over immovable property in Palestine in conformity with the Ottoman Law of Land. According to Article 46 of the British Order-in-Council of 1922,

> [T]he jurisdiction of the Civil Courts shall be exercised in conformity with the Ottoman Law in force in Palestine on November 1st, 1914, and such later Ottoman Laws as have been or may be declared to be in force by Public Notice, and such Orders in Council, Ordinances and regulations as are in force in

Palestine at the date of the commencement of this Order, or may hereafter be applied or enacted [...].[42]

Hence, instead of entirely revamping the system of land tenure, the British authorities proceeded to reform the registration of land in Palestine.[43]

The British Administration introduced a series of ordinances with the aim of formalizing the regulation of land ownership in Palestine.[44] The most sweeping process of land registration was implemented in the late twenties, on the basis of provisions of the *Land (Settlement of Title) Ordinance* (1928).[45] The settlement of title scheme was preceded by a few ordinances refining the definitions of some categories of land[46] and introducing the new category of 'public lands'.[47] Against this backdrop, the *Land (Settlement of Title) Ordinance* (1928) was introduced to examine the 'rights to land and the solution of disputes about the ownership, boundaries, category and other registerable rights in land, its cadastral survey for the purpose, and the eventual recording of the rights in Land Registers'.[48] According to Granott, the Land Settlement process in Palestine did not attempt to reform the system of land tenure inherited from the Ottomans. It focused mainly on clarifying and settling ownership rights in the land.[49] Rights recorded in the Land Registry would then be viewed as conclusive evidence of their existence and supersede all other rights or contradictory claims over land.[50] The Mandate, however, ended before all land in Palestine was accurately mapped out and registered. According to Hadawi, by the end of the Mandate, some 25 per cent of land in Palestine had been surveyed, mapped out and registered.[51] The British administration eventually published a map in 1947 and submitted it to the special inquiry committee of the UN, which eventually recommended the partition of Palestine into two independent states.[52] This recommendation was subsequently endorsed by the UN General Assembly in Resolution 181(II).[53] It is interesting to point out that most of the land surveyed fell into the part proposed for the Jewish State,[54] raising serious questions about the relationship between the settlement of title scheme and the UN's Partition Plan. As the British authorities were keen to ensure that Jewish settlers acquired a valid title to their land, they focused their settlement of title process on areas designated as 'settlement areas'. These were mostly Jewish areas, or areas subject to dispute between Jews and Arabs.[55] Hadawi summarised the double purpose of the land settlement of title operations as follows: 'the first, with which no one could argue, was to put straight a chaotic situation inherited from the Turks and to enable the cultivator to improve his land; the second had the sinister motive of facilitating and accelerating the process whereby Jews could acquire land with an accurate title in furtherance of the Balfour Declaration policy'.[56] The land settlement process was thus used to provide a valid and indisputable title to the land in predominantly Jewish 'settlement areas'.[57] Despite facilitating the Jewish settlement of land in Palestine, Israeli Law Professor, Alexander Kedar, notes that 'the expropriation potential in the process of settling title was not actualized during the Mandate'.[58]

While the Land Settlement Process was ongoing, several Commissions of Inquiry were dispatched to Palestine to evaluate the situation regarding land and Jewish immigration. According to Souad Dajani, these commissions invariably singled out unrestricted Jewish immigration and land purchases as the underlying causes of disturbances and tension between the native Arab population and the Jewish communities.[59] It is beyond the scope of this chapter to discuss the findings of these Commissions in details. It is nevertheless interesting to highlight some of the criticism levied against the JNF by the Hope Simpson report of 1930: 'the result of the purchase of land in Palestine by the Jewish National Fund has been that land has been *extraterritorialised*. It ceases to be land from which the Arab can gain any advantage either now or at any time in the future. [...] *The land is in mortmain and inalienable*'.[60] In light of the policies prohibiting any employment of Arabs in Zionist colonies, Hope Simpson considered it undesirable that large areas of land should be transferred to the JNF: 'It is impossible to view with equanimity the extension of an enclave in Palestine from which all Arabs are excluded'.[61] Notwithstanding Hope Simpson's criticism of the JNF's discriminatory use of land, the Fund continued to acquire land in Palestine during the Mandate period.[62] As will be discussed later in this chapter, the JNF also played a role in the expropriation of Palestinian refugee property in the years following the creation of the State of Israel. The Fund's use of property to the exclusive benefit of Jewish citizens of Israel remains, to this day, subject to criticism.[63]

No discussion of land policies in Mandate Palestine would be complete without mention of the 1937 *Peel Commission Report* which was the first official British document to suggest 'partition' of the territory of Palestine as a solution to the seemingly irreconcilable objectives of Jewish and Arab nationalism.[64] However, no sooner had the Report been published than Britain began a step-by-step retreat from the *Peel Commission*'s recommendations. The *MacDonald White Paper*, issued in May 1939, empowered the High Commissioner to 'prohibit and regulate transfers of land' to Jews.[65] It also curbed Jewish immigration and envisaged the creation of an independent binational state of Palestine by 1949 'in which the two in Palestine, Arabs and Jews, share authority in government in such a way that the essential interests of each are secured'.[66] With the promulgation of the 1939 MacDonald paper, Britain dropped the idea of partition and re-emphasized its responsibility over the whole of Palestine. This led to the adoption of the 1940 Land Transfer Regulations. These regulations divided the country into three zones: 'A', 'B' and 'C'. According to the Regulation, land transfers in Zones A and B, save to a Palestinian Arab, were prohibited, except in certain circumstances. In Zone C, however, transfer of land was unrestricted.[67] According to Hadawi, despite imposing restrictions on land transfers in Zones A and B, the Jewish Agency managed to exploit loopholes in the ordinance and acquire land in these areas.[68] Hadawi notes that the British authorities were aware of these prohibited transactions, but did nothing to prevent them.[69]

In sum, the British Mandate did not abolish the Ottoman system of land tenure. It adopted, instead, a series of ordinances with the aim of regulating land ownership in Palestine. The most significant development affecting land rights in Palestine during the Mandate period was the Land Settlement scheme initiated in 1928. As discussed in this section, this process had a dual purpose: on the one hand, it effectively introduced a more formal structure to the land registration system in Palestine; on the other, it was used with the more sinister motive of providing a valid and indisputable title to the land in predominantly Jewish 'settlement areas'.[70] Although Commissions of Inquiry dispatched to Palestine invariably singled out unrestricted Jewish immigration and land purchases as the underlying causes of disturbances and tension between the native Arab population and the Jewish communities, British Ordinances did little, if anything to restrict transfer of land ownership to Jews during the Mandate period.[71] Although no strict restrictions were imposed on Jewish purchases of land, maximum Jewish land holdings in Palestine on the date the State of Israel was established in 1948 stood at less than 7 per cent of the total area.[72] The next section will demonstrate how Israeli legislation was enforced in the aftermath of the 1948 war to dramatically alter the distribution of land in Palestine and effectively strip Palestinians of land they possessed from time immemorial.

1.4 Legalizing dispossession: Israeli legislation and its impact on Palestinian ownership of land (1948–)

The first Arab–Israeli war erupted on 15 May 1948, a day after the proclamation of the State of Israel. The creation of the Jewish state envisioned by the UN's

Partition Plan was accompanied by an overall transformation of the ownership of land in historical Palestine and a shift in the demographic composition of the territory on which that state was created.[73] The exact causes of the flight of the Palestinians from their homes, which Palestinians refer to as the Nakba (or catastrophe), are beyond the scope of this study and have been thoroughly examined by Palestinian and New Israeli Historians.[74] Underlying the territorial and demographic changes which accompanied the creation of the State of Israel was a declared Zionist policy aimed at creating an ethnically homogeneous state which would use land under its possession to absorb Jewish immigrants from all over the world.[75] In the furtherance of these objectives, legislation was adopted to bring land belonging to Palestinians under the control of the Jewish State. This section will discuss the various laws and regulations used by the State of Israel to expropriate Palestinian refugee property. Measures taken to prevent internally displaced Palestinian citizens of Israel from accessing their land will not, however, be examined in this chapter.[76]

Before discussing the legal mechanisms which were used to expropriate refugee land, it is important to define the extent of that land. As discussed above, the land registers left over by the Ottomans did not accurately reflect the state of land ownership in Palestine. Although the British Mandate authorities tried to remedy this situation, their land settlement of title scheme covered only some 25 per cent of the total area of Mandate Palestine and focused on 'settlement areas' (i.e. areas with a high concentration of Jewish inhabitants). This allowed Jewish settlers or settlement agencies, such as the Jewish National Fund (JNF), to have a valid, undisputed and registered title to their land.[77] On the date of the declaration of the State of Israel in May 1948, the maximum Jewish land holdings, including property owned by the JNF, stood at only 1.7 million dunums, or 6.5 per cent of the total area of Mandate Palestine.[78] At the end of the first Arab–Israeli war, the State of Israel as defined by the armistice line had a total area of 20.2 million dunums,[79] of which it owned only 1.7 million. In other words, only 8.4 per cent of the land in the nascent state of Israel was Jewish owned. It is not clear how much of the residual area (18.5 million dunums) of the State of Israel was privately owned by Palestinian landholders since the British Mandate's land settlement scheme was interrupted with the end of the Mandate. Statistics published by the Mandate administration in 1945 suggest that just over half of the land not in Jewish ownership was owned by Palestinians, and the other half was State-owned.[80] In other words, the majority of the privately owned land in the State of Israel, at the end of the 1948 war, was owned by Palestinians who were either internally displaced within Israel or refugees expelled across its borders.

The Zionist leadership was well aware of the minimal Jewish land ownership in Palestine. In the words of the first Israeli Prime Minister, Ben Gurion, 'The war will give us the land. The concepts of "ours" and "not ours" are only concepts for peacetime, and during war they lose their meaning'.[81] In line with such political statements, the State of Israel realized that a legal mechanism had to be installed to provide legal clout to what essentially amounted to the 'theft of a nation.'

The appropriation and looting of abandoned Palestinian property by individual Jewish settlers started before the state-sanctioned legal mechanism was implemented. While the battles were still being waged in war-torn Palestine, some Jews began spontaneously to move into abandoned Palestinian homes in the towns and cities, while others simply evicted the owners by force.[82] To rein in the looting and bring Arab property under its control, the Haganah[83] set up the first 'Committee for Arab Properties in the Villages' in March 1948.[84] Additional area-specific committees were created as the fighting increased and more areas were vacated.[85] Nevertheless, these committees were unable to halt the pillage and vandalism of property. Amid the chaos of war, Jewish immigrants simply proceeded to distribute the loot.[86] Entire villages were also destroyed as part of a deliberate policy aimed at preventing the refugees' return.[87] The State also proceeded to settle arriving 'olim' (Jewish immigrants) in abandoned refugee property,[88] while Jewish farmers reaped the crops of abandoned Arab arable land.[89] By destroying villages and resettling Jews in houses and land belonging to Palestinian refugees, the State of Israel was creating obstacles on the ground to the restitution of refugee property. As will be discussed in Chapter 4, the presence of secondary occupants can preclude, in some instances, the restitution of property to the rightful owners.[90] In July 1948, following the creation of the State of Israel, the State established the Ministerial Committee for Abandoned Property, which replaced all previous ad hoc committees. According to historian Michael Fischbach, '[t]he new ministerial committee decided on a plan to expropriate refugee land on August 20, 1948. [...] From now on, Israel was set to separate the refugees from legal title to their land and use it instead for permanent settlement of Jewish immigrants'.[91] Laws and regulations were subsequently adopted to bring refugee property under the control of the State, as will be outlined in this section.

The most significant and often-cited legislation affecting Palestinian refugees' property rights was the Absentees' Property Law of 5710–1950.[92] This law was initially enacted in the form of emergency regulations in 1948.[93] These regulations had the effect of confiscating the property, both moveable and immovable, of any physical or legal person falling under the legal definition of an absentee.[94] The definition potentially includes almost all Arabs, including Palestinian citizens who were temporarily out of the territory of what later became the State of Israel, even if they were away for business or leisure at the time of the adoption of the Partition Plan and were subsequently barred from returning to their homes by the nascent State of Israel.[95] More disturbingly, this definition affects Palestinian citizens who did not cross over the borders into Arab territory and fled only a few miles away from their villages *within* areas under Jewish control. When the fighting subsided, these individuals were also barred from returning to their homes and subsequently declared 'absentees'. This generated the problem of internal displacement in Israel and created the fictional legal status of 'present absentees'.[96] These Palestinians were 'absent' for the purposes of the law yet very much present in the State of Israel. In addition, while this law did not explicitly discriminate against Palestinians, regulation 28(a) of the Absentee Property Act enabled the Custodian to issue a certificate confirming that the person named therein is not an absentee if the Custodian is 'of opinion that such person has left his town or village of residence – (1) for fear that the enemies of Israel would cause him harm, or (2) not because of military operations or for fear thereof'.[97] The Custodian could therefore use the certificate to exempt Jews from the application of the law.[98] Pursuant to these regulations, 'absentee property' would vest in the Custodian of Absentee Property.[99] At this stage, the Custodian could not permanently dispose of absentee property. The Custodian's office could only lease absentee property for a period not exceeding five years.[100] It is worth mentioning that these regulations were adopted merely nine days before the United Nations General Assembly passed resolution 194 which called for the return of refugees to their homes and compensation for the losses they had incurred.[101] The United States opposed these regulations and considered them prejudicial to the refugees' rights. According to American historian, Michael Fischbach, the Americans urged the Israelis not to take unilateral action which would affect Arab absentees' property interests in Israel.[102] Nevertheless, the State of Israel was keen to sever permanently the legal ties of the refugees to their property, acquire title to it and dispose of it. In fact, as early as February 1948, Ben Gurion put forth an offer to the JNF for the sale of refugee land. The JNF was, however, interested in acquiring title to the land, not mere possession,[103] which was not then possible according to the regulations of 1948. Discussions between the State and the JNF continued with the aim of selling property to the Fund and culminated in an agreement in January 1949, in which the JNF agreed to 'purchase' one million dunums of refugee land. The JNF wanted to assure its right of ownership and insisted that land be transferred to it within one year of signing the contract.[104] This was one of the factors which prompted the State to obtain title to absentee property land.

The result was the enactment of the Absentees' Property Law of 5710/1950 by the Knesset (Israeli legislature) on 14 March 1950. Though the definition of 'absentee' remained essentially the same,[105] this Law amended the provisions of the Absentee Property Act in one very significant way: it allowed the Custodian to sell and grant long leases of absentee property to a Development Authority (DA), which had yet to be established under a law of the Knesset.[106] As mentioned above, the Custodian had already concluded a sale with the JNF prior to the enactment of the Absentees' Property Law, and more land transactions were soon to follow with the newly created DA. As will be discussed in Chapter 2, the Custodian was expected to hold property in trusteeship for the absentees until the conclusion of a peace settlement. Instead, with the enactment of the 1950s Absentees' Property Law, the Custodian in Israel was given the green light to dispose permanently of Palestinian refugee property to the DA, which in turn sold it to the JNF and the State of Israel.

The DA was created pursuant to the provisions of the Development Authority (Transfer of Property) Law of 1950.[107] The DA was given wide-ranging powers to buy, rent, develop, sell or otherwise dispose of property. These powers were not absolute. Section 3(4) of the Law provided that:

(a) the Development Authority shall not be authorised to sell, or otherwise transfer the right of ownership of, property passing into public ownership, except to the State, to the Jewish National Fund, to an institution approved by the Government, for the purposes of this paragraph, as an institution for the settlement of landless Arabs, or to a local authority; the right of ownership of land so acquired may not be re-transferred except, with the consent of the Development Authority, to one of the bodies mentioned in this subparagraph;

(b) the Development Authority shall not be authorised to sell immovable property not being land passing into public ownership, unless such property has first been offered to the Jewish National Fund, and the Jewish National Fund has not agreed to acquire it within a period fixed by the Development Authority […].

As can be seen from this section, the DA could only sell to the State, institutions approved by the government and the JNF, which even benefitted from a right of first purchase. These restrictions guaranteed that lands in Israel would remain exclusively under the control of the State and the JNF – in other words, beyond the reach of their original Palestinian owners. In fact, the overall objective of the 1950 Absentees' Property Law and the DA Law was to transform all lands taken from the Palestinians into Mekarka'ei Yisra'el [Israel Lands], thus severing the original owners' legal title to such land. According to Article 1 of the *1960 Basic Law: Israel Lands*, Israel Lands are comprised of lands owned by (i) the State of Israel, (ii) the Development Authority or (iii) the Keren Kayemet Le-Israel (Jewish National Fund). Ownership of such land cannot be transferred either by sale or by any other manner.[108] This reserved pool of land was administered by the newly created Israel Lands Administration (ILA).[109] It is estimated that Israel Lands currently form 92 per cent of the total lands in Israel,[110] of which 12 per cent belong to the JNF.[111] On 3 August 2009, the Knesset passed a new ILA Law or 'Israel Land Reform Law' which allowed the transfer of land expropriated from Palestinians from the state to private owners as well as the privatization of some of the lands of destroyed and evacuated Arab villages. As noted by Adalah, 'this privatization policy will frustrate any future possibility of returning the abovementioned lands to their original Palestinian owners, in violation of their constitutional right to property and in contravention of both domestic Israeli law and International Humanitarian Law'.[112]

In conclusion, immediately after its establishment, the State of Israel began adopting laws to bring land under its control. The Israeli State relied on 'absentee' laws to bring Palestinian refugee property under the control of a Custodian. The 1950 Absentees' Property Law enabled the Custodian to transfer title to 'absentee' land to the DA, which in turn, transferred it to the State and the JNF, following the adoption of the 1950 DA Law. There were several aims behind the adoption of these laws. On one hand, the Israeli government sought to sever the link between the original owners of the land, now refugees or internally displaced people, and their property inside Israel.[113] While the Custodian of Property theoretically had the duty to guard 'absentee' property,[114] the ILA had no such duty vis-à-vis the property's original owners. By severing the legal title to the property, the government was also undermining any chances of restituting lands to their original owners, thus promoting compensation as the only feasible remedy.[115]

1.5 Conclusion

This chapter provided a brief overview of the laws regulating land ownership in Palestine, both before and after the creation of the State of Israel in 1948, with the dual aim of providing a rounded source of information for researchers on this issue, and demonstrating how land laws were used to dispossess Palestinian refugees. The first section of this chapter began by exploring the Ottoman system of land tenure. As was demonstrated in that section, during the Ottoman Empire, the majority of land in Palestine was privately owned. This raises the question of whether the expropriation of private land is legal under international law. This question will be answered in the next chapter. The first section additionally demonstrated that the Turkish registration system was inaccurate and incomplete. As a result, Palestinian landowners had to rely on use and possession, instead of registration, to prove their acquired rights to a specific area of land. As discussed in the second section of this chapter, the British Mandatory Administration introduced a sweeping system of land registration in 1928 to remedy this situation. The Mandate, however, ended before all land in Palestine was accurately mapped and registered. The Mandatory Administration also failed to limit the transfer of land to Jews, to the detriment of the native population of Palestine. Finally, the third section of this chapter discussed Israel's use of 'absentee' laws to bring Palestinian refugee lands under the control of a Custodian. Ownership over these lands was subsequently transferred to the DA, which in turn was empowered to sell it to the State and the JNF, thus effectively dispossessing Palestinian refugees and internally displaced persons of their property. The legal implications of the use of the doctrine of enemy property to expropriate land will be explored in further detail in the next chapter. Having discussed the process by which Palestinian refugees were dispossessed of their property, the next chapter will examine the legal grounds for the Palestinian refugees' right to reparation for their property losses.

Palestinian refugee property losses: The grounds for reparation in international law

2.1 Introduction

As was discussed in the previous chapter, by the end of the first Arab–Israeli war, 726,000 Palestinians had sought refuge in neighbouring Arab countries,[1] leaving behind their houses and millions of dunams of land, many of which were privately owned. Immediately after its establishment, the State of Israel began housing Jewish immigrants in these abandoned refugee properties.[2] Laws were also adopted to transfer ownership of absentee land to the State and its related agencies, as well as to the JNF. Having established in Chapter 1 that Palestinian refugees were in fact dispossessed of their property, this chapter will provide an analysis of the grounds for the right to reparation in international law for private individual property losses. This analysis focuses on private property claims. As such, reparation for other types of material or moral damage, such as emotional suffering, physical injuries or loss of employment, fall outside the scope of this analysis. Reparation for damage or loss to public property such as schools and hospitals is also not covered by this analysis. The aim of this chapter is to define the basis in international law for the Palestinian refugees' right to reparation for loss of or damage to private immovable property, such as houses and land.

First, this chapter will define the concept of reparation in international law. This section will also argue that Israel has an obligation to repair the consequences of a breach of an international obligation for which it is responsible. The second section of this chapter will discuss how Israel's expropriation of Palestinian refugee property breached norms of international humanitarian law, the law on enemy property, UN resolutions and human rights law. Having demonstrated that the expropriation of Palestinian refugee property was a wrongful act attributable to the State of Israel, the third section of this chapter will briefly outline the consequences of a wrongful act under international law.

2.2 The legal concept of reparation

2.2.1 Clarifying the terminology

Reparation is a principle of law that has existed for centuries. In the specific context of displacement, Professor Michael Lynk notes that restitution and compensation claims of displaced persons were recognized in international treaties and state practice long before the emergence of modern human rights, humanitarian and refugee law in the immediate aftermath of the Second World War.[3] Though it has existed for centuries, the concept of reparation is ill-defined in international law.[4] Terms such as 'reparation', 'remedy', 'redress', 'rehabilitation', 'compensation' and 'restitution' have all been used interchangeably and without clear distinction.[5] The adoption in 2001 of the *International Law Commission's Draft Articles on State Responsibility* (hereinafter ILC Articles) and in 2005 of the *UN Basic Principles and Guidelines on the Right to a Remedy and Reparation for Victims of Gross Violations of International Human Rights Law and Serious Violations of International Humanitarian Law* (hereinafter Guidelines on Reparation) has, however, provided some clarification on the legal definition of these terms.[6]

'Reparation' was defined in Article 31 of the ILC Articles and Principle 15 of the UN Guidelines on Reparation. These definitions were adequately summed up by International Law Professor, Dinah Shelton. According to Shelton, 'reparation' consists of 'the various means by which a state may repair the consequences of a breach of international law for which it is responsible'.[7] Both Principle 18 of the Guidelines on Reparation and Article 34 of the ILC Articles have identified 'restitution', 'compensation' and 'satisfaction', either singly or in combination, as the main forms of reparation.[8] Principle 18 of the Guidelines on Reparation adds 'rehabilitation' and 'guarantees of non-repetition' to these three main forms of reparation. In other words, as Gabriela Echeverria suggested in a report for REDRESS, ' "reparation" refers to the *substance* of the relief afforded, such as an award for damages or a public apology'.[9] On the other hand, argues Echeverria, the term 'remedy' or 'remedies' refers to the '*procedural* means by which a right is enforced, or the means by which a violation of a right is prevented or redressed'.[10] 'Remedies' were in fact defined in Principle 11 of the Guidelines on Reparation as the right of a victim of gross violations of international human rights law and serious violations of international humanitarian law to the following: '(a) Equal and effective access to justice; (b) Adequate, effective and prompt reparation for harm suffered; (c) Access to relevant information concerning violations and reparation mechanisms.' There is no definition of the term 'remedy', nor of the term 'redress' in the ILC Articles, which suggests that these terms are generally used in the context of claims arising from human rights violations and violations of international humanitarian law, rather than interstate claims arising from general violations of international law. As for 'redress', Echeverria defines it as 'the action 'to' redress, repair, restore or remedy'.[11] In other words, redress is a concept that includes a substantive right to reparation and a procedural right to seek effective remedies. This chapter will focus on the substantive right to reparation. The procedural mechanisms which individuals or states may use to invoke a right to reparation will be discussed in Chapter 3.

2.2.2 The grounds for reparation in international law: Israel's expropriation of refugee property under the law on state responsibility

As discussed in the previous section, a state is under an obligation to repair the consequences of a breach of international law for which it is responsible. This section will therefore provide an overview of the law on state responsibility as it applies to the case of Israeli expropriation of refugee property. Applying norms of state responsibility to the confiscation of refugee land and property in Israel raises a series of issues. First, the so-called inter-temporal rule precludes the retroactive application of international law. According to this rule, which was first stated by the Permanent Court of Arbitration in the *Island of Palmas Case* in 1928, '[a] juridical fact must be appreciated in the light of the law contemporary with it, and not of the law in force at the time such dispute in regard to it arises or falls to be settled'.[12] Accordingly, the ILC Articles are only relevant to the extent that they have codified a norm of international law on state responsibility, which existed when Israel expropriated refugee property. According to the commentary to the ILC Articles, the basic principle of state responsibility which stipulates that '[E]very internationally wrongful act of a State entails the international responsibility of that State' (Article 1) was applied by the Permanent Court of International Justice (PCIJ) in a number of cases that predate the existence of the State of Israel.[13] Therefore, it can be stated that this basic principle existed in 1948 and that it can be applied to an analysis of Israel's state responsibility for land and property confiscation. The elements of a wrongful act must also be defined according to the norms of international law on state responsibility that prevailed at that time. Article 2 of the ILC Articles defines an internationally wrongful act of a State as 'conduct consisting of an action or omission [which]: (a) is attributable to the State under international law; and (b) constitutes a breach of an international obligation of the State.' According to Crawford, these elements were also enunciated by the PCIJ in the *1938 Phosphates in Morocco* case.[14] Hence, in order to prove that Israel has committed an internationally wrongful act, it is essential to establish that Israeli confiscations of private property, during and in the aftermath of the 1948 war, are attributable to the State of Israel and its agents and that these actions were in breach of an international obligation of that State.

With regards to the issue of attribution, as discussed in Chapter 1, the confiscation of Palestinian refugee property was the direct result of measures and laws adopted by the State of Israel.[15] As such, attribution is easily established in these circumstances. As for demonstrating that there was a breach of an international obligation, the inter-temporal rule requires that the conduct attributed to the State of Israel be in breach of an obligation in force for that State at that time. Since the rules on state responsibility are secondary rules of responsibility,[16] one has to look at primary obligations of international law to determine whether a breach has occurred. According to Crawford, the obligation does not have to be treaty based. It can arise from any other source of international law.[17] In the case of Israeli expropriation of refugee property, the primary obligation violated may be derived from international humanitarian law, the law on enemy property, UN resolutions and human rights law. Unless the primary obligation requires otherwise, Crawford argues that 'fault' and 'damage' are irrelevant to the notion of state responsibility in international law.[18] The next section will outline the primary obligations under international law which may have been violated by Israel when it expropriated Palestinian refugee property. It is a separate question who may invoke the responsibility arising from the breach of an obligation, more specifically whether non-state actors can invoke state responsibility and claim an individual right to reparation. The invocation of a right to reparation will be discussed in Chapter 3.

2.3 Israeli expropriation of Palestinian refugee property: A wrongful act under international law

2.3.1 Israeli damage and expropriation of Palestinian refugee property as a violation of international humanitarian law

At the time of the creation of the State of Israel, the relevant treaties and documents on international humanitarian law were the *Hague Conventions of*

1899 and 1907 and their *Regulations*.[19] The two versions of the Convention and the Regulations differ only slightly from each other with the provisions of the 1907 Hague Convention essentially replacing those of the 1899 Convention.[20] The nascent State of Israel was not, and is not today, a party to either Convention. In 1946, however, in reference to the *1907 Hague Convention on Land Warfare*, the Nuremberg International Military Tribunal stated that 'The rules of land warfare expressed in the Convention undoubtedly represented an advance over existing International Law at the time of their adoption [...] but by 1939 these rules [...] were recognized by all civilized nations and were regarded as being declaratory of the laws and customs of war'.[21] Hence, by 1948, the provisions of these Conventions and Regulations were considered declaratory of rules of customary international law and binding on all states, including those which have not ratified them. In addition, Israel's Supreme Court has also accepted the Hague Conventions and Regulations as binding customary law, enforceable in Israeli courts.[22]

The Hague Regulations, which were annexed to the 1907 Hague Convention, include provisions protecting both private and public property. These provisions fall under two different sections in the Regulations. The first two provisions protecting property rights fall under Section II of the Regulations entitled 'Hostilities'. As such, these provisions apply to protect property *during* hostilities.[23] According to Article 1 of the *1907 Hague Convention (III) relative to the Opening of Hostilities*,[24] 'hostilities between [contracting parties] must not commence without previous and explicit warning in the form of either a declaration of war, giving reasons, or of an ultimatum with conditional declaration of war'. In the case of Israel–Palestine, although Israeli forces had already invaded areas designated for the Arab state in the Partition Plan in late 1947, it can be said that hostilities officially erupted on 15 May 1948 when Syrian, Lebanese, Jordanian, Iraqi and Egyptian troops launched joint attacks to repel Israeli forces and ended in July 1949 when the last armistice agreement was signed between Israel and Syria. Hence, the provisions are relevant to an analysis of events affecting property rights which took place *during* the 1948 Arab–Israeli war. They are less relevant to the analysis of legislation that was adopted in the 1950s with the aim of expropriating refugee property, such as the 1950 Absentee Property Law or the 1950 DA Law discussed in Chapter 1. The two provisions which apply during hostilities are the following:

> **Article 23** [I]t is especially forbidden ... (g) To destroy or seize the enemy's property, unless such destruction or seizure be imperatively demanded by the necessities of war.

Article 28 The pillage of a town or place, even when taken by assault, is
prohibited.

As appears from the clear wording of Article 23(g), the destruction and seizure of
property is prohibited *unless* demanded by the 'necessities of war'. As discussed
in the previous chapter, the State of Israel was responsible for the destruction of
entire villages.[25] Israel could, however, argue that the destruction of these villages
was demanded by the 'necessities of war'.[26] Several historians have, however,
demonstrated that the destruction of villages by Jewish forces was part of an
ideologically and politically motivated military strategy aimed at displacing
Palestinians from their homes and preventing their return.[27] In other words,
there were instances when the State of Israel and its armed forces destroyed
villages without apparent military necessity. It can therefore be argued that
Israel breached Article 23(g) of the Hague Regulations. As for the prohibition
on pillage enunciated in Article 28 of the Hague Regulations, no exceptions are
made in cases of military necessity. In the case of *In re Von Lewinski*, the British
Military Court at Hamburg ruled that

> If the necessities of war were an overriding consideration to be taken into
> account in regard to all the Articles of the Convention, obviously it would be
> quite unnecessary to make a special provision to that effect in Article 23(g).
> [...] The combined effect of the preamble and the special exception in 23(g) is
> to make it clear that [...] military necessity has already been discounted in the
> drawing up of these rules.[28]

In other words, the prohibition on pillage enunciated in Article 28 is absolute.
As documented by several historians, the looting and pillaging of Palestinian
property by Jewish soldiers nevertheless occurred.[29] In his last Progress Report
to the Secretary General before being assassinated by a Jewish terrorist group,[30]
UN Special Rapporteur to Palestine, Count Bernadotte, also confirms that
'[t]here have been numerous reports from reliable sources of large-scale looting,
pillaging and plundering, and of instances of destruction of villages *without
apparent military necessity. The liability of the Provisional Government of Israel
to restore private property to its Arab owners and to indemnify those owners for
property wantonly destroyed is clear*, irrespective of any indemnities which the
Provisional Government may claim from the Arab States'.[31]

The liability of the State of Israel arises from the fact that it has violated
Articles 23(g) and 28 of the Hague Regulations. As such, Israel has committed
a wrongful act which engages its state responsibility and its ensuing obligation

to provide reparation for the damage and the destruction of property that occurred during hostilities and as a direct result of actions or omissions by the State of Israel and its armed forces. A responsible state's obligation to provide reparation was, in fact, enunciated in Article 3 of the 1907 Hague Convention: '[a] belligerent party which violates the provisions of the said Regulations shall, if the case demands, be liable to pay compensation. It shall be responsible for all acts committed by persons forming part of its armed forces.' According to Oppenheim, this Article enacts two different rules: 'firstly, that a belligerent who violates the Hague Regulations shall, if the case demands, pay compensation; and secondly, that a belligerent is responsible for all acts committed by any person forming part of his armed forces'.[32] Israel is therefore responsible for *all* acts caused by members of its forces in violation of Articles 23(g) and 28, regardless of whether the officers or organs in question have acted outside their competence.[33]

The remaining provisions of the Hague Regulations pertaining to immovable property rights fall under Section III entitled 'Military Authority over the Territory of the Hostile State'. They provide an explicit injunction against the confiscation of private property in addition to forbidding acts of pillage and damage or seizure of public property:

> **Artticle 46** Family honour and rights, the lives of persons, and private property, as well as religious convictions and practice, must be respected.
> Private property cannot be confiscated.
> **Article 47** Pillage is formally forbidden.
> **Article 56** The property of municipalities, that of institutions dedicated to religion, charity and education, the arts and sciences, even when State property, shall be treated as private property.
> All seizure of, destruction or wilful damage done to institutions of this character, historic monuments, works of art and science, is forbidden, and should be made the subject of legal proceedings.

It is important to note that the confiscation of property is prohibited in absolute terms in Article 46. No exceptions are made, not even in case of military necessity. This can be contrasted with the wording in Article 23(g), which allows the seizure and destruction of property if 'demanded by the necessities of war'.

Since the three provisions cited above fall under Section III of the Regulations, they are meant to apply in the territory of a hostile state while it is under the military authority of another state, namely an occupying power.[34]

In the 2004 Advisory Opinion on the *Legal Consequences of the Construction of a Wall in the Occupied Palestinian Territory*, the International Court of Justice found the provisions of Section III applicable to the West Bank, which is under Israeli occupation.[35] Israel could, however, challenge the applicability of these provisions to the territory of the State of Israel, in which Palestinian refugee property is located, as it is not considered occupied territory in international law. Under the current political and legal circumstances, the sovereign rights of the State of Israel within the pre-1967[36] *de facto* borders are virtually unchallenged.[37] The international community, including Arab States and the Palestine Liberation Organization (PLO), are advocating a two-state solution to the Israeli–Palestinian conflict based on the borders that existed before the 1967 War.[38] As such, there is an implicit if not explicit recognition of the State of Israel's right to claim sovereignty over seventy eight per cent of the territory of Mandate Palestine. This would enable Israel to challenge strongly the applicability of Section III of the Hague Regulations inside the *de facto* borders of the State of Israel, since it is not considered occupied territory. As a matter of fact, cases which have applied Articles 46, 47 and 56 of the Hague Regulations have all looked at the legal obligations of an *occupying* power vis-à-vis private property held in *occupied* territories.[39] For example, in the *I.G. Farben Trial*, the United States Military Tribunal at Nuremberg stated that Articles 46, 47, 52, 53 and 55 of the Hague Regulations 'are broadly aimed at preserving the inviolability of property rights to both public and private property during *military occupancy*'.[40] However, it is interesting to note that, in a working paper which interprets the wording of UNGA Resolution 194 on 'compensation to refugees for loss of or damage to property to be made good under principles of international law or in equity', the Secretariat of the UNCCP explicitly cites these provisions as prohibiting the acts of looting, pillaging and plundering of private property and destruction of property and villages without military necessity that occurred in Palestine in 1948.[41] Nothing in the Secretariat's working paper suggests that the provisions of the Hague Regulations, including Articles 46, 47 and 56, do not apply to the territory of the State of Israel within the *de facto* borders set by the 1949 armistice agreements.

In conclusion, Israel can successfully challenge the applicability of Articles 46, 47 and 56 of the Hague Regulations within its *de facto* pre-1967 borders on the grounds that these provisions apply only in occupied territories. It remains, however, bound by the provisions under Section II of the Regulations (Articles 23(g) and 28). As such, it has the obligation to provide reparation for the damage caused to property that was pillaged or destroyed, without military necessity, by Israeli troops during the 1948 war.

2.3.2 Israeli property expropriation and the doctrine on enemy property

While the previous section focused on violations of international law committed by the State of Israel *during* the war, this section will explore the Israeli State's policy towards refugee property both during and after the war. As noted by Professor Michael Kagan, civilian property was traditionally viewed as linked to sovereignty and hence considered a legitimate object of warfare (spoils of war).[42] However, as discussed earlier, the 1907 Hague Regulations introduced provisions protecting private property. These provisions effectively put a limit to the doctrine of war booty. Henceforth, immoveable private enemy property could no longer be appropriated by a belligerent under any circumstances.[43] Oppenheim, however, distinguishes between the confiscation of private property, which is prohibited under the Hague Regulations, and 'the temporary use of private land and buildings for all kinds of purposes demanded by the necessities of war'.[44] The rationale behind the latter was that civilian assets could be used to generate funds for the war effort.[45] It was also based on the presumption that, in times of conflict, a person's formal nationality will influence their political and military loyalties.[46] This led to the development of a practice in international law, which enabled a warring State to place enemy property under its administrative control in order to prevent its use for the benefit of the enemy, *without however seizing the property or depriving its enemy owner of title.*[47] The British were the first to use enemy property legislation during the First World War.[48] Britain resorted to this policy again during the Second World War by enacting the Trading with the Enemy Law of 1939, which allowed a custodian to seize land in Palestine belonging to citizens of Germany and the Axis.[49] Israel drew on this law when it enacted the Emergency Regulations on Absentees' Property of 5709/1948,[50] which were the first regulations adopted to deal with absentee property in Israel and the precursors to the Absentees' Property Law of 1950. According to Forman and Kedar, Pakistani lawmakers were also inspired by the British Trading with the Enemy Ordinance of 1939 when they drafted legislation in 1948 to deal with land permanently left behind by Hindu and Sikh refugees following the Partition of India in 1947.[51] Pakistani legislation, however, featured 'new components that facilitated not only expropriation but transfer of ownership and reallocation as well'.[52] This legislation served as a model for subsequent Israeli legislation, namely the Absentees' Property Law of 5710–1950 and the Development Authority (Transfer of Property) Law of 1950, which enabled the Custodian to dispose of absentee property instead of just holding it in trusteeship for the absentees until a peaceful settlement is reached.[53]

While the doctrine of enemy property is generally accepted, Oppenheim notes that the 'enemy' character of an individual or property remains 'to a great extent unsettled'.[54] The *Hague Convention (V) respecting the Rights and Duties of Neutral Powers and Persons in Case of War on Land of 18 October 1907* defined neutral persons according to their *nationality*.[55] This definition was accepted by all the Signatory Powers except Great Britain who signed the Convention with reservations on the definition of 'neutrals' found in Article 16. According to Oppenheim, there was no agreement as to 'whether nationality exclusively, or domicile also, should determine the neutral or enemy character of individuals and their goods'.[56] In fact, British laws on enemy property defined an enemy according to the person's residence, even if temporary, in a territory controlled by an enemy state.[57] According to Oppenheim, '[t]his treatment of foreigners resident on occupied enemy territory is generally recognized as legitimate by theory and practice'.[58] As discussed in the previous chapter, Israel similarly defined an 'absentee' according to the person's residence in territory controlled by any of the Arab armies which participated in the 1948 war, namely Lebanon, Egypt, Syria, Saudi Arabia, Transjordan, Iraq or the Yemen.[59] This process enabled Israel's Custodian to seize control of property belonging to Palestinian refugees, not just citizens of Arab states engaged in the war. At least in form, it appears that Israel followed established precedents regarding the treatment of enemy civilian property. In addition, Israel could argue that it had to use absentee property to house the thousands of incoming Jewish settlers, and hence it adopted legislation confiscating property out of necessity. However, as several authors have argued, the historical development of laws affecting absentee property suggests that the Israeli state had an ulterior motive which was to use 'law, along with other means, to impose and legitimize Jewish political and territorial domination within its sovereign space'.[60]

Several elements in the development and enforcement of Israeli legislation on absentee property suggest that Israel used the doctrine of enemy property to mask discriminatory practices aimed at permanently alienating property from its non-Jewish owners. First, Israel treated absentee property as state property, thus ignoring the temporary nature of the Emergency Regulations on Absentees' Property of 5709/1948. Israeli Agriculture Minister at the time, Aaron Tsizling, stressed the need to use law, as opposed to temporary measures and security considerations alone, to legitimize the land appropriation and reallocation to Jewish hands.[61] The need to transform temporary emergency regulations into legislation eventually led to the adoption in 1950 of the Absentees' Property Law and the Development Authority (Transfer of Property) Law. As demonstrated in Chapter 1, this two-statute mechanism enabled the Custodian to expropriate absentee property and sell it to a so-called Development Authority which would then sell it to the State or the JNF, with the aim of permanently severing the link between Palestinian owners and their property.[62] A second factor encouraging the adoption of these two laws was the sale of absentee property to the JNF in 1949, despite the fact that the 1948 Emergency Regulations prohibited selling or leasing absentee property for more than five years. According to Israeli academics Forman and Kedar, '[t]his illegal sale reflected that, despite the temporary arrangements along the way, authorities had long-term plans for the permanent use of Palestinian refugee land and the transfer of its unrestricted ownership into Jewish hands'.[63] This sale heralded the gradual transformation of lands taken from the Palestinians into Mikarki'eh Yesrael [Israel Lands] and highlighted the Custodian's discriminatory policy vis-à-vis non-Jews, since the JNF's lands are leased for the purpose of settling Jews only.[64] Further evidence of the Custodian's ethnic discrimination includes the fact that Jewish-owned property was exempted from expropriation.[65] Doubts about the objective of Israel's policy on enemy property and whether it has conformed, in both form and in principle, to established precedents were also raised when Israel's Absentee Property Law enabled the Custodian to claim the property of internally displaced Palestinians. These individuals were citizens of Israel and their assets were within the borders of the State of Israel. The expropriation of their property can hardly be justified under the enemy property doctrine as necessary measures to prevent the enemy from using civilian assets to generate funds for the war effort. As Forman and Kedar have shown, during the drafting stages of the Absentee Property Law, a Jewish–Arab coalition recognized the discriminatory nature of the statute and demanded the exclusion of internally displaced Palestinians from the definition of 'absentee'. Their motion was, however, rejected by a close vote.[66] Taken together, all of these factors cast doubts about the motives behind Israel's use of the enemy property doctrine. In a study of the perverse use of the enemy property doctrine in the Middle East, Michael Kagan reaches the conclusion that

> Israel followed the enemy property doctrine only in form. Its policies are better understood as an application of the war booty doctrine, where conquest alone

effectively led to permanent dispossession. Instead of holding refugee property in anticipation of a peace settlement, Israel transferred it for the benefit of Israeli Jews without any provision for the property to be preserved for its original owners' benefit. The enemy nationals concept hence facilitated a practice that international law had sought to ban decades earlier by providing a formal mechanism by which non-Jews could be labeled enemies (or in the Israeli legislation, 'absentees').[67]

In sum, Palestinian refugees can argue that Israel's property confiscations constituted illegal seizures from the onset. These confiscations and the subsequent alienation of refugee property for the benefit of Jews only cannot be justified under the doctrine of enemy property. The Custodian should have held the property in custody and preserved the original owner's interests in anticipation of a peace settlement. Israel's distorted use of the doctrine of enemy property is thus nothing more than a political cover to mask policies that were prohibited under international law.

2.3.3 Palestinian refugees' property rights under United Nations Resolutions

On 29 November 1947, the General Assembly adopted Resolution 181(II) (the Partition Plan). The adoption of the Partition Plan was followed by sporadic tit-for-tat incidents of violence, which rapidly spiralled out of control, escalating into an all-out regional war. It also signalled the beginning of the Exodus of Palestinians, which occurred mainly over the space of twenty months – from the adoption of the Partition Plan in November 1947 until the signing of the last Arab–Israeli armistice agreement in July 1949. Besides recommending the partition of Palestine into a Jewish and Arab State, Resolution 181 includes important provisions protecting the rights of the minorities in each state. With regards to property rights, the resolution explicitly provides that '[N]o expropriation of land owned by an Arab in the Jewish State (by a Jew in the Arab State) shall be allowed except for public purposes. *In all cases of expropriation full compensation as fixed by the Supreme Court shall be paid previous to dispossession*'.[68] The Zionist leadership accepted Resolution 181 and proceeded with its plans to establish a Jewish State. On 14 May 1948, the Jewish leaders grounded the declaration of the Jewish State of Israel 'on the strength of the resolution of the United Nations General Assembly [Resolution 181]'.[69]

Although United Nations General Assembly resolutions are generally not binding, the nascent State of Israel has accepted this resolution and relied on it when it declared its independence. A study prepared by the United Nations Committee on the Exercise of the Inalienable Rights of the Palestinian People (CEIRPP) concluded that '[s]ince, of the two states envisaged in the partition plan, Israel was the only one to come into existence, it bore the obligation of discharging the responsibilities toward its minority population as prescribed by the partition resolution'.[70] Therefore, according to the CEIRPP, Israel is bound by the provisions of Resolution 181, including the ones protecting minority rights and their property interests. As discussed in the previous section, Israel did not confiscate property for public purposes, though the housing of incoming Jewish settlers may have been one of its short-term goals. From the onset, the State of Israel had a long-term plan to permanently deprive non-Jewish owners of their property and transform their land into Israel Lands. It has therefore violated its obligations towards the Arab minority under Resolution 181.

The General Assembly's intention to protect the rights of all inhabitants of Palestine was reiterated in a working paper issued by the Secretariat on 19 February 1948. In paragraph four of the paper, the Secretariat advised the Commission, which was to assume the administration of Palestine in accordance with Part I.B.2 of Resolution 181, to define its policy by issuing a Proclamation to the peoples of Palestine. The Proclamation should make clear *inter alia* that: '[a]ll inhabitants of Palestine shall enjoy equal rights and the same treatment and security in law as well as in fact'. More importantly, the Proclamation should state that '[p]rivate rights acquired under existing law are to be respected'.[71] As noted by Kagan, further indication of the international will to safeguard the rights of the inhabitants of Palestine came in the form of Security Council Resolution 46, adopted on 17 April 1948, which called on all persons and organizations in Palestine, 'and especially upon the Arab Higher Committee and the Jewish Agency [...] to refrain, pending further consideration of the future government of Palestine by the General Assembly, from any political activity which might prejudice the rights, claims, or position of either community'.[72] This resolution was passed only a few weeks before the State of Israel was declared in May 1948. At the time, the *Haganah*, which was the main paramilitary organization, and later became the regular army of the State of Israel (the Israeli Defense Forces, or IDF) had already set in motion a military plan, which called for the 'destruction of villages' and their '[...] encirclement. In the event of resistance, the armed force must be wiped out and the population must be expelled outside the borders of the state'.[73] Land confiscations and expulsions were thus taking place in Palestine, both before and after the creation of the State of Israel. The broad language of the resolution and its clear prohibition of any activity which might prejudice the 'rights, claims, or positions of either community' should have prevented Israel from confiscating properties and from obstructing the Palestinian refugees' return to their homes. This Palestine-specific resolution, coupled with the general rules of international humanitarian law discussed earlier, strengthen the arguments that Israel violated its obligations in international law by destroying and confiscating Palestinian-owned property, both during and after the 1948 war.

As mentioned earlier, in his last Progress Report to the UNGA, Count Bernadotte condemned the pillaging and destruction of Palestinian property, in the absence of military necessity, and considered the Provisional Government of Israel liable to restitute private property to its Arab owners and to provide them with compensation for property wantonly destroyed.[74] Acting on Bernadotte's report, the UNGA adopted Resolution 194, which established a Conciliation Commission for Palestine (UNCCP) and requested it to assume the functions of the UN Mediator on Palestine, in view of reaching a final settlement of the Palestine question. More specifically, with regards to refugees, the UNCCP was instructed in paragraph 11 of Resolution 194, 'to facilitate the repatriation, resettlement and economic and social rehabilitation of the refugees.' Paragraph 11 further provides the most often cited statement in support of the right of return, restitution and compensation of Palestinian refugees in international law. According to paragraph 11, sub-paragraph 1, the General Assembly:

> Resolves that the refugees wishing to return to their homes and live at peace with their neighbours should be permitted to do so at the earliest practicable date, and that compensation should be paid for the property of those choosing not to return and for loss of or damage to property which, under principles of international law or in equity, should be made good by the Governments or authorities responsible [...]

This provision has generated a lot of controversy mostly on the right of return.[75] Since our focus is on the property rights of Palestinian refugees, the right of return will only be discussed to the extent that its implementation would lead to, or facilitate, the restitution of property. Relying mainly on UN archival documents, this section will attempt to define the different rights embodied in paragraph 11, sub-paragraph 1 of Resolution 194, in order to reach a conclusion regarding Israel's obligations to restitute property and/or provide compensation.

2.3.3.1 *Right of return and restitution*

Resolution 194 does not explicitly mention a 'right to return', nor is there any mention of a right to 'restitution'. These rights need to be deduced from the resolution's wording. In a working paper issued on 15 May 1950, the UNCCP's Secretariat clarified the meaning of the various terms in paragraph 11, based on the drafting history of Resolution 194. According to the debate which preceded the adoption of paragraph 11, the drafters agreed to use the term 'refugees' to refer to 'all refugees, irrespective of race or nationality, provided that they had been *displaced from their homes in Palestine*'.[76] Therefore paragraph 11(1) applies both to Arab and Jewish refugees who had been residing in Palestine and were displaced from their homes during the 1948 war. It does not apply to Jewish refugees who fled from other Arab countries in 1948, or later on. Nor does it apply to Arab Palestinians who lost their lands, but not their homes. This would be the case, for example, of a Palestinian residing in Gaza city who owned land in the Negev and subsequently lost it when Israel declared its sovereignty over the Negev in 1948. Interestingly, however, the drafters used the term 'refugee' to include Palestinians in Israel who were displaced from their normal place of residence as a result of the war and have come to be known as internally displaced Palestinians, as opposed to refugees.[77]

According to the wording of Resolution 194, only those refugees 'wishing to return' should do so. Debates at the General Assembly reveal that the GA 'intended to confer upon the refugees as *individuals* the right to exercise a *free choice* as to their future. The choice was between repatriation *and* compensation for damages suffered, on the one hand, or no return and compensation for all property left behind, on the other'.[78] This interpretation identifies three important features of paragraph 11(1). First, paragraph 11(1) refers to individual rights, as opposed to collective rights. Therefore, each individual refugee has a choice as to his or her future, and should not be forced into a settlement which would bargain away this individual right. Second, the use of the word 'wishing' implies free choice: '[s]uch choice would have to be made in full knowledge of the alternative conditions involved both on the physical and the political plan […]'.[79] Another important feature is that repatriation and compensation are not mutually exclusive. The choice is between repatriation to their homes *and* compensation for damages suffered, or compensation for all the property left behind. Since refugees who choose not to return are to be compensated for their property losses, by implication, repatriation would be accompanied by the restitution of property and compensation for damages incurred. In fact, paragraph 11(1) stipulates that refugees should be permitted to return 'to their homes'. According to the UNCCP's records, '[t]here is no doubt that in using this term the General Assembly meant the home of each refugee, i.e., his house or lodging and not his homeland. This is indicated by the fact that two amendments using the term 'the areas from which they have come' were rejected'.[80] In a written memorandum submitted to the UNCCP, the Legal Adviser to the United Nations Economic Survey Mission for the Middle East, Paolo Contini, reiterated the Palestinian refugees' right to restitution pursuant to principles of international law: 'Whenever it is established that, under international law, the property of a refugee has been wrongfully seized, sequestered, requisitioned, confiscated, or detained by the Israeli Government, the claimant is entitled to restitution of the property, if it is still in existence, plus indemnity for damages'.[81] Contini did not necessarily link the return of refugees to the restitution of their property. Non-returning refugees were also entitled to the restitution of their property, though he believed this would mostly apply to movable property – especially blocked bank accounts.[82]

It has been argued, however, that paragraph 11(1) did not conceive of Palestinian return, and similarly of restitution, as a right.[83] Paragraph 11(1) stipulates that refugees who freely choose to return '*and* live at peace with their neighbours *should* be permitted to do so [...] [Emphasis added]'. At first sight, this phrase seems to create a limiting condition upon the return of refugees: (i) by imposing an obligation on returning refugees to be willing to live at peace with their neighbours and (ii) by giving the authorities in whose territory the refugees will be residing a discretionary right to refuse the admission of refugees if they fail to meet that obligation. In other words, instead of having an obligation to allow refugees to return, Israel would have the right to request assurances (in the form of a written undertaking, for example) from the refugees of their intention to live at peace with their neighbours in the Jewish state. Israel would also have the right to deny the return of any refugee whose past or present actions indicate an unwillingness to integrate peacefully into Israeli society. This is one plausible interpretation of the injunction. The reverse may also be true. This injunction may actually be imposing several obligations on the Government in whose territory the refugee will be settling (i.e. Israel). In relation to refugees who choose to return and live at peace with their neighbours, Israel would have 'an obligation [...] to ensure the peace of the returning refugees and protect them from any elements seeking to disturb that peace'.[84] Returning refugees would thus have the *right* to live at peace with their neighbours rather than an obligation to provide assurances to Israel that they are able and willing to integrate peacefully. This interpretation seems to be more consonant with the historical events that led to the exodus of Palestinians from their homes in 1948. In fact, the majority of the Palestinian population did not want hostilities.[85] Furthermore, fear of Jewish reprisals and a desire to maintain economic relations prompted several Arab villages and cities to sign non-aggression pacts with their neighbouring *kibbutzims*.[86] Even the Arab village of Deir Yassin, which would become the site of a massacre in April 1948, was among the villages which had concluded peace agreements with Jewish leaders in their neighbourhood.[87] Thus, for the most part, Palestinians had the intention of living in peace with their neighbours but were not allowed to do so. Paragraph 11(1) further stipulates that refugees 'should be permitted' to return to their homes. This injunction is 'addressed primarily to the Governments in whose territory the refugees will enter [i.e. Israel]; secondarily to the Governments in whose territory the refugees actually find themselves [for instance Lebanon or Iraq]; in the third place to the Governments through whose territory the refugees might have to pass in the course of their return [for example Jordan for refugees returning from Iraq]'.[88] Despite the use of the word 'should', delegates who addressed the issue during the drafting debates at the General Assembly were consistent in either stating or assuming that Israel would be expected to repatriate.[89] In his recommendations to the General Assembly, which eventually served as a basis for Resolution 194, Bernadotte urged the United Nations to affirm '[T]he right of the Arab refugees to return to their homes in Jewish-controlled territory at the earliest possible date [...]'.[90] To dispel any ambiguity on this issue, subsequent General Assembly resolutions explicitly referred to a Palestinian return as a matter of right.[91] Finally, the host countries in which refugees reside must not influence or hinder in any way the exercise of free choice by the refugees.[92]

It was also argued that since the General Assembly resolved that refugees should return 'at the earliest practicable date', their return cannot materialize until a formal regional peace agreement is reached.[93] This was not, however, the intention of the drafters. During debates on the wording of the resolution, Guatemala had in fact submitted an amendment which would have required contending parties in Palestine to declare peace *before* refugees are permitted to return to their homes.[94] This amendment was opposed by the United Kingdom representative who noted 'the fact that it might be many years before a formal peace was established in Palestine'.[95] The United States delegate was not in favour of that amendment either. He stated in unequivocal terms that

His delegation could not accept the proclamation of peace as a prerequisite for the return of refugees and hoped that the Assembly would not make this a condition. It was recognized that the bulk of the refugees could only return in peaceful circumstances. However, they need not wait for the proclamation of peace before beginning. These unfortunate people should not be made pawns in the negotiations for a final settlement.[96]

The Guatemalan amendment was finally rejected by thirty-seven votes to seven with five abstentions. From the above, it becomes clear that the General Assembly did not have the intention of making the refugees' repatriation conditional upon the achievement of a formal peace. The Assembly believed instead that 'the refugees should be allowed to return 'when stable conditions had been established'. It would appear indisputable that such conditions were established by the signing of the four Armistice Agreements'.[97]

In sum, Resolution 194 – paragraph 11(1) provides refugees with the right to choose to return to their homes, repossess their property (restitution) and live at peace with their neighbours. They should have been able to exercise these rights as soon as the Armistice Agreements of 1949 were signed between Israel and neighbouring Arab countries. Resolution 194 provides also for the right of refugees to demand compensation for damages that they have incurred regardless of whether they choose to return to their homes or resettle elsewhere. The following section will look at the right to compensation, as provided for in Resolution 194.

2.3.3.2 *Right of compensation*

This section will look at compensation as described in Resolution 194, paragraph 11(1). Paragraph 11(1) stipulates 'that compensation should be paid for the property of those choosing not to return and for loss of or damage to property which, under principles of international law or in equity, should be made good by the Governments or authorities responsible'. This statement raises several questions: (i) who should be compensated; (ii) what damages are compensable; (iii) who should compensate and (iv) what is the standard of compensation?

With regards to the first question, as discussed in the section above, the term 'refugees' in Resolution 194 refers to 'all refugees, irrespective of race or nationality, provided that they had been displaced from their homes in Palestine'.[98] In his memorandum to the UNCCP, Contini stated that '[W]henever a loss or damage to refugee property is attributable to an action by the Israeli Government, which is wrongful under international law, the claimant is entitled to a pecuniary indemnification *in addition* to the restitution of returnable property'.[99] This statement confirms that the rights of return, restitution and compensation are not mutually exclusive. As such, both returning and non-returning refugees should be compensated. In fact, Paragraph 11, sub-paragraph 1 distinguishes between two different categories of claims based on whether a refugee chooses to return or not. These categories are (i) compensation claims for property of refugees not choosing to return; (ii) compensation claims for loss of or damage to property, which, under principles of international law or in equity should be made good. Compensation claims for war damages is a third category of claims which typically arises at the end of hostilities. This category of claims, however, was not included in Resolution 194.

The first category of claims listed above is based on the general legal principle that the confiscation of private property is illegal under international law, unless required for public purposes, or out of military necessity. In cases where property seizure can be justified, in order to be lawful, compensation must be paid to the property's rightful owner.[100] According to a working paper prepared by the UNCCP's Secretariat, this category of claim must also be 'considered in the light of the Assembly's decision that refugees should be given the choice either to return to their homes and live at peace with their neighbours or to receive compensation for their property if they choose not to return'.[101] The second category of claims is an intermediate group of claims which falls between compensation claims for non-returning refugees and compensation claims for war damages. The claims for loss of, or damage to property must in fact be distinguished from claims for ordinary war damages, as they do not directly arise out of military events in Palestine. According to the legislative history of paragraph 11(1), the cases which the General Assembly had envisaged were those of 'looting, pillaging and plundering of private property and destruction of property and villages without military necessity', which were all prohibited by the laws and customs of war on land laid down in the Hague Regulations of 1907.[102] By contrast, war damages originate in the direct consequences of military operations. It is interesting to note that during the drafting stages of paragraph 11(1), the United States, Colombia and Guatemala did not distinguish between claims for loss or damage which arise indirectly from military operations and compensation claims for ordinary war damages. Since they viewed 'the question of war damage [as] separate from the refugee problem',[103] they submitted amendments which would have omitted any reference to 'damage and loss', suggesting instead that 'adequate compensation should be paid for the property of those choosing not to return'.[104] This amendment would have limited compensation to non-returning refugees, thus depriving returning refugees from claiming compensation for loss or damage to their restituted property. These amendments were, however, rejected by the General Assembly.[105] According to paragraph 11, returning refugees can claim compensation for damage to their restituted property if they are able to repossess it. In cases where property restitution is impossible, returning refugees can still claim compensation for their loss: 'if property were not restored to the returning refugees the action of the Government of Israel would amount to a confiscation, which already, under general principles of international law, would pledge that Government to compensation'.[106] As for compensation for war damages, as a rule, any action with respect to this category of claim would be provided for in a peace treaty between the parties. The resolution of these claims is therefore contingent upon reaching a general peace settlement to the Israeli–Arab conflict.[107] By implication, there was no need to await a general peace settlement to resolve the two other claims mentioned in paragraph 11(1). This view was shared by Gordon R. Clapp, Chairman of the United Nations Economic Survey Mission for the Middle East, who argued that '[t]he Israeli Government should be urged to agree to the principle that payment of compensation for abandoned property (both movable and immovable) should be separate from a general peace settlement with the Arab states'.[108]

Nothing in the wording of Resolution 194 or its drafting history suggests that anything other than property loss or damage should be compensated. Damages for emotional suffering, death or physical injury for instance were not mentioned in paragraph 11(1). As for property, there is no justification in international law for a distinction between land and other property or between movable and immovable property. According to Contini, '[n]o such distinction was made in the resolution, and it was clearly the intention of the General Assembly that non-returning refugees should be compensated for whatever property they have left behind'.[109] This is particularly significant in the case of Palestinian refugees, as the majority were not landowners.[110] In addition, the majority of landowners were members of the Palestinian bourgeoisie. Had compensation been restricted to this class of individuals, the neediest refugees would have been left without any remedies for their displacement and their loss. The word 'property' in paragraph 11(1) thus refers to the loss of any property, which could include cattle, bank accounts, dwellings and lands.

Regarding the 'Governments or authorities responsible' for compensating refugees, Resolution 194 does not explicitly name any states. However, as discussed earlier, compensation should be provided in cases where property was confiscated by the State of Israel, or damaged by acts of pillage and wanton destruction, unwarranted by military necessity. In both cases, the claims for compensation arise out of actions which are directly attributable to the State of

Israel. Nothing in the various reports and working papers on the interpretation of paragraph 11(1) of Resolution 194 which were issued by the UNCCP suggest that the drafters expected the international community or states, other than Israel, to compensate refugees for their losses. Arab states may still have to compensate Israel for claims arising out of ordinary war damages. However, as mentioned earlier, this category of claims was not included in paragraph 11(1) of Resolution 194. Although there are no documents supporting this interpretation, this author's view is that paragraph 11(1) does not mention any specific Government because at the time this paragraph was drafted (i.e. in December 1948), Israel was still at war with neighbouring Arab countries and the outcome of that war was uncertain. Israel may well have lost that war, in which case Arab countries would have had to provide Jewish refugees who were residing in Palestine during the hostilities compensation for loss of or damage to their property. This interpretation may also explain why the drafters of paragraph 11(1) intended the word 'refugees' to include both Arabs and Jews, provided they had been displaced from their homes in Palestine.[111]

Unlike Resolution 181 which called for 'full compensation' in cases of land expropriation,[112] paragraph 11(1) does not refer to a specific standard of compensation. On the other hand, in his Progress Report to the General Assembly, Bernadotte favoured the standard of 'adequate compensation'.[113] The American, Columbian and Guatemalan drafts of paragraph 11(1) also referred to 'adequate compensation'.[114] In the final text of paragraph 11(1), the General Assembly opted, however, to drop the word 'adequate' as applied to the concept of compensation. This may indicate that the General Assembly was either in favour of 'full compensation' or uncertain about the applicable standard of compensation and chose to leave it to the UNCCP and the various Governments or authorities responsible to agree on a method of valuation, which would have to be based on 'principles of international law' or 'equity'.

2.3.3.3 *Significance of Resolution 194*

Seventy-five years after its adoption in December 1948, UN General Assembly Resolution 194 continues to be one of the most cited resolutions in support of the Palestinian refugees' rights to return, restitution and compensation. It is important to note that Resolution 194 was not intended to declare new rules of international law but rather to affirm existing ones. In fact, in his last Progress Report, UN Mediator Bernadotte called on the General Assembly to *affirm* and make effective the rights of displaced people,[115] rather than to declare these rights. This presupposes that these rights (return, restitution and compensation) were already well grounded in international law and were simply reiterated in Resolution 194. As discussed in this chapter, acts of destruction, pillage or confiscation of private property were already prohibited under existing norms of international law in 1948, namely the 1907 Hague Regulations. As such, violations of these Regulations created obligations on Israel to provide reparation (in the form of restitution and/or compensation) to land and property owners even before Resolution 194 was adopted. With regard to the right to compensation, Resolution 194 additionally attributes that right to 'principles of international law or [...] equity', thus making clear, as Luke T. Lee has argued, that the General Assembly was restating pre-existing law or equity.[116] Repeated and near unanimous reaffirmations of this resolution every year since 1948 have further strengthened the legal validity of refugees' rights.[117] According to Luke T. Lee, '[when] a resolution restates existing international law, [as is the case of Resolution 194] its binding legal force on member states rests not on the resolution, but on the declared law. The law binds all states, whether or not they have voted for that resolution'.[118] Israel is thus bound, by virtue of principles of international law restated in Resolution 194, to restitute the property of Palestinian refugees and provide compensation for damage to, or loss of, property.

According to the UN Committee on the Exercise of the Inalienable Rights of the Palestinian People, Israel's binding obligations towards Palestinian refugees flowed also from 'its specific undertaking, when applying for membership of the United Nations, to implement General Assembly resolutions 181 (II) of 29 November 1947, safeguarding the rights of the Palestinian Arabs inside Israel, and 194 (III) of 11 December 1948, concerning the right of Palestinian refugees to return to their homes or to choose compensation for their property'.[119] The Committee added that this undertaking was clearly reflected in General Assembly Resolution 273 (III), by which the General Assembly admitted Israel to membership in the UN.[120] In addition to recalling Resolution 181 and 194 in the text of Resolution 273 (III), the General Assembly took note of the declarations and explanations made by the representatives of the Government of Israel before the Ad Hoc Political Committee in respect of the implementation of these resolutions. In its declarations, Israel reiterated its views that the refugee problem was a direct consequence of the Arab-initiated war on Israel.[121] Arab states were thus entirely responsible for creating that problem. Israel also conditioned any solution to that problem on reaching a final settlement to the Israeli–Arab conflict. It also favoured the resettlement of Palestinian refugees in neighbouring Arab states over their return to Israel, though it 'did not exclude the possibility of a measure of repatriation'.[122] Furthermore, the Israeli Government announced 'its acceptance of obligations to make compensation for abandoned lands'.[123] It finally noted that the prolongation of the refugees' distress without 'alleviation and final settlement undermined the stability of the Middle East [...]'.[124]

Throughout the years, the General Assembly continued to reiterate the rights of Palestinian refugees to return, restitution and compensation. In the aftermath of the 1967 War, which caused a second wave of displacement of Palestinians from the West Bank and Gaza Strip, the United Nations began dealing separately with the right of return of the 1948 refugees and of the group displaced as a result of the 1967 war. On 14 June 1967, the Security Council adopted Resolution 237, which called upon Israel to 'facilitate the return of those inhabitants who have fled the areas since the outbreak of hostilities'.[125] General Assembly Resolution 2452 of 1968 recalled Resolution 237 in Section A on the 1967 displaced, while Section B of that resolution noted '*with deep regret* that repatriation or compensation of the refugees as provided for in paragraph 11 of General Assembly resolution 194 (III) has not been effected' and requested that the UNCCP continue its efforts towards the implementation of that paragraph.[126] Two additional Security Council resolutions, Resolutions 242 and 338,[127] were adopted in the aftermath of the 1967 war and the 1973 war, respectively, though they did not explicitly refer to Resolution 194. Resolution 242 affirmed 'the necessity [f]or achieving a just settlement to the refugee problem' while Resolution 338 simply called on parties to initiate negotiations aimed at achieving a 'just and durable peace in the Middle East' and to implement Resolution 242 in all its parts. Arguably, a just settlement to the refugee problem would have to conform to principles of international law and UN resolutions, including Resolution 194, all of which support the Palestinian refugees' rights to the restitution of their property and to receive compensation for loss of, or damage to property. In fact, at least since 1981, the General Assembly has annually adopted resolutions which specifically call for the protection of the rights, property and interests of the Palestinian refugees.[128] For instance, in the most recent resolution on Palestinian refugee property, the General Assembly reaffirmed that the 'Palestine refugees are entitled to their property and to the income derived therefrom, in conformity with the principles of equity and justice' and requested 'the Secretary-General to take all appropriate steps, in consultation with the United Nations Conciliation Commission for Palestine, for the protection of Arab property, assets and property rights in Israel'.[129] This resolution was passed by an overwhelming majority of State members (163 votes in favour, 5 against and 9 abstentions), thus confirming the broad international support for Palestinian refugees' property rights and interests. The five states which voted against the resolution were Canada, Israel, Micronesia (Federated States of), Nauru and the United States of America.

2.3.4 Palestinian refugees' property rights under human rights law

In a recent resolution pertaining to Palestinian Refugee Property, the General Assembly recalled 'that the Universal Declaration of Human Rights and the principles of international law uphold the principle that no one shall be arbitrarily deprived of his or her property'.[130] International human rights law can thus provide an additional basis for Palestinian refugee property claims in Israel. The main obstacle to a rights-based approach to these claims is the inter-temporal rule, which precludes the application of modern norms of international law to events which occurred several decades ago. Modern human rights treaties, such as the 1965 Convention on the Elimination of Racial Discrimination (CERD),[131] which include provisions protecting property rights either did not exist or were not binding on Israel in the 1940s and 1950s, when Palestinians were displaced from their homes or when Israel adopted legislation confiscating their property. The right to property and adequate housing, in particular, has only gained significance and broader appeal in the early 2000s. According to Scott Leckie, one of the world's leading global housing, land and property rights experts:

> By rapidly increasing measure, it has been accepted, and even now considered in many settings to constitute the normative baseline, for the displaced to not simply be entitled to return to their countries or be allowed some form of temporary humanitarian access to their original homes, but to have a legally enforceable right to return to, recover, repossess, re-assert control over and reside in, the homes and lands they had earlier fled or from which they had been displaced; the implementation of the process of *restitutio in integrum*. [...] [T]he emergence of [the right to housing and property restitution] as a core human rights issue for refugees and IDPs is now abundantly clear.[132]

The argument that binding norms of human rights pertaining to property were violated by Israel in 1948–50 is therefore tenuous. The only two provisions on return and property rights in international human rights law that existed at that time were Article 13 of the *Universal Declaration of Human Rights* (UDHR), which provides that '[E]veryone has the right to leave any country, including his own, and to return to his country' and Article 17(2) which stipulates that '[N]o one shall be arbitrarily deprived of his property'. The UDHR was adopted by the UN General Assembly on 10 December 1948,[133] several months after the creation of the State of Israel, but well before Israel adopted the Law on Return and the Absentee Property Law of 1950, barring the refugees' return and expropriating their property. There are no signatories, however, to the UDHR and it is not considered a source of binding obligations under international law.[134]

Although it would be difficult to establish that Israel's expropriation of property in the 1950s violated binding norms of human rights law, this does not render this body of international law irrelevant to a discussion of Palestinian refugee rights. Notwithstanding the application of the inter-temporal rule, UN studies, Human Rights Organizations and legal scholars, have argued that the rights of Palestinian refugees to return to their homes and receive compensation for their losses are based on and strengthened by norms of international human rights law enunciated in modern treaties.[135] The articles most-often cited in support of the rights of Palestinian refugees are the following:

Artticle 13 of the UDHR:
Everyone has the right to leave any country, including his own, and to return to his country.

Article 17 of the UDHR:
1. Everyone has the right to own property alone as well as in association with others.
2. No one shall arbitrarily be deprived of his property.

Article 12(4) of the ICCPR:[136]
No one shall be arbitrarily deprived of the right to enter his own country.

Article 5 of CERD:
[…]State Parties undertake to prohibit and to eliminate racial discrimination in all its forms and to guarantee the right of everyone, without distinction as to race, colour, or national or ethnic origin, to equality before the law, notably in the enjoyment of the following […](**d**)civil rights, in particular: (**ii**) the right to leave any country, including one's own, and to return to one's country; […](**v**) the right to own property alone as well as in association with others.

In an implicit criticism of the discriminatory nature of the Israeli Law of Return, the Committee on the Elimination of Racial Discrimination expressed its concern about 'the denial of the right of many Palestinians to return and repossess their land in Israel' (Article 5(d)(ii) and (v) of CERD) and urged the State of Israel 'to assure equality in the right to return to one's country and in the possession of property'.[137] More recently, in its report on Israel's Apartheid against Palestinians, Amnesty International affirms that Israel continues to deny Palestinian refugees 'their right to return to their former places of residence and property – a right, which has been widely recognized under international human rights law'.[138] Likewise, Human Rights Watch also invokes Article 12(4) of the ICCPR in support of Palestinian refugees' right to return to their homes.[139] These statements and studies demonstrate that the international community considers Palestinian refugee rights to be supported and strengthened by modern norms of international human rights law.

2.4 Consequences of an internationally wrongful act

Based on an analysis of various areas of international law and UN resolutions, this chapter demonstrated that the expropriation of Palestinian refugee property was a wrongful act attributable to the State of Israel. In the *Factory at Chorzow* case, the Permanent Court of International Justice enunciated the general obligation flowing from the commission of an internationally wrongful act: 'It is a principle of international law that the breach of an engagement involves an obligation to make reparation in an adequate form'.[140] The obligation to provide reparation was reiterated in Article 31 of the ILC Articles and Principle 15 of the Guidelines on Reparation. Therefore, Israel, as the responsible State, is under an obligation to make full reparation to Palestinian refugees for the damages they have incurred as a result of their dispossession. The question remains, however, as to whom this obligation is owed? Can individuals have a right to reparation, or is this right reserved to States only?

According to Article 33(1) of the ILC Articles, the obligations of a responsible state arising under the ILC Articles 'may be owed to another State, to several States, or the international community as a whole'[141] but not to individuals. The Commentary to Article 33(1) provides additional clarification on the scope of a responsible state's obligations. According to the Commentary, even when an obligation of reparation exists towards other states, reparation may still accrue to the individual's benefit. For instance, if a state breaches an obligation under a treaty concerning the protection of human rights, its responsibility may exist towards all the other parties to the treaty, but the individuals concerned remain the ultimate beneficiaries and, in that sense, the holders of the relevant rights.[142]

Thus, the ILC Articles only address the possibility for individuals to have a right to reparation in an incidental way, as beneficiaries of a responsible state's obligation towards another state or states. The Articles do not, however, affect 'any right, arising from the international responsibility of a State, which may accrue directly to any person or entity other than a State'.[143] An individual right to reparation could arise, for instance, where the primary obligation is owed to the individual, such as under human rights treaties, and the treaty provides for a mechanism which enables the individual to invoke the responsibility of the state on its account and without the intermediary of any state.[144] The ILC Articles thus leave the door open for the primary rule to determine whether individuals or non-state actors are able to invoke responsibility on their account. The Articles themselves do not, however, address the possibility for individuals or non-state entities to invoke responsibility without the intermediary of a state. The ILC was thus criticized for favouring expediency over comprehensiveness. According to Professor of International Law, Edith B. Weiss, 'by largely ignoring the growing and significant international practice in which individuals and nonstate entities are invoking state responsibility, the Commission produced articles that, however noteworthy, are to some extent out-of-date at their inception'.[145]

As the ILC Articles were being drafted in the early 1990s, the UN Subcommission on Human Rights (then the UN Subcommission on Prevention of Discrimination and Protection of Human Rights) appointed Professor Theo van Boven and charged him with drafting guiding principles on the right to restitution, compensation and rehabilitation of gross violations of human rights and fundamental freedoms. Several drafts of the guidelines were presented before the *Basic Principles and Guidelines on the Right to Remedy and Reparation*[146] were adopted on 19 April 2005 by the sixty-first session of the United Nations Commission on Human Rights.[147] Although there are many similarities with the reparation provisions of the ILC Articles,[148] unlike these Articles, the Guidelines on Reparation provide victims of gross violations of international human rights law and serious violations of humanitarian law with an individual right to reparation.[149] To sum up, in theory and as a matter of substantive rights, individuals and/or their representative state are entitled to reparation either under the law on state responsibility or under primary obligations included in more modern human rights instruments. In practice, however, the remedies available to individual victims will depend on the procedural means by which they, or the State representing them, can bring claims for reparation against the state responsible for an internationally wrongful act. In the case of the Palestinian refugees, it would be essential to determine whether there is a forum, either domestic or international, which would have the jurisdiction and the capacity to handle hundreds of thousands, if not millions, of claims pertaining to property losses arising in the late 1940s and early 1950s. These claims may either be espoused by a state or brought forth by individuals. The different possibilities for the invocation of the responsibility of the State of Israel for loss of or damage to Palestinian refugee property will be the subject of the next chapter.

2.5 Conclusion

The aim of this chapter was to define the grounds in international law for the Palestinian refugees' right to reparation for loss of or damage to private property. This chapter demonstrated that measures taken by Israel against Palestinian refugee property constituted an internationally wrongful act, for which Israel is responsible. As such, Israel is under an obligation to provide reparation for the injury caused by its unlawful destruction and expropriation of Palestinian refugee property. The forms of reparation for private property losses will be explored in detail in Chapter 4.

The fact that Israel has an obligation under international law to provide reparations to refugees for their losses does not necessarily mean that it will comply with this obligation. Israel may possibly deny that it has committed any breaches of international law in the first place. As discussed in this chapter, Israel may use the inter-temporal rule to reject the retroactive application of modern norms of human rights law to events which took place in 1948–50. Israel can also challenge the application of some of the provisions of the 1907 Hague Regulations (Articles 46, 47 and 56) prohibiting the pillage and destruction of property on the grounds that these provisions only apply in occupied territories. As such, they are inapplicable within Israel's *de facto* pre-1967 borders. In spite of these challenges, this chapter has demonstrated that it can still be argued that Israel has breached norms of international humanitarian law (namely Articles 23(g) and 28 of the 1907 Hague Regulations) as well as UN resolutions. Israel has also misused the doctrine on enemy property to mask the unlawful expropriation of Palestinian refugee property. Having established that Israel has an obligation to provide reparations to Palestinian refugees for the destruction and confiscation of their property, the next chapter will look at the different legal avenues which can be used by Palestinian refugees to invoke that right.

3

Invoking the right to reparation: Is there a forum for Palestinian refugee property claims?

3.1 Introduction

In the 1990s, there was a strong drive to hold state and non-state actors (such as individuals and corporations) accountable for crimes under international law. Two ad hoc tribunals, the International Criminal Tribunal for the former Yugoslavia and the International Criminal Tribunal for Rwanda were set up to prosecute persons responsible for genocide and other serious violations of international humanitarian law.[1] The Rome Statute of 1998 established the International Criminal Court and empowered it to try persons for serious crimes such as genocide, crimes against humanity and war crimes.[2] Domestic courts also played a role in the prosecution of war criminals.[3] Individual perpetrators of war crimes were not the only ones being called upon to answer for violating the law. German corporations, Swiss banks and insurance companies also faced the threat of litigation in US courts for their involvement in crimes committed against Jewish victims of the Holocaust.[4] Other reparation movements included the Japanese–American internees' claims against the US government[5] and the Black reparation movement for slavery.[6] Reparation for property losses was also the subject matter of several claims on both sides of the Atlantic. In Europe, the fall of the Berlin Wall opened the door for claims against communist-era property expropriations,[7] while negotiations aimed at restoring indigenous land rights were pursued in North America and elsewhere.[8]

For Palestinian refugees, however, the 1990s was the decade of false hopes and shattered dreams. Despite the initiation of Israeli–Palestinian negotiations in 1993, Palestinian refugee property claims remained unresolved.[9] The aim of this chapter is to draw lessons from other reparation movements in order to identify the advantages and disadvantages of the different legal avenues which were used by victims, or States, to invoke a right to reparation and, more importantly, to assess whether any of these options are available for Palestinian refugees. The first section of this chapter will look at the possibility of invoking a right to reparation before domestic courts. Drawing lessons mainly from the 1990s' Holocaust restitution movement in US courts, the section will argue that there are several procedural barriers and disadvantages to pursuing litigation in the case of Palestinian refugee property claims. This section will also outline some of the limited advantages of filing lawsuits for reparation. The second section will explore the International Court of Justice's potential role in the resolution of Palestinian refugee property claims. Finally, the last section of this chapter will identify the main features of collective claims mechanisms as the most suitable option for the resolution of Palestinian refugee property claims.

3.2 Invoking a right to reparation before domestic courts

On 3 October 1996, the Weisshaus lawsuit, a class action lawsuit against Swiss banks filed in a New York federal court, marked the beginning of the Holocaust restitution movement in the United States.[10] Three lawsuits later, the Swiss banks succumbed to the pressure and decided to come to the bargaining table in the summer of 1998.[11] Faced with additional lawsuits in California and after several months of negotiations, the Swiss banks finally agreed to settle for $1.25 billion dollars on 13 August 1998: 'at that time, the largest settlement of a human rights case in U.S. history'.[12] Meanwhile, German corporations were also being dragged to US courts by plaintiffs demanding compensation for their slave labour during the Nazi era. After close to sixty lawsuits were filed against more than twenty different German and Austrian firms for their exploitation of slave labour during the Second World War, at the initiative of German Chancellor Gerhard Schroeder, the German Economy Foundation Initiative, also known as 'Remembrance, Responsibility and the Future', was set up on 16 February 1999.[13] In return for 'legal peace', in other words, a guarantee that all German companies, including foreign affiliates and parent companies will be protected against lawsuits relating to the Nazi era,[14] the Foundation Initiative member companies assumed 'moral responsibility' on behalf of the German industry.[15] No admission of legal responsibility was ever made by the Foundation's members, in part because many of these member companies did not even exist at the time of the war and because an admission of this kind would have granted ample justification for legal action against these corporations.[16] Soon thereafter, the Austrian government and corporations followed suit and established the Austrian Fund for Reconciliation, Peace and Cooperation in November 2000.[17] The Fund was modelled on the German Foundation, and similarly, no acknowledgement of legal responsibility was ever issued by either the Austrian government or the corporations.[18]

The apparent successes of the Holocaust reparation movement in the States gave impetus to other reparation movements.[19] Even Palestinian refugees, who were at the time commemorating the fiftieth anniversary of the Nakba, sought inspiration in the successes of that movement.[20] In 2000, a Council for Palestinian Restitution and Repatriation (CPRR) was established in Washington with the aim of achieving some form of redress for Palestinian refugees.[21] For reasons unknown to the author, CPRR's existence was short-lived and amounted to naught. However, had such an organization been able to gather the support, funds and expertise necessary to mount a litigation campaign in the United States, modelled on the Holocaust restitution movement, would it have succeeded? In other words, is the litigation model a good one for Palestinians? More importantly, were the settlements solely the result of a successful litigation campaign, or were they the result of a unique set of circumstances which are unlikely to be repeated? This section will identify the pros and cons of the litigation model with the aim of determining if this model should be pursued by Palestinian refugees and, if so, for what purposes. The analysis will draw lessons mainly from the Holocaust restitution movement and other reparation movements in the United States. The reason for focusing on US courts is threefold: first, arguably the most successful and oft-cited precedent for the litigation model is the Holocaust restitution lawsuits; second, according to Professor Michael Bazyler, a leading authority on the use of American and European courts to redress genocide and other historical wrongs,[22] the American system of justice presents unique features which make the United States the most attractive, if not the *only* forum for cases involving foreign defendants and human rights abuses committed in foreign lands. Bazyler identified these unique features as follows:

1. The ability of foreign citizens to file suit in the United States for human rights abuses committed in foreign lands.
2. The recognition of jurisdiction over foreign defendants that do business in the United States, even over claims that occurred abroad.
3. The recognition of class action lawsuits.
4. The ability of lawyers to take cases on a contingency basis [...]

5. A legal culture in which lawyers are willing to take high-risk cases with a low probability of success, in order to test the limits of the law.
6. Fixed and affordable court filing fees when filing a civil lawsuit.
7. The ability to have a jury trial in civil litigation.
8. The existence of an independent judiciary that does not take 'marching orders' from the political branches of government.[23]

A third reason has more to do with the practicalities of enforcing a judgement, assuming a court in the US awards damages to Palestinian refugees and, even more unlikely, that it has the jurisdiction to issue and enforce such an award against the State of Israel or Israeli corporations. The United States is Israel's main export market and, as such, there is a considerable number of assets in the United States which could be seized to satisfy an award for compensation. For these reasons, the analysis will focus mainly on reparation cases brought before US courts.

3.2.1 The Holocaust restitution movement: A case apart

The prevalent image of the Holocaust restitution movement is that of lawyers in the US mounting successful class action lawsuits against Swiss banks and German corporations, which eventually force the defendants to agree to an out-of-court settlement. This is not, however, the entire picture. In August 1998, when the Swiss banks agreed to a settlement, and almost two years after the first lawsuits were filed against them, none of the cases had yet proceeded to trial. Defence lawyers filed motions to dismiss the suits on procedural grounds,[24] while plaintiffs argued that the suits should be allowed to proceed to trial. On 1 August 1997, after hearing the oral arguments on the Swiss Bank defendants' motions to dismiss or stay, instead of ruling on the motions, Judge Korman stalled the decisions. Hence, none of these cases ever made it to trial, and there was no ruling on the merits. Arguably, had the cases been allowed to proceed to trial, they would have failed on procedural and jurisdictional grounds. The inherent weaknesses of these claims began to surface by the time lawsuits were filed against German companies. On 13 September 1999, the Holocaust restitution movement suffered its first legal defeat when five slave-labour lawsuits were dismissed by federal judges sitting in New Jersey.[25] According to Law Professor Michael Bazyler, 'the two New Jersey federal judges did what Judge Korman declined to do: they examined the legal arguments made by both sides and ruled that the slave-labour lawsuits – and by implications every other Holocaust-era restitution suit – could not be adjudicated in the United States.'[26] The judges' reasoning in those cases was that reparations remained the province of government-to-government negotiations and fell outside the purview of domestic courts.[27] Hence, one of the first strategies deployed during the Holocaust restitution litigation movement was the stalling tactic of Judge Korman. According to Bazyler, had the judges not dismissed the lawsuits brought against German corporations 'but waited, like Judge Korman for the parties to reach a settlement, the eventual settlement amount could have been higher, and more money would have been available to the survivors'.[28]

Judge Korman's stalling tactics were not the only factors which contributed to the success of the litigation campaign and Nazi-era settlements. Morris Ratner and Caryn Becker, two lead counsels for Holocaust survivors and heirs in many Holocaust-era class action lawsuits, identified additional factors. These were European guilt at the turn of the century,[29] support of the US government[30] and media attention as well as regulatory pressure and threatened legislation.[31] Considering the long-standing bias of the US government and American media in favour of Israel,[32] it is unlikely that they would side with Palestinian refugees should they launch a reparation campaign against Israel. At the time of writing, the United States has given Israel the diplomatic cover to undertake a genocidal campaign against Palestinians in Gaza.[33] The Center for Constitutional Rights in the United States has filed a lawsuit against President Biden and other US officials for complicity in Israel's genocide of Palestinians in Gaza. The government's initial response argued that the court cannot review its policy choices and that Israel is causing the plaintiffs' injuries as an 'independent actor'. The case is ongoing.[34]

As for the regulatory pressure, at the behest of Comptroller Alan Hevesi, the chief financial officer of New York City, the Swiss banks did face the threat of financial sanctions in several states which, if imposed, would have led to colossal losses.[35] As argued by Bazyler, several factors contributed to the success of Hevesi's sanctions: they were aimed against private enterprises, not a government; they were threatened for the single limited purpose of affecting the outcome of a lawsuit; they were endorsed by high-ranked officials in various states and, if used, would have damaged the capacity of the banks to conduct business in the United States.[36] Since sanctions were used against Swiss banks, the US Supreme Court has, however, rendered a decision in 2000 severely limiting the power of states and local officials to issue them.[37] Notwithstanding this decision, as of 2024, thirty-eight states have passed bills and executive orders designed to discourage boycotts of Israel, which would make the imposition of sanctions on companies doing business with Israel even more challenging. Hence, the circumstances which contributed to the success of the campaign against the Swiss banks were unique. Judge Korman's manipulative tactics cannot easily be matched, while Hevesi's 'rolling sanctions' are unlikely to be rolled out against corporations doing business in Israel, at least not in the immediate future. The more likely scenario is that the judges will dismiss the claims on procedural grounds.

3.2.2 Facing the jurisdictional barriers: Do the property claims of Palestinian refugees stand a chance?

As discussed in the previous section, the success of the Holocaust restitution movement was owed to events and circumstances which took place outside the courtroom. As such, it can hardly be considered a 'legal precedent'. On the contrary, as Law Professor Roy L. Brooks stated in his comprehensive study of Black reparations, the Holocaust litigation precedent demonstrates 'an unmistakable judicial indisposition towards lawsuits that seek redress for past injustices. In the absence of special legislation or settlement, these lawsuits have been dismissed before the judge has had an opportunity to consider the merits of the claims at trial [...]. Every slave-redress lawsuit that has been decided thus far has met with a similar fate'.[38] These precedents essentially suggest that when cases pertaining to events which occurred in a distant past, and at times on foreign soil, are filed before domestic courts, they are likely to get dismissed on procedural grounds. There are a number of grounds which can, either separately or jointly, lead to the failure of these types of claims. Individual claims can, for instance, be precluded by a peace settlement. Slave-labour lawsuits against German corporations were, in fact, dismissed by US federal courts on the ground that the various treaties signed between post-war Germany and the Allied powers precluded individual private litigation.[39] According to Law Professor Rudolf Dolzer,

> The practice of subsuming war-related claims within the process of reparation, and thus not allowing the individual resolution of such claims by national courts, had a two-fold basis. First, it was consistent with the broader classical rules of international law under which aliens must have their claims, whether arising from wartime or peacetime events, protected by their home countries. Second, it reflected the practical necessities of peacemaking as the presence of claims controlled by individuals would further complicate the always difficult process of international peace negotiations.[40]

An 'end of claims clause' is thus likely to be included in any final settlement with the Palestinians in order to shield Israel from any further individual claims before national courts. According to the EU Non-Paper prepared by the EU Special Representative to the Middle East Process, Ambassador Moratinos, after consultations with the Israeli and Palestinian negotiators present at the Taba Talks of 2001, the 'issue of the end of claims was in fact discussed, and it was suggested that the implementation of the agreement shall constitute a complete and final implementation of UNGAR 194 and therefore ends all claims'.[41] Should such a clause be incorporated in a final peace agreement between Israel and Palestinians, domestic courts could use it to dismiss individual claims by Palestinian refugees. Until the parties reach a final peace agreement, the claims of Palestinian refugees can be dismissed on other grounds, as will be demonstrated in this section.

The doctrine of sovereign immunity is the primary ground for the dismissal of claims against a State before the domestic courts of another. In the words of Lord Denning, 'The doctrine of sovereign immunity is based on international law. It is one of the rules of international law that a sovereign state should not be impleaded in the courts of another sovereign state against its will.'[42] The doctrine of state immunity is premised on the sovereign equality of states. Traditionally, the doctrine was defined as a complete exemption from the jurisdiction of the courts of another state (i.e. absolute immunity). In recent years, a more restrictive interpretation of the doctrine was endorsed by EU, United States and UK legislation.[43] Additionally, in December 2004, the UNGA endorsed the principle of restrictive immunity by adopting the United Nations Convention on Jurisdictional Immunities of States and their Property (JISP).[44] According to the principle of restrictive immunity, there are some exceptional cases which would preclude a state from invoking immunity from the jurisdiction of another state's municipal courts.[45] Since these limited exceptions to state immunity relate mainly to transactions of a commercial nature, they would not prevent the State of Israel from claiming immunity from the jurisdiction of another state's domestic courts, should Palestinian refugees file claims for reparations for their property losses.[46] While Israel can use the doctrine of sovereign immunity to shield itself from the jurisdiction of another state's municipal courts, this immunity is only *procedural*. It does not exempt Israel from its obligations under international law to provide reparations to Palestinian refugees. It is important to distinguish, however, between the State of Israel and companies or organizations incorporated in Israel, which may have subsidiaries in other parts of the world. As with the Swiss banks and German corporations, these companies would not be able to resort to the doctrine of sovereign immunity to shield themselves from lawsuits in foreign countries. They would have to present other grounds for the dismissal of these lawsuits. The possibility of bringing claims against corporations, whether Israeli or other, for violations of international law is, however, beyond our scope, since the focus is on the State of Israel's responsibility under international law.[47]

In addition to sovereign immunity, courts may dismiss claims by individuals for reparation on the ground that individual victims lack standing to bring cases against states for violations of international law.[48] As demonstrated in Chapter 2, it was not until the Guidelines on Reparation were adopted in 2005 that victims of gross violations of international human rights law and serious violations of humanitarian law were provided with an individual right to remedies.[49] Statutes of limitations can also be used as grounds for the dismissal of claims pertaining to actions or omissions which took place several decades ago.[50] According to Roy L. Brooks, the statute of limitations was one of the main procedural obstacles to the success of slave-redress litigation in the United States.[51] The more chronologically remote the events on which the claims are based, the more likely these claims will be time barred. Additionally, when the injustice is far removed in history, it may be harder to identify a class of plaintiffs which would be entitled to recover from any settlement. This is particularly the case when the direct victims of the injustice have passed away and when the harm done was personal (physical), rather than material, as in the case of torture or slavery.[52] For instance, it would be harder to identify the direct descendants of a former slave in the United States, and to compensate them for the physical harm inflicted on their forefathers, than it would be to identify the descendants of a Jewish German refugee or a Palestinian refugee and compensate them for the property they lost when they were forced to flee in the mid- or late 1930s or 1940s.

One way to surmount these procedural barriers is to enact legislation which would overrule statutes of limitations, or other procedural impediments, and explicitly grant courts jurisdiction over claims pertaining to a very specific set of facts and a well-defined class of plaintiffs. The restitution laws adopted in Eastern Europe following the fall of the Berlin Wall present an illustration of this type of legislative creativity. In the Czech Republic, for instance, the government enacted restitution laws in the 1990s which were tailored to remedy specific cases of property expropriation.[53] According to Robert Hochstein, the Czech Republic was initially reluctant to restitute property nationalized in 1948, for fear that it would open the door for the restitution claims of the approximately three million Sudeten Germans expelled from Czechoslovakia at the end of the Second World War and who, pursuant to the Benes Decrees of 1945–6, were forced to forfeit their property to the State.[54] Eventually, the laws were passed only after the Czech government limited their scope to property confiscated under Germany's racial laws between 1939 and 1945.[55] As such, these laws effectively excluded claims of the Sudeten Germans who were expelled because of their nationality, while ensuring the restitution of Jewish property expropriated by the Nazis which had remained in the hands of the state.[56] A more famous example of a law that paved the way for the redress of a historical injustice is the 1988 Civil Liberties Act signed by former US President Ronald Reagan, in which Japanese-American interns received a formal apology in addition to financial compensation for the harm that was done to them during the Second World War.[57] Here as well, 'the bill limited redress to those Americans of Japanese ancestry who were alive on the date of the signing, a requirement inserted for a reason – to avoid a "precedent" for African Americans'.[58] These sorts of legislative developments are typically preceded by a significant historical or political event. In the case of Eastern Europe, the political and economical upheavals engendered by the fall of the Berlin Wall prompted emerging post-communist governments to repair the errors of the past. Political pressure can also be generated by the victims themselves and their supporters. It took, for instance, Japanese-Americans more than three decades to generate sufficient public and political support in favour of the 1988 Civil Liberties Act.[59] The success of the litigation model for Palestinian refugees thus hinges, in large part, on their capacity to garner sufficient economic, political and public support to effect the legislative changes necessary to remove all procedural barriers to legal action before domestic courts. Judging from the failure of the Black American Redress Movement to rally sufficient public and political support in the United States in favour of a redress Bill,[60] the challenge will not be an easy one for Palestinian refugees. Whether they decide to file suits in the United States, Israel or elsewhere,[61] Palestinian refugees and their supporters will need a dynamic leadership, a political and economic pressure strategy, time, and an unwavering and united drive to transform public opinion and force nations to revisit their past and acknowledge their guilt.

In addition to the procedural barriers outlined above, there are several disadvantages in pursuing the litigation model in the case of Palestinian refugees. First, no domestic court in the world would have the jurisdiction or the capacity to examine millions of claims.[62] Case-by-case litigation tends to function more effectively for individual claims or small class-action lawsuits. Because of the limitations of individual reparations in cases where the number of victims is large, Professor of Law Naomi Roht-Arriaza favours collective reparations in the aftermath of mass violence. According to Roht-Arriaza, such collective reparations would consist of reparations as community development, reparations as community-level acknowledgment and atonement, and reparations as preferential access.[63] She also argues that courts, domestic, regional and international, are usually ill-equipped to award collective reparations of this sort.[64] Second, if cases are filed in different jurisdictions there is a great risk that the awards will not be uniform, even when cases bear similar facts. This could lead to tension and disappointment among the refugee communities who would view these inconsistent results as yet another form of injustice.[65] Third, litigation is a costly and challenging venture. As such, better-educated and wealthier victims are more likely to access court systems than less fortunate ones. This is likely to fuel the perceived sense of inequity among the majority of the refugee population, if only the few, less needy individuals are able to file claims.[66] In fact, when UNCCP's land experts, Berncastle and Hadawi, conducted a survey in the 1960s, they discovered that about 40–50 per cent of the total value of refugee land would be distributed among less than 10 per cent of the total refugee population (the Palestinian bourgeoisie or 'effendi class') who were neither living in refugee camps, nor receiving assistance from UNRWA.[67] This indicates that large landowners constitute a small percentage of the total refugee population, and they are likely to be the only ones with the financial ability to pursue legal action. Any eventual mechanism which is set up to resolve Palestinian refugee property claims would thus have to ensure that even small owners of property receive some form of reparations commensurate with their losses. To that effect, the litigation model is more likely to enhance disparities than to achieve an equitable redistribution of wealth. Fourth, the litigation model is adversarial by nature and, as such, it is not conducive to reconciliation. The tort model can also result in an insufficient development of the historical narrative.[68] Fifth, lawsuits can raise expectations among victims while their chances of success are very limited. Legal action can also drag on for years, and time is against the ageing survivors of the Nakba. The dismissal of a lawsuit could also be misinterpreted in the court of public opinion as a case weak on merits. As such, there is a risk that an unsuccessful lawsuit could diminish public support for Palestinian refugee rights. Lastly, the tort model is susceptible to lawyer abuse, with the plaintiffs receiving only a trickle of the money, if any is awarded.[69]

3.2.3 The limited advantages of the litigation model

The tort model is not, however, entirely without merits. Writing about the Holocaust Reparations Movement of the 1990s, John Authers mentions

US civil lawsuits as one of several factors that drove Germany to agree to a substantial settlement.[70] The other factors were German internal political pressures, international civil society and external political pressure (mainly from foreign governments rather than the UN).[71] The strategic role of lawsuits was also highlighted by Georgetown Law Professor, Emma Coleman Jordan. In an analysis of the African-American Reparations movement, Coleman Jordan points out at least three arenas in which the reparations issue may be contested:

> One is the political arena. In the arena of legislation and political maneuvering, bills must be submitted for majoritarian acceptance. […] [S]uccess in the political arena requires personal and collective political activism.
>
> The second arena is legal. In this arena those wronged can bring lawsuits. […] As a lawyer, I must confess that the legal arena is probably less promising than the political arena. Although several legal precedents serve as barriers standing in the way of success in the courts, lawsuits are not, however, without value. One must simply understand their limited value.
>
> Lawsuits create the platform for the third, most important and powerful arena: the intellectual challenge to the history of racism. […] Reparations as an intellectual project is most promising because it engages us all and gives us an opportunity to challenge the idea of racism […].[72]

Filing lawsuits, even if unsuccessful, can thus be a strategy in itself. Lawsuits may not lead to a successful outcome on the merits, but they can be used to put pressure on the wrongdoing state, or on private entities associated with it, and strengthen the victims' position in an eventual negotiated settlement.[73] Looking back at the Holocaust Restitution Movement, despite the fact that the courts dismissed the lawsuits against German corporations, German negotiators clearly perceived these lawsuits as a threat and insisted on including legal peace in any settlement.[74] Legal action can also be used to raise public awareness and stimulate discussions within political and intellectual circles. In turn, a more informed public can put pressure on their democratically elected political representatives and demand the enactment of legislation on redress. The role of civil society in generating the momentum necessary for these changes must not be undermined. At the end of the Second World War, for example, Jewish advocacy organizations played a significant role in the German government's decision to initiate individual reparations. The decimated Jewish community consolidated its efforts under the banner of the Conference on Jewish Material Claims Against Germany ('Claims Conference' or 'JCC'), and the JCC became a legal signatory to the 1952 Luxembourg Agreement, which obliged the State of Germany to disburse DM 450 million to the JCC and to legislate for a national individual compensation law.[75] As argued by Andrea Armstrong, the role played by the JCC set a precedent for the participation of non-governmental groups in international state negotiations.[76] In the case of Palestinian refugees, organizations such as the International Center for Justice for Palestinians (ICJP), Adalah in Israel and Al Haq in the Occupied Palestinian Territory have already brought claims before Israeli courts or foreign courts, including the International Criminal Court to defend Palestinian rights and hold Israel accountable for violations of international law.[77] Based on the precedents discussed in this chapter, it is important to emphasize that individual lawsuits or even class actions should not be pursued with the aim of resolving millions of claims and bringing about reparation for all Palestinian refugees. They must be used as part of an overall reparation movement, with the dual objective of raising awareness and putting indirect pressure on the State of Israel. For example, lawsuits can be brought against the JNF, and its affiliated branches incorporated in the United States, UK or Canada, to highlight the JNF's discriminatory land policies and its use of tax-exempted donations to create parks, such as Canada Park, on the ruins of Palestinian villages.[78] These lawsuits can succeed in overcoming procedural barriers since they are not time barred and do not violate the principle of state immunity, because the JNF is a private entity. Lawsuits against the JNF can also raise public awareness about the Fund's state-sanctioned land policies in Israel which violate the *jus cogens* prohibition against discrimination and which, as discussed in Chapter 1, were used in the past to deny Palestinian refugees access to their land.

3.2.4 Individual claims before regional courts: The Loizidou case

Individual claims can also be brought before regional courts such as the Organization of American States (OAS), the Organization of African Unity (OAU) and the Council of Europe.[79] To enable the individual complaints mechanisms, states must become parties to the regional conventions or otherwise recognize the courts' or commissions' jurisdiction to hear individual petitions. Since Israel is not a party to any of these regional conventions, nor is it likely to consent to the jurisdiction of these bodies, none of these institutions would be able to hear the individual claims of Palestinian refugees. In addition, apart from the principle of state immunity, all other procedural obstacles and disadvantages which accompany individual claims submitted before domestic courts will also arise when similar claims are filed before regional bodies. These venues for dispute resolution will therefore not be examined in further detail.

It is nonetheless worth mentioning the European Court of Human Rights (ECtHR)'s decision in *Loizidou*,[80] which has often been cited by proponents of Palestinian refugee rights as relevant for Palestinian refugee property claims.[81] In this case, the ECtHR ruled that a Greek Cypriot refugee had retained valid title to her property in Northern Cyprus by invalidating the laws used to expropriate that property. Ms. Loizidou was a Greek-Cypriot citizen who grew up in Northern Cyprus and subsequently moved to Southern Cyprus, while retaining her property in the North. In 1974, the Turkish military intervened in Northern Cyprus. Since then, control over the island has been divided between the Government of the Republic of Cyprus in the South, with strong ties to Greece and, in the North, a Turkish Cypriot administration. Military guards continue to control the border between the two parts of Cyprus and prevent persons from crossing to the other side. In 1983, the northern administration declared itself the 'Turkish Republic of Northern Cyprus' (TRNC) and was recognized by Turkey. To date, no other state recognizes the TRNC. In 1985, the TRNC made a constitutional declaration by which all 'abandoned' property was deemed to belong to the new government. The TRNC subsequently distributed much of the property to other private persons, including Turkish Cypriots who had fled from southern Cyprus. In March 1989, Ms. Loizidou tried to cross the border along with other Greek Cypriot women. They were all arrested by Turkish Cypriot policemen and taken back to the southern Greek Cypriot area. In July of 1989, Ms. Loizidou filed an application with the European Commission of Human Rights asserting that Turkey was violating her property rights under the ECHR. The case was then referred to the ECtHR. In January 1990, Turkey accepted the ECtHR's jurisdiction and filed a preliminary objection to the jurisdiction *ratione temporis* (temporal jurisdiction) of the ECtHR.[82] Turkey argued that since Ms. Loizidou had irreversibly lost ownership of her property prior to January 1990, the ECtHR lacked jurisdiction to rule on the merits of this case. In a judgement rendered on 18 December 1996, the ECtHR dismissed Turkey's preliminary objection to the Court's temporal jurisdiction.[83] In the Court's view, since the TRNC was not recognized as a state under international law, its 1985 declaration on 'abandoned' property is not law and has no effect on the applicant's property rights.[84] Besides declaring the property 'abandoned', Turkey had no other legal grounds to expropriate the property of Greek Cypriots. Ms. Loizidou thus retained ownership of her property throughout these years, and its *de facto* expropriation constituted a wrongful act. In the Court's view, Turkey was committing a continuing violation by denying Ms. Loizidou 'total and continuous' access to her property from 1974 until the date of the judgement.[85] Owing to the continuing character of this violation ('continuing violation doctrine'), the Court had temporal jurisdiction to rule on the merits of the case.[86] The Court further dismissed Turkey's argument that Loizidou should be denied her property rights (access to the property and compensation) because her property was used to house Turkish Cypriot refugees.[87] The *Loizidou* case provided much hope to other Greek Cypriot refugees who were hoping to return to their homes and receive compensation for their losses. It also paved the way for the establishment in 2005 of the Immovable Property Commission (IPC), which provided Greek Cypriots with a mechanism to file claims for their property losses in North Cyprus.[88] Turkey had already paid Loizidou around one million euros in compensation in 2003, but it continued to deny her a right to restitution. In 2022, the Council of Europe's Committee of Ministers decided to end its 'supervision' of the execution of the ECtHR's judgement in the Loizidou case, which left her with the IPC as the only venue to enforce her claim for restitution.[89] This outcome further demonstrates the limitations of bringing individual claims for mass displacement before local and regional courts. As will be argued in Section 3.4 of this chapter mass claims tribunals, such as the IPC, provide the best venue for the resolution of refugee property claims.

3.3 Palestinian refugee claims and the International Court of Justice

The previous section of this chapter examined the main benefits and challenges of filing individual legal claims before domestic courts. The disadvantages of a case-by-case approach were highlighted, thus underscoring the need for a more appropriate legal framework to resolve mass claims. Since it began work in April 1946, the International Court of Justice (ICJ) has delivered judgements in cases and advisory opinions involving such diverse issues as territorial and maritime disputes, the legality of the use of force and the violation of consular or diplomatic rights between states.[90] It is the principal judicial organ of the United Nations and serves as 'a constant reminder to states of the availability of litigation as a means of peaceful settlement'.[91] The ICJ played a centre-stage role in the politics of the Middle East in 2004, when it issued an advisory opinion on the legality of the Wall in the Occupied Palestinian Territory.[92] It is expected to play an even more significant role in 2024 as South Africa has lodged a claim with the ICJ to examine Israel's alleged violations of its obligations under the *Convention on the Prevention and Punishment of the Crime of Genocide* in relation to Palestinians in the Gaza Strip and indicate provisional measures.[93] The Court hearing were broadcast live on 11 and 12 January 2024 and the Court has issued several provisional measures since. Public hearings on the request for an advisory opinion on the *Legal Consequences arising from the Policies and Practices of Israel in the Occupied Palestinian Territory, including East Jerusalem* also took place in February 2024 and the Court is expected to issue an advisory opinion in the summer of 2024.[94] Although the ICJ's advisory opinions are non-binding, authoritative judgements issued by courts or other legal bodies can help clarify ambiguous points in international law. While judicial interventions to obtain legal clarity might be criticized for politicizing international law, Michael Kagan argues to the contrary, observing that '[l]imiting judicial intervention does not de-politicize law; it simply surrenders the legal playing field to governments and increases the likelihood that political power rather than principle will carry the day'.[95] Can the ICJ also play any influential role in clarifying the rights of Palestinian refugees under international law and help pave the way for a resolution to their mass claims for reparations?

3.3.1 The ICJ's contentious jurisdiction and Palestinian refugees' property claims

The International Court of Justice has a dual jurisdiction.[96] It decides, in accordance with international law, disputes of a legal nature referred to it by states (jurisdiction in contentious cases). It may also render advisory opinions on legal questions submitted to it by the General Assembly and Security Council of the UN and other UN organs or specialized agencies authorized to make such a request (advisory jurisdiction). The two principal texts regulating the organization, powers and work of the Court are the UN Charter[97] and the Statute of the Court.[98] According to the Court's Statute, only States may be parties in contentious cases before the court.[99] The Court is open to use to the States Parties to the Statute (i.e. the 193 members of the UN).[100] The Court cannot, however, exercise its jurisdiction unless all the parties to the case consent to it.[101] The main obstacle to the institution of proceedings against Israel is that it has not consented to the Court's jurisdiction under Article 36(2), nor does it seem likely to grant its consent in the foreseeable future.[102] Although Israel has not consented to the ICJ's jurisdiction under Article 36(2), it may still be subject to the Court's jurisdiction under treaties it has signed. For instance, Israel is a signatory to both the 1951 Refugee Convention and the 1967 Refugee Protocol. Since Israel has not submitted any reservations to Article 38 of the Refugee Convention, which requires state parties to submit disputes relating to the interpretation of the Convention to the ICJ, Professor Susan Akram argues that Israel is subject to the ICJ's jurisdiction for Convention violations.[103] However, as stated in Chapter 2, the right to reparation of Palestinian refugees is not based on a violation of the 1951 Convention on Refugees. As such, claims for 1948 property reparations cannot be brought against Israel at the ICJ unless Israel explicitly consents to the Court's jurisdiction. As for the State of Palestine, which is considered a non-member observer state to the UN, it has consented to the jurisdiction of the Court and has deposited the following declaration in its Registry on 4 July 2018:

> 'Pursuant to Security Council Resolution 9 (1946) of 15 October 1946, which provides the conditions under which the Court shall be open to States not parties to the Statute of the International Court of Justice, adopted by virtue of its powers under Article 35 (2) of the Statute of International Court of Justice, the State of Palestine hereby declares that it accepts with immediate effect the competence of the International Court of Justice for the settlement of all disputes that may arise or that have already arisen covered by Article I of the Optional Protocol to the Vienna Convention on Diplomatic Relations Concerning the Compulsory Settlement of Disputes (1961), to which the State of Palestine acceded on 22 March 2018.
>
> In doing so, the State of Palestine declares that it accepts all the obligations of a Member of the United Nations under Article 94 of the Charter of the United Nations.'[104]

As such, the State of Palestine can bring claims against Israel for Convention violations, as South Africa has done recently. It can't rely on the ICJ though to bring a case for the right to reparation of Palestinian refugees who were displaced in 1948, as that right is not based on a violation of the 1951 Convention on Refugees and Israel has not ratified the 1899 and 1907 Hague Conventions.[105]

3.3.2 The ICJ's advisory jurisdiction and the rights of Palestinian refugees

According to Article 65 of the ICJ's Statute, the 'Court may give an advisory opinion on any legal question at the request of whatever body may be authorized by, or in accordance with the Charter of the United Nations to make such a request'. The UN Charter authorizes the General Assembly and the Security Council to refer any legal question to the ICJ.[106] It also permits other organs of the United Nations and specialized agencies, with the authorization of the General Assembly, to present requests for advisory opinions on legal questions arising within the scope of their activities.[107] In December 2003, the General Assembly submitted a request to the ICJ for an advisory opinion on the legal consequence of the construction of the Wall in the Occupied Palestinian Territory.[108] Though this was the first time the General Assembly asked the ICJ to issue an advisory opinion on a highly contentious legal issue in the Palestine–Israel conflict, the idea of resorting to the ICJ was not a novel one.

In 1947, the General Assembly constituted an Ad Hoc Committee on the Palestine Question, which in turn formed two subcommittees to recommend a solution for the future governance of Palestine. Sub-Committee 2, which was entrusted with drawing up a plan for a single Palestine state, urged the General Assembly to seek an advisory opinion from the International Court of Justice before adopting any resolution on Palestine.[109] The Sub-Committee's request for an advisory opinion was narrowly rejected by the Ad Hoc Committee.[110] The idea of resorting to the ICJ in the context of the Arab–Israeli conflict surfaced again in 1952 when Syria raised the possibility of submitting a request to the Court for an advisory opinion on a series of questions on the refugee issue.[111] Once more, the proposal failed to gather sufficient support. The idea of seeking an advisory opinion was dropped until May 1976 when the Committee on the Exercise of the Inalienable Rights of the Palestinian People submitted a report to the General Assembly, which included some significant conclusions and recommendations on the right of return.[112] The Committee proposed a two-phase programme to implement the right of return.[113] In the first phase, the Palestinians displaced in 1967 should be allowed to return to the Occupied Palestinian Territory. In preparation for the second phase, which relates to Palestinian refugees from 1948, the Committee suggested that the Security Council or the General Assembly request an advisory opinion of the ICJ, in accordance with Article 96 of the UN Charter, on certain legal aspects of the right of the Palestinians to return to their homes.[114] The Committee's report was eventually discussed by the Security Council in June 1976. A draft resolution was issued affirming 'The inalienable right of the Palestinian people to self-determination, including the right of return and the right to national independence and sovereignty in Palestine, in accordance with the Charter of the United Nations'.[115] The resolution was, however, vetoed by the US.[116] In November 1976, and again in December 1977, the General Assembly endorsed the Committee's report,[117] thereby reaffirming the right of return of the Palestinian people. Despite these endorsements, the ICJ was sidelined again and prevented from playing any role in the Israeli–Palestinian conflict.[118]

The ICJ was finally thrown into the tumultuous waters of the Middle East conflict when it issued an advisory opinion on the Wall in July 2004.[119] Professors Susan Akram and Michael Lynk have identified four main legal outcomes arising from the ICJ's Advisory Opinion on the Wall and their repercussions for the rights of Palestinian refugees.[120] First, by affirming the applicability of law to the conflict, the Court implicitly dismissed a strictly political solution to the conflict. Thus, Akram and Lynk argue that key rights of Palestinian refugees must be respected in any negotiated settlement to the Arab–Israeli conflict. Second, the Court affirmed two legal principles relevant to Palestinian refugee rights: the right to restitution of illegally expropriated property and the right to compensation for loss and damage to property.[121] Third, the Court placed an obligation on States parties to the Fourth Geneva Convention to enforce Israel's obligations under that Convention.[122] According to Akram and Lynk, this is a significant conclusion for Palestinian refugees because Article 49 of the Fourth Geneva Convention prohibits individual or mass forcible transfers and calls for the return of displaced persons to their homes, after hostilities forcing their displacement have ceased.[123] Finally, the Court ruled that all of the principal humanitarian law and human rights treaties apply in full to Israel,[124] thereby imposing substantial obligations on Israel vis-à-vis the Palestinian refugees.[125] Though it is not binding, the Wall Advisory Opinion marked a watershed in the legal history of the Israeli–Palestinian conflict. By shifting the spotlight on Israel's violations of international law, it was a source of pressure and political embarrassment for the State of Israel. The increased public support and high-level political discussions that followed the issuance of the opinion have regenerated interest in pursuing judicial action to clarify specific and fundamental legal issues that are at the core of the Israeli–Palestinian conflict. To add to these advantages, the procedure to seek an advisory opinion is relatively simple, provided there is sufficient political will on behalf of the General Assembly or the Security Council to submit a request to the ICJ.

On 30 December 2022, the General Assembly adopted UNGA Resolution 77/247 in which it requested the ICJ to give an advisory opinion on the legal consequences arising from the policies and practices of Israel in the Occupied Palestinian Territory, including East Jerusalem.[126] Public hearing will commence on 19 February 2024. It is therefore possible for the State of Palestine to eventually garner the support needed in the General Assembly to submit a request for an ICJ advisory opinion on refugee-related issues,[127] although this issue is unlikely to be prioritized while there are two pending cases related to Palestine before the ICJ. There is, however, growing momentum to hold Israel accountable for gross violations of international law and increased awareness of its historic responsibility for the ethnic cleansing of Palestinians from their ancestral land in 1948. When the time is right, the question to be referred to the ICJ for an advisory opinion would have to be carefully drafted in order to maximize the chances of getting the required majority of votes in the General Assembly. First, it would have to be drafted in neutral language in order to diffuse any concerns or criticisms about politicising the Court. As such, the Court should be asked to rule about the legal consequences of certain objective facts or to clarify the legal obligations of Israel vis-à-vis Palestinian refugees without any presumptions of Israeli wrongdoing. For example, the Court could be asked the following questions: 'What are Israel's obligations vis-à-vis Palestinian refugees?',[128] or 'Is Israel's conduct in relation to absentee property in breach of Israel's obligations under international law?' Although an ICJ advisory opinion will not provide remedies for action found to be unlawful, it has the added benefit of being a speedy and relatively inexpensive alternative to intricate contentious proceedings. It is not, however, sufficient on its own to redress past injustices. An advisory opinion can be part of a coherent strategy to affirm the rights of Palestinian refugees in international law, strengthen the negotiating position of the PLO and dismiss any political settlement of the refugee question, which would overlook these rights.

3.4 Collective settlements of mass claims

When millions of claims arising from a dispute between two or more states have to be resolved, a mechanism providing collective settlement has generally been preferred over a case-by-case approach.[129] According to Hans Das, there are three key objectives of mass claims processes, which give them an edge over a more individualistic approach.[130] First, they are aimed at providing an expeditious resolution of numerous claims. Second, when compared to protracted and expansive individual lawsuits, they offer a more cost-efficient alternative for the resolution of thousands of claims for restitution or compensation. Finally, by providing a single forum for all claimants, these processes are likely to yield more consistent outcomes with claims bearing similar facts. Collective settlements may either involve the payment of a lump sum, or the administration of claims through mass claims tribunals or a combination of both. During a 1999 conference on Palestinian refugee compensation, which was part of a series of workshops initiated by Canada to stimulate two-track diplomacy (also known as the Ottawa Process), participants found that 'a greater degree of refugee satisfaction would be generated by a regime that handles individual claims under a claims-based system, with payments made to individuals. A regime that handles per capita payments along with a collective payment paid on a lump-sum basis was seen to be more acceptable to Israeli concerns and political constraints'.[131] While making note of these considerations, the objective of this section is not to propose a detailed mechanism for the resolution of Palestinian refugee property claims, which would cater to the requirements and concerns of both Palestinians and Israelis. This section will simply identify the main features of collective settlement mechanisms, with a view to stimulating discussions among policymakers about the suitability of this option for the resolution of Palestinian refugee property claims.

There are two different means for establishing mass claims processes between states.[132] They can either be established by reaching a negotiated agreement between states or through UN Resolutions. Negotiated agreements have provided for the creation of the mixed claims commissions in Europe at the beginning of the twentieth century to oversee the exchange of minorities and the associated property claims arising from the exchange of populations between Bulgaria, Greece and Turkey.[133] More recent examples of mechanisms created pursuant to binding peace agreements include the Iran-United States Claims Tribunal (Iran-US CT)[134] and the Commission for Real Property Claims of Displaced Persons and Refugees (CRPC) in Bosnia.[135] By contrast, the United Nations Compensation Commission (UNCC) was created in 1991 by a UN Security Council Resolution[136] and was charged with processing claims and disbursing compensation for losses arising out of Iraq's invasion and occupation of Kuwait. Similarly, the Housing and Property Directorate (HPD) and the Housing and Property Claims Commission (HPCC) in Kosovo were both established pursuant to Regulation 1999/23 of the United Nations Interim Administration Mission in Kosovo (UNMIK). The Directorate was charged with providing overall direction on property rights in Kosovo, while the HPCC was charged with settling private non-commercial disputes pertaining to residential property.[137]

The main objective in setting up all of these mass claims processes was to resolve a multitude of claims in a timely and efficient manner. Yet when it came to achieving this objective, some of these processes were more successful than others. For instance, at the end of June 2005, the Iran–US CT had only been able to finalize a total of 3,936 cases,[138] which stands in stark contrast to the 2.6 million claims resolved by the UNCC in an even shorter period of time.[139] As argued by John R. Crook, agent for the United States at the Iran–US CT and former US representative to the UNCC, the explanation for these very divergent results lies mainly in the different processing methods adopted by these various commissions.[140] The Iran–US CT attempted to resolve claims on its docket using case-by-case arbitration of disputes, which eventually proved to be expensive, slow and time-consuming.[141] In fact, the Iran–US CT's processing mechanism was so inefficient that a lump sum settlement had to be concluded in 1990 to settle certain small claims pending before the Tribunal, almost nine years after its establishment and close to twelve years after the losses were incurred.[142] According to Judge Brower, who served as a full-time Judge on the Iran–US CT from 1984 to 1988, the tedious claims-processing scheme adopted by the Iran–US CT can be attributed to the circumstances behind its establishment. Since the Tribunal was the result of a negotiated compromise between Iran and the US,[143] every aspect of this Tribunal was subject to negotiations and agreements between the two parties. Brower argues that the need to ensure mutual consensus and equality between the parties on every aspect of the process stalled the adjudication of claims.[144] Despite these impediments to efficient and timely adjudication of claims, the Iran–US CT was able to resolve about 95 per cent of all the claims submitted to it by the two governments and their respective nationals. Judge Brower argues, however, that the Tribunal could not have achieved this 'astonishingly good record were it not for the fact that the Tribunal involved two nations, rather than a multitude of them; that a rather modest number of claims were filed (4,000); and that something over 2,500 of those claims have been settled between the two governments and a substantial additional number settled involving private claimants'.[145]

Despite the difficulties involved in a case-by-case arbitration of claims, in the face of a significantly higher number of potential claims than the paltry four thousand claims filed before the Iran–US CT, the claims commissions established in both Kosovo and Bosnia still opted for this method of adjudication. In Kosovo, the HPD and its judiciary affiliate, the HPCC, were established in 1999, at a time when hundreds of thousands of people had been dispossessed of their homes or were internally displaced.[146] Yet each claim filed before the HPD was individually researched. To resolve a claim, the HPD conducted interviews, verified submitted documents and, where appropriate, undertook mediation. If mediation failed, the claim was presented to the HPCC for adjudication.

Notwithstanding this intricate processing mechanism of claims, by January 2006, the HPD had decided a total of 29,160 individual claims, which was roughly 99.7 per cent of the claims filed before it.[147] A case-by-case adjudication of claims was also favoured by the CRPC in Bosnia, where the number of actual claims filed was at least ten times higher than in Kosovo.[148] A few months following Bosnia's declaration of independence in 1992, there were close to 2.6 million refugees and displaced persons.[149] It was estimated that the number of claims would be in the hundreds of thousands. Despite this potentially large number of claims, the CRPC, which was established pursuant to Annex 7 of the Dayton Agreement of 1995,[150] was granted the mandate to receive individual applications and 'decide any claims for real property in Bosnia and Herzegovina, where the property has not been sold or otherwise transferred voluntarily since 1 April 1992, and where the claimant does not now enjoy possession of that property'.[151] In 2003, the CRPC wrapped up its work and handed over its mandate to local authorities in Bosnia and Herzegovina.[152] Throughout its operation, the CRPC issued over three hundred thousand final and binding decisions concerning ownership, possession, occupancy or other property rights. It is estimated that close to one million people benefitted from the CRPC's decisions.[153]

The successful precedent established by the CRPC demonstrates that even when there is a potentially large number of claimants, it is still possible to review claims individually and provide remedies accordingly. While feasible, a case-by-case adjudication of claims remains a time-consuming process. It took the CRPC eight years to render its decisions. With over 5.9 million Palestinian refugees worldwide, more than twice as many as there were Bosnian refugees when the CRPC was established, the number of claims for property losses is also likely to be at least two times higher than it was in Bosnia and hence require over twice as many years to process, all other things being equal. It will, therefore, be up to the various parties involved in the negotiations over Palestinian refugee property rights to determine whether the level of refugee satisfaction generated by an individual adjudication of claims is likely to overcome the frustration and anguish which will ensue from a protracted process. The timeliness and efficiency of the claims-processing mechanism is particularly crucial in the case of Palestinian refugees as the events leading to their dispossession occurred seventy-five years ago. The survivors of the Nakba may not even be alive to witness the signature of a peace agreement, let alone the resolution of their property claims. Besides being time-consuming, case-by-case consideration of claims is also very costly. Sometimes, the 'institutional costs of individualized consideration – both of arbitrator and staff time and of opportunities foregone – could exceed many times over the value of the claim.'[154] All of these considerations have to be borne in mind by the parties involved in devising a suitable mechanism to resolve Palestinian refugee property claims.

For decision-makers, choosing between case-by-case arbitration and a speedier processing mechanism is essentially a choice between creating a judicial mechanism and establishing an administrative organ, with limited quasi-judicial functions. Faced with a staggering number of claims, claimants with multiple nationalities and the pressure of providing expeditious relief, the United Nations Compensation Commission (UNCC), which was established in 1991 to handle claims arising from Iraq's invasion and occupation of Kuwait, adopted rules of procedure to meet these realities. Javier Perez de Cuellar, the United Nations Secretary General at the time, described the Commission as being 'not a court or an arbitral tribunal … [but] a political organ that performs an essentially fact-funding function of examining claims, verifying their validity, evaluating losses, assessing payments and resolving disputed claims. It is only in this last respect that a quasi-judicial function may be involved'.[155] A total of 2.6 million claims were filed before the UNCC. As Crook notes, with the exception of some large claims, 'the UNCC's processes consciously abandoned the model of individualised case-by-case adjudication. […] [T]he UNCC instead emphasised identifying large groups of claimants with common characteristics and similar losses'.[156] The procedure implemented by the UNCC consisted of two main steps, which differentiated the UNCC from the claims commissions in Bosnia and Kosovo. First, individuals did not have the capacity to directly bring claims before the UNCC. Instead, claims were brought to the UNCC by states on behalf of their nationals and residents.[157] For individuals who were not in a position to have their claims filed by a government, such as stateless Palestinians who were previously residing in Iraq, international organizations were empowered to bring claims on behalf of these individuals.[158] This has been labelled 'a truly novel procedure'[159] and is a particularly significant precedent for future claims of Palestinian refugees. Second, the UNCC did not directly disburse its awards to the individual claimants. States were in charge of collecting the awards and distributing them to their respective nationals or residents.[160]

Having foregone the model of case-by-case adjudication of claims, the UNCC additionally divided all claims into six different categories designated by the letters 'A' through 'F'. These comprise four categories of claims of individuals (A to D), one for corporations (E) and one for governments and international organizations (F), which also includes claims for environmental damage.[161] Given the humanitarian urgency of claims falling under categories A to C, these claims were fast-tracked. Instead of issuing compensation awards for the exact amount of losses incurred by each individual, the UNCC awarded individual claimants a fixed sum of money for successful claims falling under categories A and B. Claims falling under these categories pertained to relatively small losses, and awards were similarly limited to modest sums of money ranging between US$2,500 and US$10,000. Approximately 930,000 claims under these categories were filed and resolved within one year of their submission. Claims under category C were more complex. They were made for damages of up to US$100,000 each and involved twenty-one different types of losses. The Commission took close to five years to resolve approximately 420,000 category C claims. All awards under categories A to C were paid in their entirety by the end of September 2000,[162] almost six years after they were submitted to the UNCC. Efficiency, however, comes at a price. When a commission adopts the model of case-by-case adjudication of claims, each individual case is evaluated on its merits, with the aim of providing 'absolute justice' to claimants. On the other hand, as Caron and Morris have argued, mass claims-processing models, such as the one used by the UNCC, offer 'practical justice': 'that is, a justice that would be swift and efficient, yet not rough'.[163] However, not all cases can be fast-tracked. Having promptly resolved the larger number of claims falling under categories A to C, the UNCC shifted its focus, during the second phase of its work, to the fewer, yet larger and more complex D, E and F claims.[164] Of these claims, only category D claims pertain to losses incurred by individuals. The most common types of losses claimed under category D are the loss of personal property, real property and the loss of income and business-related losses. However, damages claimed under this category had to exceed US$100,000 each.[165] As such, these claims called for a more assiduous review and stricter rules of procedure than claims for smaller losses falling under categories A to C.[166] The Commission's mandate ended in February 2022, nearly thirty-one years after its establishment.[167] Overall, the UNCC's administrative nature and its collective resolution of claims enabled it to provide relief to millions of claimants worldwide.[168] According to Caron and Morris, the Commission's accomplishments were unparalleled in the history of mass claims commissions.[169]

From this brief overview of the UNCC, Palestinian refugees can draw important lessons. First, when dealing with a significant number of potential claims, a case-by-case adjudication of claims may not necessarily be practicable, at least not for all claims. Palestinian refugee property claims may also be categorized. For instance, the claims of Palestinian refugees residing in refugee camps may have to be fast-tracked because of their humanitarian urgency.

These refugees' losses would not be evaluated on an individual basis. Instead, each claimant, individual or family would receive a fixed amount of money as a form of compensation for lost or damaged property. Although this solution is likely to fall short of the refugees' expectations, from a practical perspective, it may still provide a better alternative to a more just, yet lengthy and inefficient, case-by-case adjudication of claims. Case-by-case adjudication of claims may still be required for a limited number of claims pertaining to substantial losses of property. The large landowners of the 1940s in Palestine belonged to the Palestinian elite and are likely to be living in much better conditions in exile then camp dwellers. As such, their claims might not be deemed urgent on humanitarian grounds, and they may be more willing to wait for their claims to be adjudicated on an individual basis. Second, the UNCC highlighted the role that can be played by states and international organizations in the submission of claims as well as in the collection and distribution of awards. This is particularly relevant for Palestinian refugees as, by definition, they all reside outside their country of origin (historical Palestine before it was partitioned in 1947) and are either stateless or have acquired the citizenship of another state. Their country of residence or nationality may thus assist in the submission of claims on behalf of these refugees. International organizations may also assist in the submission of these claims. This two-step process allows for an initial screening of all claims by the various countries involved in this procedure before their submission to the claims commission. By weeding out inaccurate or incomplete applications, this initial screening process will reduce the number of claims filed before the commission and enable it to complete its work more promptly. The role of these third parties will not be limited to the submission of claims. Governments and organizations could also assist the commission by collecting and disbursing the awards to claimants.

On a practical level, the UNCC's accomplishments were no doubt outstanding. The UNCC has, however, been criticized for its highly political character and its absolute exclusion of Iraq from the reparation proceedings. Iraq's resounding defeat in the 1991 Gulf War removed all bargaining power it may have had to negotiate a fair deal, leaving the victorious coalition members in the UN to dictate the terms of the agreement.[170] As David Bederman's work has shown, historically, not all international claims tribunals were reciprocal in the character of the claims brought.[171] As was seen in the Iran–US CT, sometimes parity between all parties involved in the conflict can even hamper the processing of claims. Nevertheless, the UNCC's structure, composition and procedure were blatantly unfair towards Iraq. According to Bederman, most commissions were at least 'fair insofar as the real decision-making power of the tribunal was left to an ostensibly neutral arbitrator who was not a national of either of the litigants and who, moreover, was satisfactory to both parties'.[172] By contrast, Iraq had no role in choosing the individual commissioners who were to process claims brought against it. These decisions were also reviewed by the UNCC's Governing Council, which was 'the alter-ego of the Security Council which waged war against Iraq'.[173] These serious shortcomings 'call into question not only the UNCC's fairness in general, but also its validity as an example for future reparation mechanisms in similar post-war situations'.[174] Bederman argues that it is 'unlikely that a potential respondent state would agree to the type of coercive, multilateral lump-sum settlement employed by the UNCC unless it had been the subject of an international enforcement action by the United Nations'.[175] Considering the lack of political will to enforce the rights of Palestinian refugees over the course of the past seventy five years and the obstructionist role played by the US, Israel's strongest ally, in the Security Council, it is hard to foresee a mechanism, modelled on the UNCC, being imposed on Israel to resolve the claims of Palestinian refugees. Historically, a UN agency, the United Nations Conciliation Commission for Palestine (UNCCP), was instructed to 'facilitate the repatriation, resettlement and economic and social rehabilitation of the refugees and the payment of compensation [...]'.[176] The UNCCP failed to achieve this objective, and at least since the signature of the Oslo Accords in 1993, it has become apparent that any commission created to resolve Palestinian refugee property claims in the future is likely to be the result of bilateral or multilateral negotiations,[177] rather than a UN Security Council Resolution. Although a commission for Palestinian refugee property claims is likely to be established under different circumstances than the UNCC, on a practical level, the lessons learned from the UNCC's time-efficient collective processing of claims may still apply, at least with regard to claims for compensation. Claims for the restitution of property may still require case-by-case adjudication.

In addition to the different circumstances which gave rise to the establishment of the UNCC, it must also be noted that the UNCC was essentially a war reparations undertaking. As discussed in an earlier chapter, the drafters of UNGA Resolution 194 intended for war reparations to be dealt with separately from Palestinian refugees' claims for compensation.[178] As such, any commission created to resolve these claims would require a narrower mandate than that of the UNCC. In order, however, to implement Resolution 194, paragraph 11, in its entirety, the mass claims commission which would result from a peace treaty signed between Israel and the Palestinians would have to be granted the mandate to implement the twin rights of restitution and compensation. As mentioned above, the UN General Assembly intended for the UNCCP to facilitate the implementation of both rights. In this regard, the Commission for Displaced Persons and Refugees in Bosnia, subsequently renamed CRPC, provides an interesting precedent. According to Annex 7 of the Dayton Agreement, the Commission was empowered to receive claims for the 'return of the property or just compensation in lieu of return'.[179] It succeeded in rendering decisions confirming real property rights for displaced persons and refugees, which enabled these individuals to regain possession of their homes. It failed, however, to award any compensation to claimants as the Refugees and Displaced Persons Fund, which it was supposed to administer in order to settle claims for compensation, was never established because no resources were made available.[180] Any mechanism set up in the future to resolve property claims for Palestinian refugees would have to overcome the shortcomings of the CRPC and ensure that both rights, restitution and compensation, receive equal support and funding.

3.5 Conclusion

This chapter outlined the main advantages and drawbacks of a variety of fora and mechanisms which can be used, or have been used in the past, to invoke a right to reparation. The first section demonstrated the shortcomings of the litigation model for the resolution of mass claims while highlighting some of the limited advantages of this model, namely how lawsuits can be used to raise public awareness or put pressure on the wrongdoing state. The second section explored the possibility of seeking an advisory opinion from the ICJ to clarify Israel's legal obligations vis-à-vis Palestinian refugees.

Finally, the last section of this chapter identified some of the main features of collective settlement mechanisms. Compared with the other fora discussed in this chapter, mass claims tribunals seem to offer the best venue for the resolution of Palestinian refugees' property claims. According to Crook, '[m]ass claims processes work best (i) where there are large numbers of similarly situated people; (ii) who have suffered similar injuries; (iii) where some responsible organ has made an authoritative judgment that such injuries entitle the victims to compensation; and (iv) where there is an underlying political consensus and adequate resources supporting the institution and its work'.[181] Palestinian refugees are a similarly situated group of people who have suffered similar injuries. They could resort to the ICJ for an advisory opinion to get an authoritative judgement which would affirm the principles of restitution and compensation – as well as the principle of return. They may also use other fora, such as domestic courts, to raise public awareness of such rights for the Palestinians in the hope of strengthening their negotiating position and garnering sufficient public, political and financial support to implement the rights of refugees. As will be discussed in Chapter 5, peace proposals have, indeed, suggested the establishment of mass claims mechanisms for the resolution of Palestinian refugee claims. Having identified the most suitable avenue for the resolution of these claims and before delving into Israeli–Palestinian negotiations on the refugee issue, the next chapter will outline the forms of reparation for private property losses and the legal obstacles to the implementation of Palestinian refugee property rights.

Forms of reparation for private property losses and legal obstacles to the implementation of Palestinian refugees' property rights

4.1 Introduction

As discussed in the previous chapter, the 1990s was the decade of reparation. For refugees, the 1990s was also the decade of repatriation. From Mozambique,[1] to Cambodia,[2] Afghanistan[3] and Bosnia,[4] repatriation was occurring on a scale unforeseen in previous decades. It is estimated that up to 12 million refugees returned to their homes during the 1990s.[5] Refugee return became the cornerstone of several internationally negotiated peace agreements during that period and 'the *sine qua non* for reconstruction, reconciliation, and democratic government to proceed'.[6] While these agreements paved the way for hundreds of thousands of refugees to return to their homes, the ill-fated Oslo process relegated the refugee issue to final status negotiations which never materialized.[7] Palestinian refugees saw no end in sight to their exile as Israeli officials continued publicly to deny their right to return to the homes that had been theirs before 1948. During the height of the negotiations, in an interview with the Palestinian newspaper *Al-Quds* on 5 January 2001, Yossi Beilin, then Justice Minister in Ehud Barak's government, stated in unequivocal terms that 'refugees, in their large masses, will not return to their places of residence, because this is impractical and unrealistic'.[8] Demographic, ideological and legal arguments were deployed to demonstrate the impracticality, if not the absurdity, of the right of return and the restitution of refugee property.[9] It is beyond the scope of this analysis to discuss the feasibility of a massive return of refugees in terms of its impact on the State of Israel's ethnic demographic composition, economy or its use of natural resources.[10] Instead, this chapter will focus solely on the main *legal* obstacles to the implementation of Palestinian refugees' property rights.[11]

This chapter will begin by discussing the two main forms of reparation available under international law to remedy private property losses: restitution and compensation. It will demonstrate that restitution is the preferred form of reparation. Compensation is only considered a suitable alternative remedy when restitution is 'factually impossible'. The second section of this chapter will outline some of the legal issues which are likely to impede the implementation of Palestinian refugee property claims. It will argue that none of these obstacles is insurmountable.

4.2 Forms of reparation for private property losses

Before discussing the legal obstacles to the implementation of Palestinian refugees' property rights, it is important to identify the forms of reparation available following private property losses. In the *Factory at Chorzow* case, the Permanent Court of International Justice (PCIJ) declared it 'a principle of international law that the breach of an engagement involves an obligation to make reparation in an adequate form'.[12] The Court in that case had to determine the forms of reparation available for the expropriation of German factories by Poland. The Court went on to define the content of the obligation of reparation and outline the two main forms of reparation for the expropriation of property:

> reparation must, so far as possible, wipe out all the consequences of the illegal act and reestablish the situation which would, in all probability, have existed if that act had not been committed. Restitution in kind, or, if this is not possible, payment of a sum corresponding to the value which a restitution in kind would bear; the award, if need be, of damages for loss sustained which would not be covered by restitution in kind or payment in place of it – such are the principles which should serve to determine the amount of compensation due for an act contrary to international law.[13]

The PCIJ thus identified restitution and, if restitution is not possible, compensation as the two main forms of reparation awarded following an expropriation of property. As demonstrated in Chapter 2, drawing on these existing norms of international law, the General Assembly reaffirmed the twin rights of restitution and compensation in Resolution 194 and applied them specifically to expropriations of property, which accompanied the mass displacement of refugees during the 1948 Arab–Israeli war.[14] Since this resolution was adopted, there have been many developments in the law on state responsibility and reparation. This raises the question of whether the inter-temporal rule precludes the application of modern legal standards on reparation on the ground that the expropriation of Palestinian refugee property occurred in 1948.

As discussed in Chapter 2, the inter-temporal rule precludes the retroactive application of international law. The rule was enunciated first by Judge Huber in the 1928 *Island of Palmas* arbitration. This rule contains two elements. The first element of the rule stipulates that '[a] juridical fact must be appreciated in the light of the law contemporary with it, and not of the law in force at the time such dispute in regard to it arises or falls to be settled'.[15] The second element of this doctrine affects rights which have already been acquired. According to Judge Huber, 'a distinction must be made between the creation of rights and the existence of rights. The same principle which subjects the act creative of a right to the law in force at the time the right arises, demands that the existence of the right, in other words its continued manifestation, shall follow the conditions required by the evolution of law'.[16] This effectively means that rights which were acquired at the time of their creation must be maintained and interpreted according to the evolution of international law.[17] In Chapter 2, Israel's state responsibility under international law was established according to norms which prevailed at the time the wrongful act occurred – in other words when Palestinian refugee property was expropriated or damaged. Thus, Israel has an obligation to provide reparation to Palestinian refugees for the losses they have incurred. The forms of reparation available for these private property losses can, however, be defined according to norms of international law which exist at the time reparation is actually awarded to refugees. Hence, it is possible to look at modern standards of international law for guidance on the right to restitution and the right to compensation for expropriation of private property.

4.2.1 The right to restitution

Resolution 194 reaffirmed the refugees' right to return to their 'homes' and hence to repossess their property. As discussed in Chapter 2, the adoption of the ILC Articles in 2001 and the Guidelines on Reparation in 2005 confirmed, respectively, the right of a state and the right of individual victims to receive reparation following a breach of international law, gross violations of international human rights law and serious violations of humanitarian law.[18] Restitution was included among the forms of reparation available under Article

34 of the ILC Articles and under Principle 18 of the Guidelines on Reparation. These two instruments outlined some of the general rules on reparation. More specific standards pertaining to the right to property restitution of refugees and displaced persons were adopted on 11 August 2005 by the then UN Sub-Commission on the Promotion and Protection of Human Rights (UN Sub-Commission).[19] The so-called Pinheiro Principles were the culmination of a seven-year process which was initiated when the UN Sub-Commission adopted resolution 1998/26 on *Housing and Property Restitution in the Context of the Return of Refugees and Internally Displaced Persons.*[20] This resolution signalled the Sub-Commission's growing interest in restitution as a fundamental human right. In 2002, the Sub-Commission appointed Paulo Sergio Pinheiro as the Special Rapporteur on Housing and Property Restitution for Refugees and Internally Displaced Persons and entrusted him with the task of drafting guidelines on housing and property restitution.[21] A final draft was adopted in 2005. The Pinheiro Principles are not a treaty and, therefore, are not formally binding. Nevertheless, the Principles have persuasive authority and are firmly grounded within existing norms of international human rights, refugee and humanitarian law.[22] They were also inspired by national restitution policies, programmes and practices, including those developed for Afghanistan, Bosnia-Herzegovina, Cyprus, Guatemala, Kosovo, Rwanda and South Africa.[23] The Principles were designed to provide states, as well as international and national organizations, with specific policy guidelines to address the legal and technical issues surrounding the implementation of the right to housing and property restitution.[24]

Principle 2 of the Pinheiro Principles outlines the forms of reparation available to remedy property losses following displacement:

2.1   All refugees and displaced persons have the right to have restored to them any housing, land and/or property of which they were arbitrarily deprived, or to be compensated for any housing, land and/or property that is factually impossible to restore as determined by an independent, impartial tribunal.

2.2   States shall demonstrably prioritize the right to restitution as the preferred remedy for displacement and as a key element of restorative justice. The right to restitution exists as a distinct right, and is prejudiced neither by the actual return or non-return of refugees and displaced persons entitled to housing, land and property restitution.

In line with the principles of international law stated in the *Factory at Chorzow* case, this principle reaffirms restitution and compensation as the two forms of reparation used to remedy an expropriation of property. Following up also on the norms enunciated in the *Factory at Chorzow*, this principle prioritizes restitution as the preferred remedy in cases of property expropriations and presents compensation as an alternative only when restitution is 'factually impossible'. This view was endorsed by the European Court of Human Rights (ECtHR) in a few decisions, namely in the *Papamichalopoulos* case[25] and the *Loizidou* case.[26] In the *Papamichalopoulos* case, the Court found that the applicants had retained ownership, under national law, of the land to which they were denied access by the Greek government. Since this deprivation of property constituted an illegal taking, the Court favoured the restitution of the property to its rightful owners and awarded compensation for damage and loss of use of property, as well as other non-pecuniary damages.[27] As discussed in Chapter 3, in the *Loizidou* case, the ECtHR found the plaintiff had retained ownership of her land by invalidating the abandonment laws of the TRNC based on the TRNC's status under international law.[28] The Court additionally awarded compensation to Ms. Loizidou for the loss of use and enjoyment of her property as well as for non-pecuniary damages such as anguish, helplessness and frustration.[29]

The primacy of restitution was also confirmed in Article 35 of the ILC Articles which stipulates that

> A State responsible for an internationally wrongful act is under an obligation to make restitution, that is, to re-establish the situation which existed before the wrongful act was committed, provided and to the extent that restitution: (a) is not materially impossible; (b) does not involve a burden out of all proportion to the benefit deriving from restitution instead of compensation.

Recalling the principles on reparation set out in the *Factory at Chorzow* case, the ICJ reaffirmed the primacy of restitution as the required remedy for wrongful property expropriation in its Advisory Opinion on the Wall. The Court found that Israel was under an obligation to return the land, orchards and other immovable property seized from the Palestinians in order to build the illegal Wall.[30] Compensation would be considered as an alternative in the event that restitution proves to be 'materially impossible'.[31] According to Professor Michael Dumper, restitution has not only been favoured by the courts: 'In reviewing postconflict agreements, it is noteworthy, despite the difficulties involved, the extent to which the preferred option of international law – restitution is employed'.[32] Housing and property rights expert Scott Leckie argues that the formulation of housing and property restitution rights in voluntary repatriation agreements concerning refugees indicates 'the growing acceptance of norms recognizing that the right to return and voluntary repatriation includes the right to return to one's original home and lands from which they were originally displaced.'[33] In 2004, the UNHCR Executive Committee took notice of these developments and issued a conclusion addressing the importance of restitution in post-conflict refugee repatriation and reconciliation. The Executive Committee's 66 member states unanimously endorsed a statement in which they

> Recogniz[ed] that refugees, in exercising their right to return to their own country, should in principle, have the possibility to return to their place of origin, or to a place of residence of their choice, subject only to restrictions as permitted by international human rights law; and, in this context, *notes* the importance of efforts that seek to mitigate the likelihood that returning refugees could become internally displaced; [...]

> Recogniz[ed] that, in principle, all returning refugees should have the right to have restored to them or be compensated for any housing, land or property of which they were deprived in an illegal, discriminatory or arbitrary manner before or during exile; *notes*, therefore, the potential need for fair and effective restitution mechanisms, which also take into account the situation of secondary occupants of refugees' property; and also *notes* that where property cannot be restored, returning refugees should be justly and adequately compensated by the country of origin [...].[34]

Adopted in 2005, the Pinheiro Principles were thus grounded in existing norms of international law and reflected a growing trend in post-conflict agreements to recognize the right to restitution as a preferred remedy for unlawful property expropriations.

In addition to reaffirming the primacy of restitution as a remedy for displacement and dispossession, Principle 2 of the Pinheiro Principles explicitly distinguishes between a refugee's right to restitution and his or her right to choose a durable solution. The three durable solutions identified by the UNHCR are voluntary repatriation, which UNHCR promotes as the 'preferred solution, where feasible',[35] local integration and resettlement to a third country. According to Principle 2.2, the right to property restitution is not prejudiced by the refugee's actual return or non-return. This point is particularly significant in the case of Palestinian refugees. As discussed in Chapter 2, Resolution 194 does not explicitly refer to a right to restitution. The right to restitution has to be inferred from the wording in Resolution 194 paragraph 11, which provides for the return of refugees to their 'homes'. As we have seen in Chapter 2, according to the UNCCP's records, the General Assembly rejected two amendments which would have used the term 'the areas from which they have come' to replace 'homes'.[36] As such, the General Assembly clearly intended for returning refugees to repossess their homes. In the wording of Resolution 194, the two rights, return and property restitution, were intertwined. Instead of being presented as two distinct rights, property restitution was viewed as a corollary to return. Interestingly, in a memorandum submitted to the UNCPP, the Legal Adviser to the United Nations Economic Survey Mission for the Middle East, Paolo Contini refrained from linking the return of refugees to the restitution of their property. According to Contini, non-returning refugees were also entitled to the restitution of their property, though he believed that this would mostly apply to movable property – especially blocked bank accounts.[37] Hence, the lack of clarity in the wording of Resolution 194 generated the wrongful assumption that the two rights are inseparable. By contrast, Principle 2.2 draws the line between property restitution, which is a form of reparation under international law for unlawful property expropriations, and return, which is a form of restitution for displacement,[38] a distinct right under international law[39] and also one of three durable solutions available for refugees. The confusion between durable solutions and remedies, in this case voluntary repatriation and property restitution, was further aggravated by the Arab governments' and the PLO's unequivocal rejection of any durable solution for Palestinian refugees, other than return to their homes,[40] under the pretext that local integration or resettlement in a third country would negate the Palestinian refugees' right to repossess their original homes. This need not be the case. Palestinian refugees can choose *not* to return *without* losing their right to the restitution of their property.[41] In Jordan, for instance, Palestinian refugees were exceptionally granted citizenship and most have successfully integrated into Jordanian society.[42] Some of these refugees may *voluntarily choose* not to return to their homes in what is now Israel, yet they may wish to retain ownership over their ancestral home in Israel because of its personal and emotional value. In other words, the implementation of the refugees' right to property restitution need not be accompanied by the physical return of refugees to their homes. While the return to and repossession of one's original home should remain the main objective of any restitution process, restitution can be implemented in different ways depending on the specific circumstances of each conflict: 'A particular restitution process may involve a combination of return, facilitated sales of properties to which refugees voluntarily did not wish to return but which they retained rights over, and where appropriate forms and amounts of compensation were provided'.[43] There can therefore be creative ways to implement the right to restitution in the Israeli–Palestinian context. Nevertheless, it must be emphasized that, in order to conform to the Pinheiro Principles' legal standards on restitution, any prospective restitution mechanism would have to ensure that '1. Refugees and displaced persons have a *preferential* right to housing and property restitution as a legal remedy; 2. Any divergence from this should be exceptional and fully justifiable in terms of the relevant law and; 3. All refugees and displaced persons must be able to access durable solutions in conformity with their rights'.[44]

While refugees can choose property restitution as a remedy, without opting for voluntary repatriation as a durable solution, the opposite can also be true. Refugees can choose voluntarily to repatriate to their country of origin, in the case of Palestinians the historical land of Palestine from which they fled during the Nakba, without necessarily having their property restituted to them. This scenario is likely to arise in the case of Palestinians, particularly villagers. Having spent over seventy-five years in exile living in cities or urban camps, these refugees might have lost the skills to engage in agricultural labour. Their descendants may be even more eager to relocate to a city in Israel–Palestine, instead of a destroyed and unpopulated village.[45] These refugees may therefore choose voluntary repatriation as a durable solution, but elect compensation, instead of restitution, as a remedy for their property losses. There may also be instances where refugees have no other choice but to accept compensation as an alternative to restitution. As discussed above, according to precedents and existing norms of international law,[46] compensation is considered a suitable alternative remedy whenever restitution is 'factually impossible'. The difficulty, however, lies in defining when restitution is not 'factually' possible.

According to Principle 21.1 of the Pinheiro Principles, 'restitution is only deemed factually impossible in exceptional circumstances, namely when housing, land and/or property is destroyed or when it no longer exists, as determined by an independent, impartial tribunal'. The mere destruction of property does not, however, exempt it from restitution claims, nor does it preclude claimants from seeking and obtaining restitution or compensation.[47] Palestinian refugees whose homes and villages were destroyed during the 1948 war may still wish to regain possession of their property, albeit in ruins, and receive financial compensation for the damages incurred, which may eventually be used to rebuild the demolished structures.[48] The situation would be different, however, if their original land or home has been put to the use of the general public or if it generates considerable economic benefit to the area concerned.[49] Restitution would be 'factually impossible' if the land of Palestinian refugees has been transformed during their absence into an airport, a university or an industrial zone which benefits the wider public. The repossession of individual property in these circumstances is likely to generate a 'burden out of all proportion to the benefit deriving from restitution'.[50] There may also be circumstances where Palestinian refugee property has been used to house Israeli citizens. This raises the complex issue of the rights of secondary occupants and whether these rights supersede the Palestinian refugees' right to property restitution.[51] These conflicting rights and other legal obstacles to the implementation of the Palestinian refugees' right to restitution will be examined in detail at a later stage in this chapter. Suffice it at this point to state that compensation is an acceptable remedy to property expropriation only when restitution is deemed 'factually impossible' by an impartial tribunal or when those possessing restitution rights choose to receive financial compensation *in lieu* of restitution.

4.2.2 The right to compensation

In Resolution 194, paragraph 11(1), the General Assembly referred to two categories of claims only: (i) compensation claims for property of refugees not choosing to return and (ii) compensation claims for loss of or damage to property, which, under principles of international law or in equity, should be made good.[52] As discussed in Chapter 2 , since compensation for war damages was to be provided for in a peace treaty, this category of claims was intentionally excluded from paragraph 11 of Resolution 194. Additionally, claims for non-material damages were omitted from paragraph 11. The emphasis was entirely on property loss or damage, though no distinction was made between movable and immovable property. It is not uncommon, however, for regional courts and mass claims tribunals to award compensation for non-pecuniary damages.[53] In addition, paragraph 11 provided that compensation should be paid to both returning and non-returning refugees and for loss of property as well as for damage to repossessed property. As such, the General Assembly clearly perceived compensation as a complementary right, rather than as a substitute for return and restitution.[54]

To conclude, there are two forms of reparation for private property losses: restitution and compensation. They are not mutually exclusive, nor do they depend on the refugees' choice of durable solutions. According to international law, restitution remains the preferred remedy for displacement and dispossession.

When restitution is 'factually impossible' to implement, or when it is not enough on its own such as when the repossessed property has been damaged and is in need of repair, compensation in cash or in kind can either supplement restitution or substitute for it. The next section will explore some of the most significant legal obstacles to the implementation of Palestinian refugee property rights.

4.3 Legal obstacles to the implementation of Palestinian refugee property rights

Resolving the property claims of victims of mass displacement and dispossession is one of the most difficult issues arising in the aftermath of ethnic conflicts. The challenges to reparation and the restoration of property rights are compounded in protracted refugee situations. According to refugee expert Jeff Crisp, 'refugees can be regarded as being in a protracted situation when they have lived in exile for more than five years, and when they still have no immediate prospect of finding a durable solution to their plight by means of voluntary repatriation, local integration, or resettlement'.[55] The definition of protracted refugee situations is best illustrated in the case of Palestinian refugees. Over seventy-five years after their initial displacement from their homes, Palestinian refugees are still without a solution.[56] The majority of these refugees live within proximity of their homes in historical Palestine, a fact which, Abu-Sitta argues, is indicative of their strong attachment to their places of origin.[57] The lack of political will to resolve the refugee issue has unnecessarily prolonged their forced exile. Meanwhile, this lapse of time was being translated with dramatic changes inside Israel, some of which might now be deemed irreversible. As discussed in Chapter 1, before the ink had dried on the armistice agreements signed between Israel and neighbouring Arab countries in the aftermath of the 1948 war, Israel had already proceeded to install an intricate system of laws to deny Palestinian refugees access to their land, denationalize them and sever their title to their property. Changes were also occurring on the ground. Hundreds of Palestinian villages were reduced to ruins, while incoming Jewish settlers occupied the homes of Palestinian refugees.[58] The transformation of Israel's landscape and ethnic composition since 1948 has lent weight to arguments against the repatriation of Palestinian refugees and the restitution of their property.[59] The existence of abandonment laws, secondary occupants and other legal obstacles to the implementation of refugee property rights are not unique to the Palestinian refugee case, and there are many lessons to draw from other precedents on how to address these challenges.

4.3.1 Repealing laws

Dismantling the intricate web of laws used to legitimize the expropriation of refugee property along discriminatory grounds ranks among the first priorities of any process aimed at reversing the results of ethnic conflicts. Bosniaks, Serbs and Croats all adopted property laws during and in the aftermath of the Bosnian war with the aim of furthering ethnic cleansing.[60] Property belonging to ethnic minorities displaced during the war was declared abandoned by wartime regimes and used to settle displaced persons belonging to the majority ethnic group.[61] According to Cox and Garlick, the reallocation of property was initially declared as a temporary humanitarian measure aimed at reducing the hardships of internally displaced persons.[62] Over time, local authorities dropped the pretence that these laws represented a legitimate humanitarian concern and began using abandoned property as war booty.[63] As discussed in Chapter 1, a similar situation arose in Israel in the aftermath of the 1948 war. The State of Israel initially adopted emergency regulations on absentee property with the aim of using the property to accommodate the growing needs of incoming Jewish settlers. Emergency regulations were gradually replaced by the 1950 Absentees' Property Law and other related laws which allowed the transfer of refugee property from the Custodian to the State of Israel, with the intention of permanently severing the refugees' title to their property.[64] However, unlike the situation in Israel–Palestine, the adoption by the parties to the Bosnian conflict of discriminatory property legislation was not left unremedied. The internationally-brokered Dayton Agreement required the parties to the agreement to repeal domestic legislation and administrative practices with discriminatory intent or effect.[65] Laws on abandoned property were considered as violating the rights to return and property enshrined in Annex 7 of the Dayton Agreement and 'one of the most significant obstacles to the return of displaced persons and refugees to their pre-war homes'.[66] Largely as a result of the international community's threats to interrupt reconstruction aid if these laws were not revised, the Federation of Bosnia and Herzegovina (Federation) and the Republika Srpska (RS) finally agreed in 1998 to amend their laws to conform to Annex Seven.[67] According to Eric Rosand:

> the international community's persistent efforts to remove this obstacle to return is just one example of the world's commitment in Bosnia to enforcing the right to return of hundreds of thousands of people on the ground. Ever since hostilities commenced in 1992, the international community has remained steadfast in its belief that all dislocated persons – in the end numbering more

than two million- not only have the right to return to their pre-war homes, but that they should be able to exercise this right.[68]

The amended property laws were met with heavy resistance at the municipal level. None of the local authorities was eager to evict members of their own ethnic group in favour of returning minorities. The initial lack of cooperation on the local level prompted international agencies working in the field – mainly the UNHCR, the Organization for Security and Cooperation in Europe (OSCE) and the Office of the High Representative (OHR)[69] – to set up an extensive network to oversee the implementation of the laws across all 149 municipalities.[70] The international community thus continued to exert pressure at the domestic level, even after the adoption of the amended property laws.[71] This continuous effort reflected the international community's commitment to reversing ethnic cleansing in Bosnia-Herzegovina.[72] In the absence of a similar international commitment in the case of Israel–Palestine, Israel has had a free rein to adopt laws and policies aimed at denying displaced Palestinians access to their land.[73]

The need to repeal discriminatory laws affecting property rights was reiterated in Principles 18.1, 19.1 and 19.2 of the Pinheiro Principles:

18.1 States should ensure the right of refugees and displaced persons to housing, land and property restitution is recognized as an essential component of the rule of law. States should ensure the right to housing, land and property restitution through all necessary legislative means, including through the adoption, amendment, reform, or repeal of relevant laws, regulations and/or practices. States should develop a legal framework for protecting the right to housing, land and property restitution which is clear, consistent and, where necessary, consolidated in a single law.

19.1 States should neither adopt nor apply laws which prejudice the restitution process, in particular through arbitrary, discriminatory, or otherwise unjust abandonment laws or statutes of limitations.

19.2 States should take immediate steps to repeal unjust or arbitrary laws and laws that otherwise have a discriminatory effect on the enjoyment of the right to housing, land and property restitution, and should ensure remedies for those wrongfully harmed by the prior application of such laws.

In the aftermath of conflict, a newly established political authority can use legislative amendments as a tool to distance itself from the discriminatory practices of its predecessors and promote a society built on the rule of law. Effecting dramatic legislative reforms is not, however, without challenges. The difficulty in implementing legislative changes affecting property rights increases if the previous laws had been in force for a significant amount of time. The need to take into consideration the rights of secondary occupants becomes even more acute under these circumstances.

4.3.2 Dealing with secondary occupants

The phenomenon of secondary occupants is one that arises in all post-conflict situations, and it has been considered a significant impediment to the return of refugees and displaced persons. Despite hampering return efforts in different parts of the world,[74] there are currently no specific guidelines on how to resolve conflicting rights between returning refugees and secondary occupants,[75] nor even an accepted definition of 'secondary occupants'. According to the Handbook on the Pinheiro Principles, '[s]econdary occupants are persons who take up residence in a home or on land after the legitimate owners or users have fled due to, *inter alia*, forced displacement, forced eviction, violence or threat of violence, natural or human-made disasters'.[76] As such, they do not necessarily have to own the property but they must be residing in it. The problem of secondary occupants is of particular significance in the case of Palestinian refugees. More than seventy-five years after their dispossession, Palestinian refugees continue to pass on the deeds and keys to their original homes from generation to generation. By clinging on to these relics, they demonstrate their profound attachment to their right to return and restitution. The restitution of property provides a unique sense of justice to victims of displacement and dispossession – a sense of justice which has certainly been overshadowed by 'pragmatic' concerns in most discussions on Palestinian refugee rights.[77]

Despite restitution's significance to the victims of dispossession, international law does recognize situations where restitution is 'factually impossible' and where refugees are forced to accept an alternative form of reparation. In some situations, the presence of secondary occupants may in fact impede the restitution of property belonging to returning refugees and displaced persons. However, the magnitude of this problem has largely been exaggerated in the case of a large-scale return of Palestinian refugees since most of the land belonging to these refugees remains vacant. According to Palestinian researcher Salman Abu-Sitta, 86 per cent of Israel, which is largely the land and home of Palestinian refugees, is inhabited by about two hundred thousand rural Jews who make up roughly 22 per cent of all Jews in Israel.[78] Hence, most pre-1948 Palestinian villages remain uninhabited. While it is true that several hundred Palestinian villages were destroyed during or in the aftermath of the 1948 war, as stated earlier, the mere destruction of property does not preclude restitution claims over it. Therefore, Palestinian refugees originating from areas in Israel which remain vacant can demand the restitution of their land and property without interfering with the rights of secondary occupants.[79] The first task of any restitution programme would have to include a comprehensive survey of land and property in Israel to determine the extent to which the issue of secondary occupancy arises in case of a large-scale return of Palestinian refugees.

In cases where secondary occupants have been residing in Palestinian refugee property or where land belonging to refugees has been used to build permanent structures accommodating Israeli citizens or benefitting the wider public, the right to property restitution of Palestinian refugees will conflict with the rights of secondary occupants.[80] The Pinheiro Principles have addressed the issue of secondary occupants in Principle 17. There are some key features to this Principle. With regard to the rights of secondary occupants, the Principle identifies three main rights. The first is the right to be protected against 'arbitrary or unlawful forced eviction' through safeguards of due process (Principle 17.1). The second right is to be provided with alternative housing and/or land in cases where eviction is 'justifiable and unavoidable' (Principle 17.3). The third concerns third parties who have purchased the property in good faith from a second occupant (Principle 17.4). These individuals may be entitled to receive compensation if they were bona fide purchasers. While secondary occupants are entitled to rights and procedural safeguards, Principle 17.2 states clearly that these safeguards 'do not prejudice the rights of legitimate owners, tenants and other holders to repossess the housing, land and property in question in a just and timely manner'. Thus, the underlying notion in Principle 17 is the primacy of the right to restitution over the rights of secondary occupants. The restoration of displaced persons' property rights is particularly required when the secondary occupation was an integral part of ethnic cleansing.

The precedents in Bosnia and Kosovo demonstrate the international community's endorsement of this principle in the aftermath of ethnic conflicts. Notwithstanding the presence of secondary occupants, the emphasis in Bosnia was on the restitution of property as a means of reversing ethnic cleansing. The Commission for Displaced Persons and Refugees in Bosnia, subsequently renamed the CRPC, was established by Annex 7 of the Dayton Agreement, to receive claims for the 'return of the property or just compensation in lieu of return'.[81] The compensation fund[82] failed, however, to materialize due to lack of support from donors. According to Eric Rosand, the right to compensation enunciated in Annex 7 'has been largely ignored for fear that a refugee or displaced person's ability to receive compensation might interfere with the primary goal of ethnic reintegration'.[83] While promoting restitution, the High Representative in Bosnia did acknowledge that secondary occupants, who were often themselves displaced, are entitled to temporary, humanitarian shelter until they were able to return to their homes or another durable solution was found to their displacement.[84] In practice, the implementation of the right to restitution encountered some difficulties as alternative accommodation was lacking and local authorities were not exercising sufficient efforts to assess the needs of current occupants.[85] It was only a matter of time before the property repossession process began gaining momentum as well as broader support within Bosnian society. According to Cox and Garlick, '[a]s the social environment began to normalize with the passage of time, it became clear that most people were uncomfortable with the idea of living in someone else's home, and the level of voluntary compliance with the laws increased over time'.[86]

Similarly, in Kosovo, the UN Security Council endorsed the right of all refugees and displaced persons to return to their homes.[87] In 2000, the UN Interim Administration Mission in Kosovo (UNMIK) adopted a regulation governing property restitution.[88] This regulation provided, among other things:

2.2 Any person whose property right was lost between 23 March 1989 and 24 March 1999 as a result of discrimination has a right to restitution in accordance with the present regulation. Restitution may take the form of restoration of the property right (hereafter 'restitution in kind') or compensation. [...]

2.5 Any refugee or displaced person with a right to property has a right to return to the property, or to dispose of it in accordance with the law, subject to the present regulation. [...]

13.2 The Directorate shall deliver an eviction order issued by the Commission to the current occupant of the claimed property. The Directorate may at its discretion, delay execution of the eviction order for up to 6 months, pending resolution of the housing needs of the current occupant, or under circumstances that the Directorate deems fit.

Like Bosnia, to enable the restitution of property to its rightful owners, secondary occupants in Kosovo were expected to move out. According to section 13.2, eviction could not be delayed for more than six months. The international community was thus encouraging the prompt repossession of property in order to facilitate the return of displaced persons and refugees.[89]

In Kosovo and Bosnia, it was possible to foresee the eviction of secondary occupants as they had only been residing in vacant properties for a few years. The peace agreement in Rwanda suggests, however, that restitution may be harder to implement when longer periods of time have lapsed. Since the end of colonial rule in 1959, Rwanda's Tutsi minority have been repeatedly targeted by the Hutu-dominated government in 1959, 1963 and 1973.[90] Each of these conflicts caused the forcible displacement of thousands of Rwandans, mainly Tutsis. In 1990, the Rwandan Patriotic Army (RPA), which was formed mainly by exiled Tutsis, launched a war against the Hutu-dominated government during which more than 2 million Hutu Rwandans fled to neighbouring countries.[91] The RPA succeeded in taking over the country in 1994 and declared their intention to abide by the 1993 Arusha Accords, which were a series of agreements signed to bring an end to the Rwandan civil war. According to Article 1 of the Protocol to the Arusha Accords, 'the return of Rwandese refugees to their country is an inalienable right and constitutes a factor of peace, national unity, and reconciliation'.[92] Article 2 of the Protocol affirmed the right of refugees to settle down in any place of their choice inside the country, *so long as they do not encroach on the rights of other people*' [emphasis added], presumably secondary occupants. While affirming the right of refugees 'to repossess their property on return', Article 4 specifically addressed the rights of secondary occupants by stating that 'in order to promote social harmony and national reconciliation, refugees who left the country more than ten years ago should not reclaim their properties, which might have been occupied by other people. The Government shall compensate them by putting land at their disposal and shall help them to resettle'. The parties to the Protocol thus considered the right of return of refugees as an essential factor to reconciliation while acknowledging that, for the sake of reconciliation as well, the rights of secondary occupants might supersede the refugees' right to restitution if the initial displacement occurred more than ten years ago. Returnees who were unable to repossess their land under this rule were entitled to receive compensation in the form of alternative accommodation from the Government in order to settle in other parts of Rwanda. Former UNHCR officer in Rwanda Lisa Jones notes that 'the 'ten-year rule' was painfully negotiated primarily as a pragmatic (and political) solution for achieving 'peaceful return'.[93] Though 'political' or 'pragmatic' concerns prevailed over legal principles in Rwanda, the 'ten-year rule' has been criticized by Pinheiro as 'yet another example of how unjust policies often serve to deny certain persons their right to restitution, in this case through the imposition of arbitrary and discriminatory time limitations'.[94] The rule was even challenged by a small number of returnees who actively sought to regain possession of their properties, though only a few were successful.[95] Additionally, according to a UNHCR Report on land and ownership in repatriation operations, the '10 year-rule' applied in Rwanda derives essentially from local customary law.[96] As such, it cannot be viewed as a general precedent on property restitution. To avoid the use of this rule as a precedent, Principle 10.2 of the Pinheiro Principles provides that the refugees' right to return to their former homes, lands or places of habitual residence 'cannot be abridged under conditions of State succession, nor can it be subject to arbitrary or unlawful time limitations'.

Determining a lawful cut-off date for restitution will depend on the circumstances of each conflict. In South Africa, for instance, property rights have been affected by centuries of colonialism and apartheid's discriminatory policies. Since the Dutch traders' invasion of South Africa in 1652, the distribution of land in the country has been inequitable.[97] British imperialism, which began in 1870, deepened the gaps between white and black ownership of land by creating a number of reserves for the native inhabitants of South Africa.[98] Discriminatory land policies persisted after South Africa proclaimed independence in 1910. The Natives Land Acts, passed in 1913, precluded native blacks from acquiring non-agricultural land.[99] When apartheid was abolished in 1991, South Africa's Restitution of Land Rights Act 22 of 1994 and its Constitution of 1996 recognized the right to restitution of a person dispossessed of a right in land. Though discriminatory land policies had been in place for centuries, both the Act and the Constitution set the cut-off date for restitution claims in 1913.[100] According to Section 25(7) of the South African Constitution: 'A person or community dispossessed of property after 19 June 1913 as a result of past racially discriminatory laws or practices is entitled, to the extent provided by an Act of Parliament, either to restitution of that property or to equitable redress'.[101] The drafters of the Constitution drew the line in 1913 out of concern that indigenous title claims would 'create a number of problems and legal-political complexities that would be impossible to unravel'.[102] Though the right to restitution was enshrined in the country's constitution, the restitution programme in South Africa has not escaped criticism, mainly for inefficiency.[103] NGOs have additionally criticized the State for failing 'to integrate restitution properly with the broader land reform programme, and in the process los[ing] the opportunity to shift the skewed racial patterns of land ownership in South Africa'.[104]

As evidenced by these precedents, although the passage of time and the presence of secondary occupants have made the implementation of restitution more difficult, they have not made it impossible. Even in Rwanda, where an arbitrary time limitation to restitution claims was imposed, refugees and displaced persons were still entitled to return to the areas from which they were displaced and receive alternative accommodation for the land or property they were unable to repossess.[105] In none of these precedents were refugees expected to resettle in another country and accept financial compensation as an alternative to both return and restitution. This stands in stark contrast to the situation of Palestinian refugees who, generation after generation, continue to be denied their right to return to their former homes and villages.

4.3.3 Rights of descendants

Due to the protracted nature of the Palestinian refugees' situation, it is important to clarify the rights of subsequent generations of refugees. As has been demonstrated, the rights to restitution and compensation are not favours, or humanitarian gestures, bestowed by Israel on Palestinian refugees. These rights are grounded in international law, and Israel has an obligation to enforce them. Under UNRWA's working definition 'Palestine refugees are persons whose normal place of residence was Palestine between June 1946 and May 1948, who lost both home and means of livelihood as a result of the 1948 conflict. [...]' UNRWA's definition of a refugee also covers the descendants of fathers fulfilling the definition.[106] This situation is not peculiar to Palestinian refugees falling under UNRWA's definition. The UNHCR also recognizes the refugee status of a refugee's dependents.[107] Like refugees the world over, Palestinian refugees retain their status as refugees until a durable solution is agreed.[108] In addition, property rights, in both municipal and international law, are one of the few rights which are inherited. Principle 18.2. of the Pinheiro Principles restates the position of international law on this matter by urging states to include in their property laws all claimants legally entitled to the restitution of their housing, land and property, including subsidiary claimants, such as 'resident family members at the time of displacement, spouses, domestic partners, dependents, legal heirs and others who should be entitled to claim on the same basis as primary claimants'. According to the Handbook on the Pinheiro Principles, even '[i]n cases of long term displacement where the original and legitimate holders of housing and property restitution rights have died, heirs do maintain and 'inherit' these restitution rights if they themselves have not accessed any other durable solution and as long as they expressly indicate their continued assertion over the rights associated with the housing or property under consideration".[109] As such, international law recognizes the refugee status and property rights of descendants of Palestinian refugees originally displaced in 1948. The rights of descendents of refugees to demand the restitution of property is also supported by precedents. Members of the family household and heirs of natural persons with a legal interest in the claimed real property were entitled to submit claims before the CRPC in Bosnia,[110] the HPD in Kosovo[111] and the Commission on Restitution of Land Rights in South Africa.[112]

4.4 Conclusion

This chapter outlined the two main forms of reparation for property losses: restitution and compensation. It also demonstrated that restitution is the preferred form of reparation under international law. Compensation can only be considered an alternative to restitution if the refugees voluntarily choose compensation over restitution or when restitution is 'factually impossible'. The second section of this chapter presented some of the main legal issues which could impede the restitution of Palestinian refugee property. Although these legal issues can complicate the restitution of property claims to Palestinian refugees, it was argued that they do not necessarily render the restitution of property 'factually impossible'. In other words, Israel's resistance to implement return-based restitution, and the international community's unwillingness to support restitution rights, do not automatically make compensation an acceptable alternative to property restitution.[113]

This is particularly true when the displacement and dispossession of refugees were part of a wider campaign of ethnic cleansing. In these circumstances, every effort to secure return-based restitution and reverse ethnic cleansing must be exhaustively exercised before pursuing any subsequent efforts which may rely on compensation-based durable solutions to displacement. The international community adopted this approach to resolve refugee crises arising from conflicts worldwide, most recently in Bosnia and Kosovo.[114] There is, therefore, 'growing recognition […] in both law and practice, of the necessity of consciously undoing the effect of human rights violations and other causes of displacement through reliance on the principles governing the emerging right to housing and property restitution. This has been accompanied by an understanding that return without restitution can only ever provide an incomplete durable solution to displacement'.[115] Equally, restitution without return is an incomplete remedy for displacement and dispossession, unless refugees *voluntarily* choose not to exercise their right to return to their original homes and lands. This situation arose in Bosnia where the international community's strong commitment to property restitution did not suffice to calm refugees and displaced persons' fears of returning to an area where they would form the minority ethnic group.[116] Concerns over safety and stability arise in the context of nearly every mass refugee return. Although these concerns require carefully planning the implementation of refugee repatriation, they do not constitute a barrier to return and property restitution.[117] As in other conflict resolution situations, legal measures to restore property rights will have to be accompanied by societal changes, confidence-building measures and efforts at promoting reconciliation between Palestinians and Israelis who will have to learn to live together after decades of enmity. The next chapter will examine whether and how Israeli and Palestinian negotiators have attempted to address property claims in official agreements and peace initiatives.

Palestinian refugee property claims in Israeli–Palestinian negotiations

5.1 Introduction

As demonstrated in the previous chapter, Palestinian refugees have a right to reparation for the property losses they incurred both before and in the aftermath of the 1948 Arab–Israeli war. Nevertheless, since the creation of the refugee issue in 1948, the political will to implement the Palestinian refugees' right to return, restitution and compensation has been lacking. On the other hand, over the years, there has been no dearth of proposals, conferences and initiatives to resolve the intractable Israeli–Palestinian conflict. The objective of this chapter is to provide a critical analysis of the proposed solutions to the Palestinian refugee issue, which resulted from official Israeli–Palestinian talks, two-track negotiations and peace initiatives. It is not the aim of this chapter to provide a comparative analysis of the role of international law and human rights in the negotiation, drafting and implementation of a peace agreement.[1] Nor will this chapter discuss the concepts of 'justice' and 'peace'[2] and the trade-offs between the two which might be necessary to achieve a breakthrough in Israeli–Palestinian negotiations on the refugee issue. Instead, this chapter will demonstrate that the refugee issue in general, and property claims in particular, were largely ignored in Israeli–Palestinian negotiations. It is also the aim of this chapter to demonstrate that the law-based or rights-based approach to the refugee issue[3] was dismissed in the negotiations process and in peace initiatives as 'unrealistic'. It was replaced with an approach that called for a 'pragmatic' or 'politically feasible' solution to the refugee issue.[4]

This chapter will begin by arguing that there was an international consensus in favour of a law-based approach to the resolution of the refugee issue, which prevailed until the inauguration of the Madrid Peace Conference in 1991. The next section of this chapter will discuss the launch of the Madrid

Peace Conference and the initiation of bilateral, multilateral and two-track negotiations aimed at resolving the intractable Middle East conflict (Section 4.3). This section will demonstrate that the law-based approach that prevailed in the 1980s was abandoned in Madrid. Section 4.4 of this chapter will focus on the Declaration of Principles on Interim Self-Government Arrangements (DOP), which was signed by Israel and the PLO on 13 September 1993 and heralded the beginning of official bilateral negotiations between Israel and the PLO in what has come to be known as the Oslo Peace Process (OPP). This section will demonstrate how the negotiating parameters set by the DOP have led to the marginalization of refugee rights throughout the negotiations process and the abandonment of a law-based approach to the resolution of the refugee issue in second-track negotiations which have emerged from the OPP. Section 4.5 will examine final status negotiations in Camp David II and Taba in 2000 and how these negotiations have addressed the issue of Palestinian refugees. This section will put emphasis on the Palestinian proposal at Taba, which marked a return to the law-based approach to the resolution of the refugee issue. It will also provide an overview of the Clinton Parameters' position on the refugee issue. Section 4.6 will discuss peace initiatives which have been promoted after the collapse of official negotiations between Israel and the PLO in the aftermath of Taba. Starting with a brief discussion of the Arab League's 2002 Peace Initiative and the Road Map, this section will focus on peace proposals generated by track-two negotiations, namely the 2002 Nusseibeh–Ayalon Agreement and the 2003 Geneva Accords. This section will demonstrate how these proposed solutions failed to meet international legal standards on reparation.

5.2 From the Nakba to Madrid: The emergence of an international consensus in favour of a law-based approach to the resolution of the refugee issue

From the creation of the Palestinian refugee issue in 1948 until the inauguration of the Madrid Peace Conference and the signature of the DOP in the early 1990s, the international community, through the UN and its organs, was charged with the task of facilitating the resolution of the Middle East conflict. As discussed in Chapter 2, Resolution 194, which was adopted in the aftermath of the 1948 Arab–Israeli war, established the UNCCP and instructed it to 'facilitate the repatriation, resettlement and economic and social rehabilitation of the refugees and the payment of compensation.[5] In an effort to conciliate between the parties to the conflict, the UNCCP convened a Conference in Lausanne in April 1949. Several proposals were tabled to deal with the return and compensation of refugees, but the Arab and Israeli positions were irreconcilable.[6] In another attempt to reconcile the parties, the UNCCP convened a conference in Paris between September and November of 1951.[7] Again, this Conference failed to bridge the gap between the parties to the conflict. This prompted the UNCCP to suspend its mediation efforts and focus instead on technical matters, namely the identification and valuation of refugee property.[8]

As such, there was relatively little diplomatic activity throughout the fifties and sixties. In the aftermath of the 1967 war, the UNSC adopted Resolution 242, which affirmed the necessity of achieving a 'just settlement of the refugee problem'.[9] Unfortunately, the adoption of this Resolution was not followed by diplomatic initiatives to bring the parties to the conflict to the negotiating table. It was not until the eruption of the 1973 Arab–Israeli war that the UN reinvigorated its interest and active involvement in the Middle East conflict. On 22 October 1973, the Security Council adopted Resolution 338 in which it decided that 'immediately and concurrently with the cease-fire, negotiations shall start between the parties concerned under appropriate auspices aimed at establishing a just and durable peace in the Middle East'.[10] With the UNCCP's mediation efforts suspended, the Secretary-General invited Egypt, Israel, Jordan, the US and the Soviet Union to a peace Conference in Geneva on 21 December 1973. The Conference was convened under the auspices of the UN.[11] Again, the Conference failed to yield any substantive results that could bring an end to the Arab–Israeli conflict.[12] What is relevant for the purposes of this chapter is the adoption by the GA, almost a year later, of a resolution in which it reaffirmed that the inalienable rights of the Palestinian people include their right to self-determination and their right to national independence and sovereignty.[13] The GA proceeded also to reaffirm the 'inalienable right of the Palestinians to return to their homes and property from which they have been displaced and uprooted'.[14] In the same resolution, the GA emphasized that 'full respect for and the realization of these inalienable rights of the Palestinian people are indispensable for the solution of the question of Palestine'. As such, the GA acknowledged that the Palestinian people's rights to self-determination and national independence do *not* preclude individual Palestinians from returning to their homes and repossessing their property inside what is now the State of Israel. According to the GA, all of these inalienable rights must be respected and implemented in order to resolve the question of Palestine. This position was reiterated in subsequent UNGA resolutions.[15] As will be demonstrated later in this chapter, this law-based approach to the resolution of the Israeli–Palestinian conflict in general, and the refugee issue in particular, was abandoned in the post-Oslo era. Instead, as will be argued in Section 4.4, the negotiations process initiated by the DOP separated the rights of the Palestinian refugees to return and restitution from the collective aspiration of the Palestinian people to declare a state in the OPTs and presented these two sets of rights as contradictory and mutually exclusive.

It was not until 1981 that the GA reaffirmed the need to convene an international conference on the question of Palestine.[16] An international conference was eventually convened in Geneva, under the auspices of the UN, from 29 August to 7 September 1983.[17] Though the Conference did not culminate in the signature of any peace agreements, it adopted by acclamation a series of guidelines in which it reasserted the importance of the legitimate inalienable rights of the Palestinian people, 'including the right to return, the right to self-determination and the right to establish its own independent State in Palestine'.[18] Furthermore, the 1983 UN Conference 'consolidated an international consensus with regard to the responsibility and duty of the world community, and particularly of the United Nations, to bring about a solution to the [Middle East] problem'.[19] The adoption of UNGA Resolution 38/58 C, shortly after the Conference ended, 'clearly demonstrated that an international consensus had emerged regarding the idea of resolving the Middle East problem through the convening of an international conference on this issue under the auspices of the United Nations'.[20] The idea of holding an international conference, under UN auspices, to resolve comprehensively all aspects of the Israeli–Arab conflict was endorsed by an overwhelming majority of states in annual GA resolutions.[21] In these resolutions, the GA reaffirmed the necessity of establishing 'a comprehensive, just and lasting peace in the region' based on UN resolutions and 'full respect for the Charter and the principles of international law'.[22] A number of resolutions were even more specific and affirmed the need to resolve, among other issues, the 'problem of the Palestine refugees in conformity with General Assembly resolution 194 (III) of 11 December 1948, and subsequent relevant resolutions' in order to achieve a 'comprehensive peace'.[23] There was, therefore, a near consensus that a law-based approach was necessary for a comprehensive resolution of the conflict, including the refugee issue, and that an international conference convened under the auspices of the UN was the most appropriate forum to guarantee that such a solution is reached. It is important to note, however, that Israel and the United States both rejected this consensus by repeatedly and consistently voting against these resolutions. The Secretary General at the time perceived 'the inability of the Government of Israel as a whole to agree on the principle of an international conference under United Nations auspices' as the 'major obstacle' to the convening of that conference.[24] As a consequence, despite benefitting from widespread international support, the UN was unable to convene another conference under its auspices. Following the victory of the US-led coalition forces in the 1991 Gulf War, the United States emerged as the new regional power in the Middle East and began intensive diplomatic efforts to initiate peace negotiations between Israel and its Arab neighbours. The time was ripe for another Middle East peace conference, but with the US replacing the UN as host, the rules of the negotiations were about to change.

5.3 The Madrid Framework

5.3.1 The Madrid Peace Conference – a new approach to peace negotiations in the Middle East

As demonstrated in the previous section, in the 1980s, there was a near international consensus on the need to convene a conference under UN auspices to resolve the Middle East conflict, including the refugee issue, in a comprehensive way and on the basis of full respect for the Charter, UN Resolutions and general principles of international law. The Madrid Peace Conference of 1991 signalled a departure from this international consensus. The Conference was the result of intensive diplomatic efforts initiated by former US Secretary of State, James Baker, in the aftermath of the 1991 Gulf War. It opened on 30 October 1991. Unlike previous international peace conferences on the Middle East, the Madrid Conference was co-hosted by the United States and the former Soviet Union, instead of by the UN or one of its agencies. In a Letter of Assurances to the Palestinians, the US outlined the envisaged role of the UN as follows:

> With regard to the role of the United Nations, the UN Secretary-General will send a representative to the conference as an observer. The co-sponsors will keep the secretary-general appraised of the progress of the negotiations. Agreements reached between the parties will be registered with the UN Secretariat and reported to the Security-Council, and the parties will seek the Council's endorsement of such agreements. Since it is in the interest of all parties for this process to succeed, while this process is actively ongoing, the

United States will not support a competing or parallel process in the United
Nations Security Council.[25]

According to Professor Quigley, the US construed the last sentence broadly
to the point that it opposed Security Council condemnation of unlawful
acts committed by Israel against the Palestinians, with respect to matters on
which the two parties were supposed to negotiate.[26] Quigley contrasts the US's
stance with that of most other UN member states, which 'have taken a view
of the post-Madrid process that is more multilateralist, and more in keeping
with the approach taken in the 1980s'.[27] By marginalizing the role of the UN
in the Madrid Conference, the United States in fact wanted to promote a new
approach to negotiations between Israel and neighbouring Arab countries.
Instead of the UN hosting multilateral negotiations with all of the parties to
the conflict with the aim of reaching a comprehensive solution, the Madrid
Conference separated the parties to the negotiations and fragmented the issues
to be negotiated. It inaugurated parallel tracks of bilateral and multilateral
negotiations (Madrid Framework).[28] Bilateral negotiations were scheduled to
begin four days after the opening of the conference and were aimed at reaching
separate peace agreements between Israel and its regional neighbours (Jordan,
Syria and Lebanon).[29] Multilateral negotiations were to be convened two weeks
after the opening of the conference with the aim of focusing on region-wide
issues, including refugee issues.[30] Dividing the Arab parties in negotiations was
a strategy aimed at weakening them to the advantage of the Israeli negotiators.
Isolating the Palestinians in the negotiations from other Arab countries, and
marginalizing the UN from the process, was a particularly effective way of
weakening the Palestinians who were deprived of their 'historical' allies, the UN
and Arab states, even if their support had only been verbal throughout the years.

The position of the Palestinians in the Madrid Conference was further
undermined by their limited participation. While the Guidelines adopted
at the 1983 UN-sponsored Conference affirmed the right of the PLO, as the
representative of the Palestinian people, 'to participate on an equal footing
with other parties in all efforts, deliberations and conferences on the Middle
East',[31] Israel imposed several conditions on the representation of Palestinians in
Madrid as a result of which a joint Jordanian–Palestinian negotiating team was
formed.[32] In addition, negotiations between Israel and the Palestinians had to be
conducted in phases beginning with talks on self-governing arrangements, which
were to be followed by permanent status negotiations. The Madrid Framework's
incremental approach to conflict resolution resulted in the fragmentation of the

different aspects of the conflict. The focus was first on interim arrangements affecting the rights of residents of the Occupied Palestinian Territory (OPT). Then, at some later date, hard issues (including the core of the original conflict, the refugees) were to be negotiated. This delinking of the various issues in the conflict stands in stark contrast to the UN's efforts in previous decades to do the exact opposite; in other words, to link the right of return to the right of self-determination and to view the full respect and realization of *all* the inalienable rights of Palestinians, both as individuals and as a people, as 'indispensable for the solution of the question of Palestine'.[33] As will be discussed later in this chapter, the DOP was to accentuate even further the separation between the rights of refugees and the right of the Palestinian people to declare a State in the OPTs, to the extent of presenting these two rights as contradictory and mutually exclusive.

The marginalisation of the UN, the fragmentation of the conflict into separate issues and the isolation of the parties in bilateral negotiations were all factors that demarcated the Madrid Framework from the UN-endorsed comprehensive, multilateral approach to conflict resolution that prevailed in the 1980s. In addition, as discussed in the previous section, the international consensus in the 1980s affirmed the necessity of establishing 'a comprehensive, just and lasting peace in the region' based on UN resolutions and 'full respect for the Charter and the principles of international law'.[34] This law-based approach was also abandoned in Madrid. According to the US–Soviet Letter of Invitation to the delegations to Madrid, permanent status negotiations between Israel and the Palestinians as well as the negotiations between Israel and Arab states were to be based on Resolutions 242 and 338.[35] Besides these two Resolutions, there was no reference to norms of international law or explicit specifications of the rights to be protected.[36] As discussed in Chapter 2, these Resolutions were drafted in general terms and do not explicitly refer to UNGA Resolution 194, which is the principal resolution on refugee rights. Resolution 242 affirmed 'the necessity [f]or achieving a just settlement to the refugee problem', while Resolution 338 simply called on parties to initiate negotiations aimed at achieving a 'just and durable peace in the Middle East' and to implement Resolution 242 in all its parts. Arguably, a just settlement to the refugee problem would have to conform to principles of international law and UN Resolutions, including Resolution 194, all of which support the Palestinian refugees' rights to the restitution of their property and to receive compensation for loss of, or damage to, property. However, as will be discussed in the next section, Israel and the US dismissed attempts by the Palestinians to raise the issue of Resolution 194 in the multilateral talks on refugees. The omission of any reference to Resolution 194 clearly exposed the intentions of the United States and Israel to reject a law-based approach to the refugee issue. The dismissal of the law-based approach was facilitated by the fact that the Madrid Framework had marginalized the UN and limited its ability to ensure that an agreement would remain within the bounds of what is required by international norms. As Professor Quigley noted, the 'Madrid approach gave more play to the power relationship between the two parties and brought the risk that Israel, as the stronger of the two parties, might force acceptance of its entire agenda'.[37] The following sections will demonstrate that, in the absence of specific references to Resolution 194 and to norms of international law, the rights of refugees were not addressed in the multilateral talks of the Refugee Working Group or in track-two negotiations. Instead, under the banner of 'political realism', these negotiations proposed solutions that undermined the rights of Palestinian refugees.

5.3.2 The Refugee Working Group (RWG)

Several multilateral working groups were created within the Madrid Framework with the aim of focusing on 'region-wide issues such as arms control and regional security, water, refugee issues, environment, economic development, and other subjects of mutual interest'.[38] Five working groups were officially established in Moscow in January 1992 to deal with these issues. Canada was invited to chair the Refugee Working Group (RWG), which was composed of the 'core parties' (Israel, Jordan, Egypt and the PLO), the co-sponsors (the United States and Russia), the co-organizers of the multilateral track (EU and Japan), and a number of Arab and non-Arab states which recognized the importance of the refugee issue and were committed to the multilateral process.[39] The RWG held five coordination meetings between 1996 and 1999. Its prospects of achieving a breakthrough in negotiations were diminished from the onset by Syria's and Lebanon's decisions to boycott the meetings, which they considered as 'normalization' with Israel.[40] According to a study on Canada's involvement in the Palestinian refugee issue, progress in the multilaterals was further impeded by the participating parties' divergent views on the aim of the talks: 'While the Palestinians were anxious to highlight the refugee issue, the Israelis had only accepted the existence of the RWG as part of the broader package deal that gave birth to the Madrid process. Israel was anxious to keep the RWG from addressing sensitive political issues'.[41] The RWG ultimately reduced the refugee issue to a humanitarian crisis. It was not empowered to reconcile the views of the parties on such thorny issues as the implementation of the refugees' right to return, restitution or compensation as per Resolution 194 and norms of international law.[42] Elia Zureik, a member of the Palestinian delegation to the RWG, notes how repeated efforts by the Palestinians 'to raise the issue of Resolution 194 at the RWG have been met with Israeli admonishments not to 'politicize' the meetings and with reminders that the RWG's purpose is to address the refugee issue from a scientific and technical standpoint'.[43] Israel's dismissal of Resolution 194 was seconded by the United States, which 'repeatedly pointed out that Resolution 194 has "no place" in the RWG deliberations'.[44] The US's resistance to Resolution 194 was expressed even outside the confines of the RWG meetings when, in December 1993, and for the first time since 1948, the US under the Clinton administration abstained from voting on a UNGA resolution that reaffirmed Resolution 194.[45] This shift in the US's position on Resolution 194 is very significant, particularly since the United States became the lead peace broker in subsequent Israeli–Palestinian bilateral negotiations, with President Clinton personally playing a prominent role in final status negotiations, as will be discussed later in this chapter.

With its mandate restricted to humanitarian issues, the RWG decided to focus its activities on six main themes: child welfare, databases, economic and social infrastructure, family reunification, human resources development, job creation and vocational training, and public health. Its activities were, however, overshadowed by the bilateral dynamics of the OPP, which was launched with the signature of the DOP in 1993.[46] The eruption of the second Intifada in September 2000 suspended the RWG's meetings indefinitely. With the formal track of the RWG on hold, a small group of Canadian officials and academics met in 1997 to stimulate second-track negotiations, which gave rise to the 'Ottawa Process'.[47]

5.3.3 The Ottawa Process

The Canadian-sponsored track-two process consisted of three sets of activities:

> First, Canada supported a sustained, non-public dialogue among a small group of Palestinian and Israeli experts, former officials, and officials. This 'core group' ultimately produced a joint paper on resolving the Palestinian refugee issue. The core group also provided input into other second-track activities.

> Second, Canada convened a series of expert workshops on key aspects of the refugee issue, and generally supported greater cooperation among Arab, Israeli, and other researchers. Public dialogue activities were also supported.

These non-public and public activities, in turn, had broader ripple effects, facilitating both official policy planning and unofficial research activities by others.[48]

The 'core group' held a total of ten meetings between 1997 and 2000 during which it identified eight areas of strategic research and policy analysis that might be undertaken to facilitate future Palestinian–Israeli refugee negotiations. These were as follows: 'the relationship of refugee issue to other final status issues; refugee absorption in the WB/Gaza; family reunification in Israel; the situation in present host countries; third party refugee absorption; compensation; the future of UNRWA; and interim measures.'[49] Interestingly, the core group did not list the property claims of Palestinian refugees among the issues requiring the attention of policymakers working on Israeli–Palestinian refugee negotiations, which indicates the extent to which this issue had been marginalized. This was no oversight. On the contrary, the identified areas of interest reveal an implicit agreement among the members of the core group as to what *they* viewed as the 'pragmatic' and most likely outcome of final status negotiations on the refugee issue, even before these negotiations had commenced. This 'pragmatic' solution would not involve a return-based restitution of property located in areas within the State of Israel. This is revealed by the core group's focus on the absorption of refugees in the West Bank and Gaza Strip (i.e. the territory on which the Palestinian state was likely to be established), in host countries and by third parties (i.e. resettlement countries). The potential admission of a limited number of refugees to Israel is examined under the heading of 'family reunification', rather than the right of return. Property restitution, whether accompanied by the refugees' return or not, does not seem to warrant the attention of policymakers. Compensation, on the other hand, was listed among the areas of strategic interest for negotiators. To sum up, the following are the parameters of the 'pragmatic' solution envisaged by the core group: (i) the majority of refugees will be absorbed in the future Palestinian state, host countries and third countries of resettlement; (ii) a limited number of refugees would be admitted into Israel on humanitarian grounds (i.e. family reunification); (iii) there would be no property restitution; and (iv) compensation will be the favoured remedy for the losses incurred by refugees. As will be demonstrated later in this chapter, these four parameters delineate the framework of all the solutions to the refugee issue, which have been presented in official peace talks and initiatives as 'pragmatic' and politically feasible. Supporters of this 'pragmatic' solution resorted to the notion of 'political realism' throughout the Oslo Peace Process to create the false dichotomy between politically feasible solutions and law-based solutions to the refugee issue. As a consequence, the protection and implementation of the rights of Palestinian refugees under international law was to be dismissed as 'unrealistic'. Meanwhile, the contours of the 'pragmatic' solution identified by the Ottawa Process remained virtually unchallenged. They were simply reformulated, with more or fewer details, repackaged and remarketed in subsequent negotiations and peace initiatives as the only 'pragmatic' solution to the refugee issue.

5.4 The Oslo Peace Process

As demonstrated earlier in this chapter, the convening of the Madrid Conference in 1991 announced the beginning of a new approach to the resolution of the Middle East conflict in general and the refugee issue in particular. This new approach consisted of the isolation of the parties to the conflict in separate bilateral tracks of negotiations, the fragmentation of the issues to the conflict, an incremental resolution of the Israeli–Palestinian conflict, a limited role for the UN in the negotiations process and the abandonment of a law-based approach to the resolution of the refugee issue. While the parties at Madrid could have walked away from the Conference, leaving it to fail like previous conferences convened under UN auspices, for a variety of political reasons, which are outside the scope of this analysis, the Madrid Conference eventually led to the signature of the DOP. As discussed in this chapter, Israel initially refused to negotiate directly with the PLO at the Madrid Conference. Months of negotiations eventually led 'the Rabin government to the conclusion that only a PLO team, directly authorized by Yasir Arafat, could make the hard concessions and choices that the negotiations required'.[50] Two years after the bilateral talks were launched, a back-channel negotiation track convening in Oslo resulted in a breakthrough in Israeli–Palestinian relations. On 9 September 1993, Israel and the PLO exchanged mutual letters of recognition.[51] Four days later, on 13 September 1993, the DOP[52] was signed at a public ceremony in Washington, DC. The Declaration was celebrated as an historical event marking the end of an era of conflict in the Middle East. The General Assembly expressed its full support for the DOP and considered it 'an important initial step in achieving a comprehensive, just and lasting peace in the Middle East'.[53] Thirty years later, the Oslo Peace Process has all but died.[54] At the time of writing, Israel is facing accusations before the ICJ for committing a genocide against Palestinians in Gaza,[55] and there are wider risks of an escalation into a regional war. It is beyond the scope of this chapter to discuss all of the inherent flaws of the DOP that have ultimately led us to the current impasse.[56] This section will focus solely on the impact this agreement has had on the rights of Palestinian refugees.

5.4.1 The DOP and the marginalization of the refugee issue

The DOP heralded the beginning of a two-stage process consisting of a transitional period not exceeding five years that would eventually lead to 'a permanent settlement based on Security Council Resolutions 242 and 338'.[57] During the transitional phase, a Palestinian Self-Governing Authority (PA) and an elected Council for Palestinians living in the West Bank and Gaza Strip would be established and assume some limited authority in parts of the West Bank and Gaza Strip following the phased redeployment of Israeli forces from these areas.[58] In addition, the following Committees were established on 13 October 1993, the day of the DOP's entry into force:[59] a Joint Israeli–Palestinian Liaison Committee (Article X), an Israeli–Palestinian Economic Cooperation Committee (Article XI) and a Quadripartite Committee for regional cooperation with Egypt and Jordan (Article XII). Among the tasks of the latter Committee was the constitution of a Continuing Committee, which was to decide by agreement between Israel, Jordan, Egypt and the Palestinian representatives 'on the modalities of admission of persons displaced from the West Bank and Gaza Strip in 1967, together with necessary measures to prevent disruption and disorder'.[60] The creation of this Committee demonstrated the intention of Israel and the PLO to distinguish between the status and rights of Palestinians displaced from the West Bank and Gaza Strip in the aftermath of the 1967 war (1967 displaced persons) and the refugees displaced between 1947 and 1949 from areas that fell under Israel's sovereignty in the aftermath of the 1948 war (1948 refugees). The Continuing Committee was given the mandate to oversee the admission of 1967 displaced persons to the OPTs during the transitional phase, while the rights of 1948 Palestinian refugees were relegated to permanent status negotiations.[61]

Addressing separately the rights of 1967 displaced persons and of 1948 refugees is not a novel idea. As far back as 1976, the CEIRPP proposed a two-phase programme in which the implementation of the right of return of 1967 displaced persons was envisaged separately from that of 1948 refugees.[62] The programme was to start with an initial phase during which Palestinians displaced in 1967 would be allowed to return immediately and without any conditions to the territories which have been under Israeli military occupation since 1967.[63]Additionally, preparations would be undertaken during this first phase for the eventual resolution of the 1948 refugee issue. These preparations would include, *inter alia*, the '[D]esignation or creation of a competent agency to be entrusted with the organizational and logistical aspects of the mass return of displaced Palestinians. [...]'[64] Additionally, in anticipation of the second phase, the Report suggested that the Security Council or General Assembly seek an advisory opinion from the ICJ on certain legal aspects of the right of the Palestinians to return to their homes, such as whether the return of Palestinian refugees would infringe Israel's sovereignty or whether certain laws enacted by Israel since 1948 – such as the Law of Return, or the Absentees' Property Law – are compatible with the provisions of the Partition Plan contained in General Assembly resolution 181 (II).[65] As such, while the CEIRPP proposed a phased implementation of the rights of displaced Palestinians, starting with the return of 1967 displaced persons and then with the resolution of the 1948 refugee issue, by suggesting a number of preparatory measures in the first phase, the CEIRPP ensured that the rights of 1948 refugees would not be marginalized from the process or shelved to a later date. On the contrary, the preparatory measures in the interim phase were meant to pave the way for the implementation of the rights of 1948 refugees. Additionally, the CEIRPP suggested that the 1948 refugee issue would be resolved 'on the basis of the relevant resolutions of the General Assembly and the Security Council and by agreement between the parties involved'.[66] This would presumably include UNGA Resolutions 181 (the Partition Plan) and 194 which, as discussed in Chapter 2, provide the grounds for the Palestinian refugees' right to reparation. The incremental or phased approach suggested in the CEIRPP's report thus contained guarantees for the rights of 1948 Palestinian refugees, both in the interim phase and in the final phase of implementation.

Provided the rights of refugees are protected throughout the different phases of implementation, an incremental approach to the resolution of the refugee issue seems appealing, if only for practical or logistical reasons. Commenting on the DOP's phased approach to the refugee issue, Salim Tamari, a member of the Palestinian delegation to the RWG and the Continuing Committee, highlighted several reasons why the separation of the issue of displaced persons from that of 1948 refugees would be to the Palestinians' advantage:

> First, separation would preempt claims that the settlement of displaced persons in the West Bank and Gaza is part of a final package, thereby precluding their further claims to rights inside Israel. This is particularly relevant to the status

of displaced persons who are also 1948 refugees. Second, because the issue of displaced persons is discussed in the context of the Quadripartite Committee, a purely Arab-Israeli committee, Palestinians would derive greater benefit from the participation of the international community (in particular UN organizations), with the multilaterals continuing to work on solutions for the 1948 refugees. Third, the QPCDP [Quadripartite Committee on Displaced Persons] has been discussing the status of persons who lost their residency or permanent IDs but who are technically neither refugees nor 'displaced persons', which include deportees. Besides, it would only overload the work of the final status negotiations if these categories were transferred to the final status negotiating committee.[67]

With the benefit of hindsight, it is possible to state today that Tamari was overly enthusiastic about the involvement and influence of the international community, particularly the UN, in the multilateral talks on refugees.[68] Moreover, a few years after the signature of the DOP, it became apparent that the Continuing Committee would not succeed in implementing the return of 1967 displaced persons to their homes inside the OPTs.[69] Considering that the OPP's methodology of shelving the hard issues (including the refugee issue) to a later date is drawn from conflict resolution literature, which promoted confidence-building measures to be introduced in incremental steps,[70] the Committee's failure to implement the rights of 1967 displaced persons left very little hope for the successful implementation of the rights of 1948 refugees at a later stage. Instead of leading to incremental improvements, the OPP's incrementalism led to incremental neglect and despair.

Unlike the CEIRPP's two-phase approach to the implementation of the right of return, the DOP's phased approach to the resolution of the refugee issue, and the conflict in general, postponed the resolution of that issue to final status talks without providing any guarantees that the rights of refugees would be safeguarded in the interim phase. As discussed in this chapter, the multilateral talks of the RWG evaded any discussion of the rights of refugees or the steps necessary to implement them. Furthermore, none of the interim agreements that succeeded the DOP contained any provisions on refugees,[71] or other final status issues for that matter, and no efforts were made in preparation for these final status negotiations. According to Christine Bell, mediators are sometimes inclined to dismiss human rights and postpone legally charged issues in order to find the lowest common denominator that would bring the parties to the negotiating table.[72] For human rights advocates, however, ignoring human rights in the short term cannot lead to peace in the long term.[73] Amr Sabet criticized the PLO for agreeing to the OPP's phased approach to conflict resolution which fails to prioritize the core issues:

> The Palestinian leader thus committed a serious strategic mistake by signing interim agreements that deferred to a later stage such fundamental issues as Jerusalem, refugees, and Jewish colonies – in other words, by signing agreements emphasizing the process of interaction rather than the content of the negotiating positions. [...] Within the framework of a confidence-building process (as opposed to one based on content), priority goes to current and ad hoc problems of whatever magnitude at the expense of long-term strategic considerations, in essence resulting in a policy that gives equal weight to all issues. Indeed, this process-oriented framework actually leads to a confusion of priorities, and if priorities are confused, no long-term national interest strategy can be focused upon, nor decisions about the channeling of resources made. Process becomes an end in itself rather than the means it is supposed to be.[74]

From the perspective of international law, Christine Bell also notes the danger of adopting a process-oriented approach as it may make mediators 'more complacent as regards compromising 'justice' for 'peace' because they consider that, over time, an initial agreement can change the political climate even so as to enable justice to be delivered'.[75] The risk, however, is that the political climate may never be ripe for justice to be delivered, thus leaving the parties lost in the process of negotiating endless interim agreements and avoiding all the core issues.

To conclude, while Tamari has highlighted some limited procedural advantages to adopting a phased approach to the resolution of the conflict and to separating the issue of 1967 displaced persons from that of 1948 refugees, in practice, the incremental approach adopted in the DOP worked to the detriment of Palestinian refugees by removing them entirely from the negotiations process. The exclusion of the refugee issues from the OPP also raised the expectations of the Israelis that this issue was off the table of negotiations and that it would disappear without them having to deal with it. As far as refugees were concerned, their marginalization from the OPP was not the only negative outcome of the DOP. As will be discussed in the next section, the DOP also laid the ground for the eventual negotiation of a solution to the refugee issue which would ignore their rights under international law and promote instead a political settlement whereby, in return for the creation of the State of Palestine, Palestinian refugees would have to relinquish their right to return to their homes inside Israel and accept compensation for their property losses in lieu of restitution.

5.4.2 The DOP: Abandoning a law-based approach to the resolution of the refugee issue

As discussed in the previous section, the CEIRPP suggested that the 1948 refugee issue be resolved on the basis of relevant GA and SC resolutions,[76] which presumably would have included Resolutions 181 and 194. By contrast, the DOP does not make any reference to these Resolutions or to general norms of international law. Article one of the DOP sets out the aim of the negotiations as follows:

> The aim of the Israeli-Palestinian negotiations within the current Middle East peace process is, among other things, to establish a Palestinian Interim Self-Government Authority, the elected Council (the 'Council'), for the Palestinian people in the West Bank and the Gaza Strip, for a transitional period not exceeding five years, leading to a permanent settlement based on Security Council Resolutions 242 and 338.

> It is understood that the interim arrangements are an integral part of the whole peace process and that the negotiations on the permanent status will lead to the implementation of Security Council Resolutions 242 and 338.

As stated in this article, and as agreed upon at the Madrid Conference, the ultimate objective of the negotiations is to reach a permanent settlement to the Israeli–Palestinian conflict based on UNSC Resolutions 242 and 338. According to Kathleen Lawand, '[t]his reference to resolutions 242 and 338 commits the parties to no more than an obligation to negotiate in good faith a permanent agreement with respect to the refugee problem'.[77] As discussed in Chapter 2, neither UNSC Resolution 242 nor 338 makes any reference to UNGA Resolution 194.[78] Although it can be argued that a just settlement to the refugee problem would have to conform to principles of international law and UN Resolutions, including Resolution 194, by not explicitly making any references to these norms and resolutions, the parties to the DOP, notably Israel, have not committed themselves to their implementation. The law-based approach to the resolution of the refugee issue which was advanced by the UN in the 1980s, thus seems to have been abandoned in the DOP. It is important to note, however, that Israel has committed itself to resolving the issue of refugees and displaced persons 'in accordance with international law' in Article 8 of the Israeli–Jordanian Peace Treaty, though again, no reference was made to Resolution 194 in that treaty. As discussed earlier in this chapter, Israel also rejected attempts by Palestinians to raise the issue of Resolution 194 in the multilateral discussions of the RWG.

It can thus be argued that there was a deliberate attempt by Israel to exclude Resolution 194 from the Madrid Framework and the OPP and to lower the refugees' expectations of having their rights enforced.

Although none of the interim agreements signed as part of the OPP has addressed the refugee issue, second-track negotiations produced a series of unofficial proposals that suggest that final status negotiations between the PLO and Israel are unlikely to resolve the refugee issue on the basis of Resolution 194 or general principles of international law. As discussed in this chapter, the 'pragmatic' solution identified in the Ottawa Process discarded the right to restitution and redefined the right to return, so as to exclude any repatriation of refugees to their homes inside Israel. Under the guise of 'political realism', additional track-two initiatives in the 1990s sought to promote similar solutions that undermined Palestinian refugee rights under international law. Between 1994 and 1995, an Israeli–Palestinian Joint Working Group met at Harvard to draft general principles for a comprehensive final Israeli–Palestinian agreement.[79] In 1998, they published a paper in which they identified the gaps between the Palestinian position and the Israeli position on the Palestinian refugee problem and the Right of Return.[80] According to this paper, 'at the *practical* level, the core of the solution involves four components: a 'return', however defined, of a limited number of refugees to Israel proper; return of a larger number to the Palestinian state; permanent absorption in host countries (notably Jordan); and compensation'.[81] Thus, the Working Group at Harvard identified the same parameters of the 'pragmatic' solution envisaged by the core group of the Ottawa Process. The return of refugees was reinterpreted as a return to a *homeland* (i.e. the future Palestinian state), rather than a return to the *homes* inside Israel from which the refugees were displaced in 1948. This interpretation of the right of return goes against the terms of Resolution 194. Additionally, as discussed in Chapter 4, this solution contradicts principles of international law and precedents which favour voluntary repatriation as a durable solution for refugees and prioritize restitution as the form of reparation for property losses. No mention is made of the Palestinian refugees' right to *choose* a durable solution and the form of reparation. Instead, refugees are expected to forego their rights under international law for the sake of practicality, 'pragmatism' or 'political realism'. As such, they will have to accept local integration in Arab host countries or resettlement in third countries for a durable solution and compensation *in lieu* of restitution for their losses.

At the same time that the Harvard group was meeting, the head of the PLO's Negotiations Affairs Department, Mahmoud Abbas (Abu Mazen), and Israel's minister of justice, Yossi Beilin, were drafting a secret document outlining the framework for the conclusion of a final status agreement between Israel and the PLO, which came to be known as the Beilin–Abu Mazen document. Though the document was never officially signed, considering the influential position of its drafters, it gave an indication of the most likely outcome of final status negotiations on permanent status issues. Since the two parties failed to reach a consensus on the refugee issue, the document's article on refugees opens with each side's views on the rights of Palestinian refugees:

> 1. Whereas the Palestinian side considers that the right of the Palestinian refugees to return to their homes is enshrined in international law and natural justice, *it recognizes that the prerequisites of the new era of peace and coexistence, as well as the realities that have been created on the ground since 1948, have rendered the implementation of this right impracticable.* The Palestinian side, thus, declares its readiness to accept and implement policies and measures that will ensure, insofar as this is possible, the welfare and well-being of these refugees.[82]

Here again, the Palestinian side concedes that the implementation of refugee rights is no longer practical. Moreover, the abandonment of the inalienable rights of Palestinian refugees is presented as a necessary prerequisite of the '*new era of peace and coexistence*'. This position can be contrasted with that of the Arab states at the UNCCP's Lausanne Conference in 1949 when these states, with the exception of Transjordan, 'were not prepared to enter into general peace negotiations with Israel until the solution of the refugee problem had been found, at least in principle – i.e., until Israel had recognized the right of the refugees (as laid down in paragraph 11 of the General Assembly Resolution) to return to their homes and regain their property for those who wished, and the right to receive indemnity for losses sustained for those who did not wish to return'.[83] Forty years later, following the signature of the DOP, the mere process of entering into negotiations with Israel became the priority, rather than the substance of these negotiations and the likelihood that they would lead to the safeguard and implementation of internationally sanctioned rights.[84] While Abu Mazen recognized that Palestinian refugees have rights under international law, by agreeing to compromise these rights for the sake of achieving a 'practical' or 'pragmatic' solution to the refugee issue, he was essentially suggesting that a law-based solution to the refugee issue was not a politically feasible one. As such, the Palestinian leadership itself contributed to the erosion of the 1980s consensus, which perceived the full respect for and the realization of the inalienable rights of the Palestinian people as 'indispensable' for the solution of the question of Palestine.[85]

The Israeli position on the right of return lends further weight to the argument that the law-based approach to the refugee issue was abandoned following the signature of the DOP. Contrary to the wording of Resolution 194, in the Beilin–Abu Mazen document, Israel redefines the right of return as a return to a future Palestinian state: 'Whereas the Israeli side acknowledges the moral and material suffering caused to the Palestinian people as a result of the war of 1947–9. It further acknowledges the Palestinian refugees' right of return to the Palestinian state and their right to compensation and rehabilitation for moral and material losses'.[86] As such, this return would not be accompanied by the restitution of the refugees' property inside the State of Israel. Compensation and rehabilitation for both moral and material losses were to be awarded instead.

While the statements on the right of return in the Beilin–Abu Mazen document were fairly general, for the first time since the signature of the DOP, this document provided some details on the mechanisms necessary to implement the agreed-upon solution to the refugee issue. The parties agreed to establish an International Commission for Palestinian Refugees (ICPR) in order to settle all aspects of the refugee issue.[87] As discussed in Chapter 3, a mass claims tribunal is the most suitable vehicle for the resolution of Palestinian refugees' property claims. The ICPR envisaged by the Beilin–Abu Mazen document was to adjudicate *individual* claims for material losses.[88] Additionally, each refugee family was to be entitled to compensation for their moral loss.[89] The ICPR also provided financial support for the rehabilitation and resettlement of refugees.[90] No mention is made of the refugees' right to the restitution of their property, which is the preferred remedy for these types of losses under international law.[91] Furthermore, the Commission was to 'explore the intentions of Palestinian refugees on the one hand and of Arab and other countries on the other, concerning wishes for emigration and the possibilities thereof'.[92] It was also to 'explore with Arab governments hosting refugee populations, as well as with these refugees, venues for absorption in these countries whenever mutually desired'.[93] In other words, refugees were only to be able to choose between local integration in an Arab host country or resettlement in a third country. Voluntary repatriation, which is the favoured durable solution under international law,[94] would not be available to refugees. The envisaged solution to the refugee issue suggested in the Beilin–Abu Mazen document can be contrasted with the position of international law on the rights of Palestinian refugees as restated in the CEIRPP's 1976 report:

The opinion was expressed that whatever modalities or procedure were envisaged for the implementation of the right of return of the Palestinians – whether such return would be carried out by phases or by quotas according to a definite time-table - that right should be absolute for every Palestinian and must have priority over any other form of substitute arrangements, such as compensation. *The Palestinians should be afforded the widest practical opportunities to exercise their right of return, in regard both to the time element and to procedural conditions. Only those Palestinians who would choose not to avail themselves of those opportunities after a pre-determined period of time should be considered as opting for compensation instead of actual repatriation.*[95]

This statement demonstrates that the right of return, which was understood as a return to one's home in accordance with Resolution 194, was given priority over compensation. What is also important is the emphasis put on the right of Palestinian refugees to *choose* their durable solution and not to have a solution imposed on them. Unfortunately, the Beilin–Abu Mazen document failed to acknowledge this fundamental right of all refugees to choose their durable solution, which must include voluntary repatriation to their homes. Instead, refugees were offered the choice between local integration and resettlement, while their return was dismissed as impracticable.[96] Israel only committed to enable family reunification and to 'absorb' (not repatriate) a limited number of refugees under specially defined cases.[97] As a consequence of being denied return, the Palestinian refugees' right to the restitution of their property was entirely overlooked. Compensation was the only form of reparation envisaged by the Beilin–Abu Mazen document to address material and moral losses incurred by Palestinian refugees. The document also included an end-of-claims clause which, as discussed in Chapter 3, is normally included to preclude individuals from bringing any additional claims.[98]

The Beilin–Abu Mazen document was neither a detailed agreement nor a formal one. Nevertheless, bearing in mind that the drafters of this document were high-ranking officials in both the Israeli government and the PLO, this document revealed the extent to which each of these parties was willing to go to sign a peace agreement. On the one hand, the Palestinian negotiators were willing to compromise refugee rights in order to reach a comprehensive peace agreement with Israel, which would include the creation of a Palestinian state in parts of the West Bank and Gaza Strip.[99] As such, they were using the individual rights of Palestinian refugees, the full implementation of which was considered '*impracticable*', as bargaining chips in order to realize the collective goal of Palestinian statehood. As discussed earlier, the consensus in the 1980s was that full respect for and realization of *all* inalienable rights of Palestinians are indispensable to resolve the question of Palestine. Thus, the rights of Palestinian refugees should not be sacrificed for the right of the Palestinian people to self-determination. On the other hand, Israeli negotiators displayed the traditional intransigence on the refugee issue by dismissing the right of return and, with it, the right to property restitution. Their position was that refugees should be compensated for their losses and resettled anywhere *except* in Israel. As argued by Professor Joseph Massad, what is common about the proposals on the refugee issue that have resulted from second-track negotiations since the signature of the DOP, 'is the discourse of 'pragmatism' and 'realism' which they deploy. The definition of pragmatism in this discourse is one wherein everything Israel rejects is 'not pragmatic', while everything it accepts is 'pragmatic'. What this means is that the Palestinians are the only party being asked to be 'pragmatic', as Israeli positions function as base referents and are therefore deployed as 'pragmatic' a priori'.[100] The prevalence of the discourse of 'pragmatism' in the circle of academics, policymakers and negotiators throughout the 1990s was to carry its influence into final status negotiations.

5.5 Final status negotiations: From Camp David II to Taba

The OPP's official negotiations suffered a setback following the assassination of Israeli Prime Minister Yitzhak Rabin on 4 November 1995. News of Rabin's death came only four days after Beilin and Abu Mazen had finished drawing up the framework for the conclusion of a final status agreement between Israel and the PLO. Shimon Peres succeeded Rabin for a few months during which he was unable to achieve any breakthroughs in the negotiations with the PLO.[101] He was defeated by Benjamin Netanyahu, the leader of the right-wing Likud Party, in the May 1996 elections. Netanyahu, a fervent critic of the Oslo agreements, reluctantly agreed to negotiate with Arafat.[102] Under US pressure, the Wye River Memorandum was signed on 23 October 1998. The agreement was another interim arrangement providing for the redeployment of Israeli forces from parts of the West Bank.[103] After an initial phase of redeployment, the process was suspended by the Israeli cabinet as Netanyahu prepared for early elections. The elections in May 1999 brought the Labour Party back into power under the leadership of Ehud Barak who was elected on a 'platform for peace'.[104]

Negotiations between Israel and the PLO resumed soon after Barak's victory, and a series of low-level talks took place in the months leading up to the Camp David talks. The most significant among them were the negotiations in Stockholm in May 2000 during which the parties exchanged a 'non-paper' entitled 'Framework Agreement on Permanent Status'. The refugee question was discussed for the first time in Article 7 of the Agreement: 'Taking into consideration the suffering caused to [P: Palestinian refugees] [I: individuals and communities] as a result of the 1948 [I: Arab-Israeli] War and recognizing that a just, humane, political, and realistic solution to their right. The Parties are determined to put an end to their suffering based on UNSCR 242 [P: and leading to the implementation of UNGAR 194] is essential to put an end to the Israeli-Palestinian conflict'.[105]

There are two interesting points worth highlighting about this article: first, there is once again the discourse on the need to find a 'political, and realistic' solution to the plight of refugees, as opposed perhaps to a legal one. Second, there is the reference to Resolution 194, which was added by Palestinian negotiators. This is the first time that Resolution 194 was explicitly referred to in a jointly negotiated document, albeit a non-official one.[106] The reference reflects a growing awareness on the part of Palestinian negotiators of the importance of acknowledging and reaffirming the legal basis of the rights of Palestinian refugees in a prospective final status agreement, even though they may still perceive the *full* implementation of these rights to be unrealistic. It also reveals that, in the PLO's view, a 'just settlement to the refugee problem' in accordance with UNSC Resolution 242 would have to lead to the implementation of UNGA Resolution 194. According to Omar Dajani, in the early negotiation rounds, 'the Palestinian negotiating team took the position that international norms were mandatory rules that required resolution of disputed issues in particular ways, declining to discuss Israeli proposals until the parties reached consensus about the boundaries of the zone of lawfulness within which they were operating'.[107] However, Dajani adds, over time, Palestinian negotiators began invoking law in a different way, treating norms as default rules from which the parties could agree to depart.[108] As will be demonstrated in the next section, by the end of the Camp David talks, Palestinian negotiators were in fact willing to bargain with the rights of Palestinian refugees in order to achieve concessions on other final status issues.

Furthermore, in the 'non-paper' exchanged at Stockholm, Israeli and Palestinian negotiators proposed to create an international commission and an international fund for compensation. The commission would be entrusted with the task of ascertaining the wishes of refugees while the fund would disburse monetary awards to refugees. Here again, Palestinian negotiators displayed greater attention to the entitlements of Palestinian refugees under international law. In a form which was to be sent out by the Commission to individual refugees to ascertain their wishes among a list of options, Palestinian negotiators inserted the option for refugees to 'return to their *homes* in Israel *with* compensation'.[109] The wording of this option, which was not approved by Israeli negotiators, included an implicit acknowledgement of the right to property restitution, which was to accompany the refugees' return to Israel. It also included an affirmation that the rights of Palestinian refugees to return, restitution and compensation are not mutually exclusive. By contrast, Israeli negotiators dismissed the right of return and insisted that Israel would have the discretion to admit refugees on the basis of family reunification.[110] Despite breaking the lull in negotiations, which had persisted during Netanyahu's time in office, the talks at Stockholm did not result in a signed agreement between the parties.[111] A breakthrough was envisaged at Camp David in July 2000, which was the first time the PLO and Israel came together under US auspices for official negotiations on the final status issues.

5.5.1 Camp David II

The Camp David summit was held between the 11th and the 24th of July 2000. There are no official records of the negotiations at Camp David. The only means of gathering information about the substance of the negotiations is through 'non-papers', as well as published accounts of individuals who were present at the summit or had had direct contact with the negotiators.[112] As such, there are many versions of the talks and different interpretations of the proposals which were tabled by the participants. Nevertheless, an overview of some of these accounts reveals that the refugee issue was not negotiated in depth at Camp David and no agreements were reached on this matter.[113] An analysis of these records also indicates that though there were some differences of opinion among Palestinian and Israeli negotiators, the contours of the most likely solution to the refugee question remained essentially the same as the ones identified in second-track negotiations, from the Ottawa Process to the Beilin–Abu Mazen agreement.[114] In other words, the implementation of the right of return of refugees to their homes inside Israel was considered impracticable. According to Dennis Ross, chief Middle East peace negotiator under Clinton's administration, 'Painful concessions were required on each side. Historic myths would have to give way to political necessity and reality on each side […]. For their part, the Palestinians had to give up the myth of 'right of return' to Israel'.[115] As such,

Israel would only admit a limited number of refugees on the basis of family reunification. The remaining refugees would have to be absorbed in the future Palestinian state, Arab host countries and resettlement countries. Refugees would also be awarded compensation for their losses, in lieu of restitution. The negotiations thus revolved mainly around technical issues such as the number of refugees admitted back into Israel,[116] the amount of money awarded as compensation for the refugees' losses[117] and the mechanisms created to process their claims.[118] Although Israeli and Palestinian negotiators held different views on these matters, the most difficult aspect of the negotiations on the refugee issue was whether Israel would recognize the right of return in an eventual final agreement.

Proposals on the refugee issue were tabled from Day One of the negotiations to bridge the gap between the parties.[119] According to Balaban, 'Clinton proposed absorbing about 100,000 Palestinians over several years (about 15,000 per year), within a family reunification scheme, without recognizing "the right of return".'[120] In response, Arafat stated that he wanted 'the principle of the right of return to be laid down [...]' first, and then talk about 'the practical details of its implementation'.[121] A few days into the summit, the Americans presented a 'non-paper' which stated in part as follows:

> As part of the international effort Israel will [I: as a matter of its sovereign discretion] facilitate the phased entry of _____ refugees to its territory [P: per year on the basis of the refugees' exercise of their right of return] [I: on humanitarian grounds provided they join their families in their present place of residence in Israel, accept Israeli citizenship, and waive their legal status as refugees.] In addition, in the context of pledges made by the international community, Israel will make an annual financial and/or in-kind contribution [of $_____] to the international program and/or to Palestinian efforts to deal with the refugee problem.[122]

As evidenced by the comments inserted in the American proposal, the Israeli and Palestinian positions on the recognition of the right of refugees to return to their homes inside Israel remained significantly different. Both sides rejected the American 'non-paper' and resumed negotiations on the refugee issue in subsequent days.[123] Clayton E. Swisher reports that some Palestinians conceded after Camp David, off the record, 'that Arafat had been willing to accept a limited right of return, in all likelihood within the symbolic strictures of 'family reunification' entertained at Stockholm, so long as the Palestinians received recognition of that right and a viable state with Palestinian sovereignty over

East Jerusalem and the Haram al-Sharif/Temple Mount'.[124] Palestinians were thus willing to bargain away the rights of Palestinian refugees in order to draw concessions from the Israelis on other issues, such as Jerusalem and the borders of the Palestinian state.[125] The larger the Palestinian state, the argument would go, the greater its capacity to absorb millions of refugees. According to several Israeli delegates, the Palestinian negotiators' strategy was to save the refugees' right of return as the final card in the negotiations. They were not going to concede on this point until the parties had concluded agreements on all other remaining issues.[126] Having accepted that the implementation of the right of return to Israel would be constrained by Israel's demographic needs, the Palestinians at Camp David wanted to shift the discussion to technical issues, such as the creation of a fund for the compensation and rehabilitation of refugees.[127] According to Michael Fischbach, Palestinian negotiators held the position that the refugees still owned legal title to the land.[128] As such, they demanded that Israel hand over the accumulated funds generated from the property over years. In response, Elyakim Rubinstein, the lead Israeli negotiator on the refugee issue stated that 'these funds no longer exist. We have used them up. It is up to the international community to create funds for this'.[129] Swisher notes that most of the Israelis at Camp David agreed with Rubinstein that Israel should not finance the international fund for the compensation of refugees as this could be construed as an implicit Israeli acknowledgment of culpability for the refugee problem, thus making it legally vulnerable.[130]

What transpires from this overview of the information available on the Camp David talks is that the Palestinians once again adopted the so-called 'pragmatic' approach to the resolution of the refugee issue. Under the guise of political realism, they were willing to bargain away the refugees' right of return and restitution in order to gain concessions from Israel on other issues. By so doing, they undermined the law-based approach to the resolution of the refugee issue. Despite exhibiting considerable flexibility, Palestinian negotiators collided with the Israelis on the issue of the recognition of the right of return as enshrined in Resolution 194. Galia Golan notes that Israel preferred to avoid any reference to Resolution 194.[131] The uncompromising position of Israeli negotiators at Camp David was not surprising. In fact, as he was departing to the Camp David summit, Barak reassured the Israeli public that 'Israel will not recognize any moral or legal responsibility for the refugee problem'.[132] He further indicated that any agreement signed at Camp David 'should be signed as a replacement of 242 or 338, 194 and 181'.[133] Barak's logic was that the Israelis could then 'go to the international bodies and tell them that the agreements are instead of these resolutions, according to the will of both parties. The implementation of the decisions is written here, and there are no further demands on either party. Then Arafat will need to go to his people and tell them in Arabic that he has abandoned the claim to the right of return'.[134] In other words, Barak wanted to achieve a political settlement at Camp David which would terminate the legal claims of Palestinian refugees.

The extent to which the refugee issue played a role in the failure of the Camp David talks will remain subject to debate:[135] the talks ended on 24 July without the parties signing any agreements. The negotiations process was halted after Camp David, as Barak and Clinton laid the blame for the summit's failure squarely at Arafat's door.[136] Official negotiations were brought to a halt after the eruption of the Second Intifada in September 2000. They resumed on 10 December, a day after Barak resigned as Israel's Prime Minister.[137]

5.5.2 The Clinton Parameters

Israeli and Palestinian negotiators arrived in Washington on 19 December for another round of talks. A few days into the talks, on 23 December, President Bill Clinton presented the negotiators with a proposal to bridge the gap between the parties on key issues. This proposal became known as the Clinton Parameters.[138] On the issue of refugees, Clinton believed that 'the remaining gaps are more in formulations than in the practical realities'.[139] Clinton confirmed his commitment to the two-state solution as a means to end the Israeli–Palestinian conflict. This solution would lead to the creation of a Palestinian state 'as the homeland of the Palestinian people, just as Israel was established as the homeland of the Jewish people'. Clinton thus believed that the Palestinian refugees who 'choose to return to the area' would have to return mainly to the future Palestinian state. Clinton did not rule out the possibility that Israel would absorb some refugees, at its own discretion. He believed the parties needed to adopt 'a formulation on the right of return that will make clear there is no specific right of return to Israel, itself, but that does not negate the aspirations of Palestinian refugees to the area'.

In line with previous proposals to resolve the refugee issue, like the Beilin–Abu Mazen agreement, and contrary to principles of international law, the Clinton Parameters reinterpreted the right of return of refugees as a return to one's homeland, rather than a return to the homes from which the refugees were displaced. As such, the refugees' right to the restitution of their property was entirely overlooked in the Parameters. Nevertheless, Clinton's proposal to bridge the gaps between the parties on the refugee issue was met with Israeli condemnation,[140] while Palestinians denounced the Parameters' 'wholesale adoption of the Israeli position that the implementation of the right of return be subject entirely to Israel's discretion'.[141] The Palestinian side also noted the Parameters' failure 'to provide any assurance that the refugees' rights to restitution and compensation will be fulfilled'.[142] Though Clinton's Parameters were dismissed by both sides, they did not vanish completely. They were to resurface indirectly in the track-two Geneva Initiative of 2003, which will be discussed later in this chapter.

5.5.3 The Taba negotiations

Despite having all odds set against their success, Palestinian and Israeli negotiators convened again at Taba in a final attempt to conclude an agreement before the end of Clinton's term in office. The talks were held from 18 to 27 January 2001.[143] Contrary to Camp David, where the Americans played a significant role, no outsiders participated in the Taba talks. As in the case of Camp David though, there is no single official version of the content of the negotiations. Notes taken by EU envoy, Miguel Moratinos, were accepted by both sides as an accurate record of what took place.[144] Moratinos was the only outsider present at Taba, although not at the meetings themselves. He compiled his report from interviews he conducted with the negotiators. The parties also released a joint statement on 27 January 2007 in which they declared that 'they have never been closer to reaching an agreement'.[145] In addition, a draft Palestinian proposal on the Palestinian refugees was published by *Le Monde Diplomatique* in the summer of 2001 along with the Israeli private response to it.[146] According to Badil, the Palestinian Proposal 'is consistent with the Palestinian national consensus concerning a durable solution for refugees and provides an agenda for advocacy and lobbying, as well as the foundation for future negotiations on the refugee issue'.[147] There are several reasons why Badil deemed this proposal to be consonant with principles of international law. First, it makes explicit reference to Resolution 194 and stipulates from the onset that a 'just settlement of the refugee problem, in accordance with United Nations Security Council Resolution 242, must lead to the implementation of United Nations General Assembly Resolution 194'.[148] According to the Moratinos 'non-paper', the Israeli side concurred with this statement.[149] This statement was meant to dispel the ambiguity created by the vague wording of the DOP in which Resolution 194 was not explicitly mentioned.

While Israel's reference to Resolution 194 was a significant step forward, opinions differed as to what would constitute an implementation of this Resolution. In the furtherance of the two-state solution, the Israelis listed five different possibilities for the implementation of the refugees' 'wish to return':[150] return and repatriation to Israel, to the Palestinian state or to territory swapped from Israel to the Palestinian state. Alternatively, refugees would be able to rehabilitate in host countries or relocate to third countries. Palestinian negotiators stressed that these options 'shall be subject to the individual free choice of the refugees and shall not prejudice their right to their homes in accordance with its interpretation of UNGA Resolution 194'.[151] This was the first time that Palestinian negotiators clearly indicated their support for the refugees' right to *choose* a durable solution, as opposed to having one imposed upon them. In addition, it demonstrated the Palestinians' understanding of and commitment to the principles of international law discussed in Chapter 4, which distinguish between a refugee's choice of a durable solution and his or her right to receive reparation for property losses, whether in the form of restitution or compensation.[152] The Palestinian proposal at Taba was in fact the first time that the Palestinian side officially raised the issue of the restitution of refugees' real property:

27. Real property owned by a returning refugee at the time of his or her displacement shall be restored to the refugee or his or her lawful successors.

28. In cases where, according to criteria determined by the Repatriation Commission, it is impossible, impracticable or inequitable to restore the property to its refugee owner, the refugee shall be restituted in-kind with property *within Israel*, equal in size and/or value to the land and other property that they lost [emphasis added].

Again, these provisions reveal the Palestinian side's commitment to principles of international law according to which restitution is the preferred remedy for property losses.[153] As demonstrated in Chapter 4, compensation, in-kind or monetary, can only substitute for restitution when the latter is deemed 'factually impossible' by an impartial tribunal or when those possessing restitution rights choose to receive financial compensation *in lieu* of restitution. The Palestinian proposal thus subscribed to principles of international law on reparation for property losses. According to the Moratinos non-paper, the Israeli side rejected the Palestinians' proposal on the restitution of property and no mention is made of that right in the Israeli private response to the Palestinian refugee proposal.[154]

In addition to proposing solutions that safeguard the rights of Palestinian refugees under international law, Palestinian negotiators suggested mechanisms for the implementation of these rights. As was the case in the Dayton Agreement, the Palestinian proposal suggested the creation of two commissions: a Repatriation Commission charged with guaranteeing and managing the implementation of the right of return[155] and a Compensation Commission established to evaluate the Palestinian material and moral losses and to administer and adjudicate claims of real property by refugees.[156] To avoid a repeat of the shortcomings of the CRPC in Bosnia,[157] if both Commissions are created, they should receive equal support and funding to enable them to fulfil their mandate and guarantee the implementation of *all* the rights of refugees. To further that aim, the Palestinian proposal suggested the establishment of an International Fund.[158] According to the Moratinos 'non-paper', both sides only agreed to the establishment of 'an International Commission and an International Fund as a mechanism for dealing with compensation in all its aspects'.[159] No mention is made of a Repatriation Commission in the Moratinos 'non-paper' or in the Israeli private response to the Palestinian refugee proposal. Both sides also agreed that some claims would be subject to 'fast-track' procedures, which might have been inspired by the UNCC's processing of compensation claims pertaining to small losses.[160]

As had already been suggested in the Clinton Parameters, the parties also proposed giving preference to Palestinian refugees in Lebanon in the implementation phase.[161] In a marked departure from their historical position on this issue, the Israeli side agreed to delink the claims of Jewish refugees from Arab countries from those of Palestinian refugees.[162] The parties also discussed an end-of-claims clause, and it was suggested that the 'implementation of the agreement shall constitute a complete and final implementation of UNGAR 194 and therefore ends all claims'.[163] While several gaps in the positions of the parties on the refugee issue were bridged at Taba, divergent opinions were expressed on the future role of UNRWA as well as on the narrative pertaining to the events of 1948. Regarding UNRWA, the Israelis favoured the phased termination of the Agency within five years, while the Palestinians suggested a possible adjustment to that period.[164] As for the narrative of 1948, the sides failed to reach an agreement on the responsibility of Israel for the creation of the refugee issue.[165]

Overall, it can be said that the refugee issue was on the table of negotiations for the first time at Taba. After being marginalized for years throughout the OPP, both parties finally acknowledged that 'the issue of the Palestinian refugees is central to Israeli-Palestinian relations and that a comprehensive and just solution is essential to creating a lasting and morally scrupulous peace'.[166] Despite achieving significant progress on this issue, the main difference in the Israeli and Palestinian positions was one of approach. The Palestinians reverted back to the law-based approach to the resolution of the refugee issue, having spent several years undermining it by adopting the slanted discourse of 'pragmatism' and 'political realism' championed by the Israeli and American sides. According to Badil, the 'Palestinian proposal provides a legal framework for a durable solution that is consistent both with the terms of UN General Assembly Resolution 194 as well as international law and practice relative to durable solutions for refugees'.[167] By contrast, the Israeli response 'provides a political framework, components of which are inconsistent with Resolution 194 as well as international law and practice relative to durable solutions for refugees'.[168] Notwithstanding these differences, the proposals on the refugee issue at Taba remain the most comprehensive and detailed to date. As noted by Gali Golan, '[G]iven the context of the talks, namely both the escalating violence and especially the Israeli elections due in a matter of days which were expected to oust Barak from power, little more could have been expected from Taba'.[169]

5.6 Peace initiatives

On 6 February 2001, Ariel Sharon, leader of the right-wing Likud party, won a landslide victory over Barak. His election brought the peace process to an effective standstill. Since then, there has been no real progress in the official tracks of negotiations despite efforts by the Arab League and the US to breathe some life into the OPP. On 28 March 2002, the Arab League adopted Saudi Crown Prince Abdallah's peace proposal, also known as the Arab Peace Initiative, at its summit in Beirut.[170] The initiative endorsed the two-state solution and called upon Israel to affirm the '[A]chievement of a just solution to the Palestinian Refugee problem to be agreed upon in accordance with UN General Assembly Resolution 194'.[171] The Israeli government ignored the initiative altogether.[172] It was not until 30 April 2003 that another attempt was made to revive the peace process. This time, it was George W. Bush's administration, in cooperation with its partners in the Quartet (Russia, the EU and the UN) that put forth 'Elements of a Performance-based Road Map to a Permanent Two-State Solution to the Israeli-Palestinian Conflict' (the Road Map).[173] The Road Map was not a detailed peace plan. It was more accurately described in an International Crisis Group report as a 'a set of vital, well-crafted and balanced exhortations to the parties: end the violence; halt settlement activity; reform Palestinian institutions; accept Israel's right to exist; establish a viable, sovereign Palestinian state; and reach a final settlement on all issues by 2005'.[174] As with the DOP, the Road Map relegates the refugee issue to final status negotiations and it was another unsuccessful attempt to relaunch the OPP.

In the meantime, track-two negotiations resulted in a couple of proposals which aimed to fill the void created by the interruption of official negotiations. The first was a proposal for peace signed in July 2002 between Dr. Sari Nusseibeh, a Palestinian intellectual from the West Bank, and Amy Ayalon, former head of Israel's internal security service (Shin Bet).[175] The Nusseibeh–Ayalon Agreement, also known as the People's Voice,[176] is not a detailed proposal. It contains only five provisions, which can be spelled out on a single page. It contains a provision on borders, one on Jerusalem and a provision on refugees, which stipulates the following:

> Right of return: Recognizing the suffering and the plight of the Palestinian refugees, the international community, Israel, and the Palestinian State will initiate and contribute to an international fund to compensate them.
>
> Palestinian refugees will return only to the State of Palestine; Jews will return only to the State of Israel.
>
> The international community will offer to compensate toward bettering the lot of those refugees willing to remain in their present country of residence, or who wish to immigrate to third-party countries.[177]

This provision totally undermines the right of Palestinian refugees and absolves Israel of any responsibility towards them. It denies the refugees the right to return to their homes inside Israel and, by so doing, denies their right to the restitution of their property. Instead, it reinterprets the right of return as a return to a 'homeland', and promotes compensation as the *only* form of reparation available to refugees and even then, only to those who elect to stay in exile in Arab host countries or third countries. In addition, although the responsibility for the displacement of Palestinian refugees and the expropriation of their property lies primarily with Israel, Israel is only expected to be a contributor, one among others, to an international fund for the compensation of refugees. The international community is expected instead to foot the bill for the rehabilitation of refugees in host countries and their resettlement to third countries. The Nusseibeh–Ayalon Agreement garnered little support and was soon overshadowed by the more publicized Geneva Accords (or Geneva Initiative) signed on 12 October 2003.

Talks leading to the signature of the Accords began after the failure of the Taba negotiations in 2001. They were conducted between teams of Israeli and Palestinian professionals led by Dr Yossi Beilin, on the Israeli side, and Yasser Abed Rabbo, on the Palestinian side. The Geneva Initiative (GI) was the most detailed proposal to emerge from track-two negotiations. It endorsed a two-state solution based on UNSC Resolutions 242 and 338.[178] Article 7 of the GI addresses the refugee issue. The parties began by recognizing that 'an agreed resolution of the refugee problem is necessary for achieving a just, comprehensive and lasting peace' between Israel and the Palestinians. The resolution of that issue was also deemed central to 'stability building and development in the region'.[179] The parties then described the implementation of Article 7 of the GI as fulfilling the rights of refugees as stipulated in UNGA Resolution 194, UNSC Resolution 242 and the Arab Peace Initiative. As noted by Karma Nabulsi, however, the 'substance of Article 7 is, in very clear terms, a refutation' of the principles enshrined in Resolution 194.[180] Like the Israeli Proposal at Taba, the Article suggests that refugees shall be able to choose a permanent place of residence (PPR) from among five options: (i) the future State of Palestine; (ii) areas in Israel transferred to that State in land swaps; (iii) third countries; (iv) the State of Israel and (v) current host countries.[181] While refugees can select any of the first two options as of *right*, the three remaining options are subject to the discretion of the state admitting the refugees. This approach essentially absolves Israel of any responsibility to repatriate the refugees to their homes, as per Resolution 194 and principles of international law. Israel is treated no differently than host countries and third countries of resettlement. Although the parties recognize that the refugees' choice of their PPR shall be on the basis of a free and informed decision,[182] they do not recognize that these refugees have a *right* to choose to repatriate voluntarily to their homes inside Israel.

In addition to not recognizing the refugees' right to choose, Article 7 of the GI overlooks the issue of property restitution for refugees. By ignoring the refugees' right to restitution, this Article does not conform to standards of international law on reparation, nor does it implement the principles included in paragraph 11 of Resolution 194. The parties focus instead on compensation which shall be awarded both for 'refugeehood' and loss of property and 'shall not be prejudiced by the refugee's permanent place of residence'.[183] The parties also agree to create an International Commission to implement Article 7 in all its parts. As such, the Commission would be in charge of overseeing the process by which the refugees determine and realize their choice of a PPR. The Commission would also be in charge of overseeing the disbursement of compensation for refugees and their rehabilitation in host countries.[184] As suggested at Taba, compensation claims for property below a specified value would be fast-tracked.[185] The Commission would also accept individual claims for immovable property or other assets exceeding a certain amount.[186] The categorization of claims according to the value of the losses incurred seems inspired by the processing mechanisms employed by the UNCC. Additionally, the Commission would oversee the operation of the Refugeehood Fund, which would be established to disburse funds to refugee communities in UNRWA's areas of operations.[187] An International Fund would be created to finance the activities of the International Commission.[188] Israel would contribute to the International Fund by paying an agreed-upon 'lump-sum', which would constitute the aggregate sum of property compensation owed to refugees. The payment of that lump sum would preclude other financial claims arising from the refugee problem from being raised against Israel.[189] By expecting Israel to contribute to the International Fund a sum equivalent to the property losses incurred by the refugees, the parties seem to agree that Israel does, in fact, bear some responsibility for the expropriation of refugee property, although not necessarily for their displacement. The parties call upon the international community to participate fully in the resolution of the refugee problem in accordance with the GI.[190] Unlike any of the previous proposals discussed in this chapter, the GI included a provision on reconciliation programmes, which would, *inter alia*, lead to the creation of 'forums for exchanging historical narrative and enhancing mutual understanding regarding the past'.[191]

In sum, although the GI provided the most detailed *agreed-upon* proposal on the refugee issue, it approached the refugee issue in a very technical way. The parties sought the lowest common denominators, which, in this case, were imposed by the strongest party in the negotiations, Israel. Hence, since Israel was unwilling to accept that the refugees have a right to return to their homes inside Israel and to repossess their property, their admission into Israel was made subject to that state's discretion, while their right to restitution was completely disregarded. The parties focused instead on the refugees' absorption in the future Palestinian state or in other countries and, in the process, ignored the refugees' *right* to choose voluntarily to repatriate to their homes in accordance with principles of international law. Also contrary to international law, compensation was presented as the *only* form of reparation available to refugees. The GI thus abandoned the law-based approach to the resolution of the refugee issue in favour of the so-called 'pragmatic approach', which had emerged from second-track negotiations and has been repeatedly reformulated and represented as the *only* feasible, realistic solution to the refugee issue. Despite the incredible publicity that surrounded the signature of the Initiative in Geneva in December 2003, and the fact that it was endorsed by such prominent figures as former US president, Jimmy Carter, the Initiative failed to succeed.

In the last two decades since the GI, attempts at reviving official peace negotiations have all but failed.[192] Israel has consolidated its stronghold over the Occupied Palestinian Territory prompting leading human rights organizations, as well as the former UN Special Rapporteur on the situation of human rights in the Palestinian Territory occupied since 1967, Professor Michael Lynk, to accuse it of the crime of apartheid.[193] At the time of writing, Israel is waging a genocidal war against Palestinians in Gaza and ramping up its raids in the West Bank and East Jerusalem, in the most devastating assault on Palestinians since 1948. Israelis are also reeling from Hamas's attacks on 7 October 2023, in which 1,200 people were killed, making it the deadliest day for Israelis since the State's creation. The unprecedented scale of death and destruction of the past 100 days and counting will likely take decades to heal, leaving behind it a trail of trauma and pain that make peace a distant and elusive mirage.

5.7 Conclusion

This chapter demonstrated that there was a near international consensus on the need to convene a conference under UN auspices to resolve the Middle East conflict, including the refugee issue, in a comprehensive way and on the basis of full respect for the Charter, UN Resolutions, and general principles of international law. The Madrid Peace Conference of 1991 announced the beginning of a new approach to the resolution of the Middle East conflict in general and the refugee issue in particular. This new approach consisted of the isolation of the parties to the conflict in separate bilateral tracks of negotiations, the fragmentation of the issues to the conflict, an incremental resolution of the Israeli–Palestinian conflict, a limited role for the UN in the negotiations process and the abandonment of a law-based approach to the resolution of the refugee issue.

This approach was perpetuated with the signature of the DOP. The DOP marginalized the refugee issue by relegating it to final status negotiations. It also dismissed as 'unrealistic' any attempt to resolve the refugee issue in accordance with principles of international law. The prevalence of the discourse of 'pragmatism' in the circle of academics, policymakers and negotiators throughout the 1990s was to carry its influence into final status negotiations. Under the guise of 'political realism', Palestinian negotiators at Camp David seemed willing to bargain away the refugees' rights of return and restitution in order to gain concessions from Israel on other issues. By so doing, they undermined the law-based approach to the resolution of the refugee issue. Fortunately, at the Taba talks, Palestinian negotiators reverted to the law-based approach and issued the most comprehensive and detailed proposals on the refugee issue to date.

With the exception of the Palestinian proposal at Taba, all other proposed solutions resulting from track-two negotiations dismissed the law-based approach as 'impractical' or 'unrealistic'. As discussed in this chapter, the so-called 'pragmatic' solution to the refugee issue denies Palestinian refugees their right to choose voluntary repatriation as a durable solution and to choose restitution as a form of reparation for their property losses. Organizations such as Human Rights Watch and Amnesty International have warned against the dismissal of individual refugee rights for the sake of political expediency.[194] Similarly, Article 22(4) of the Pinheiro Principles urges '[I]nternational organizations, including the United Nations, [...] to ensure that peace agreements and voluntary repatriation agreements contain provisions related to housing, land and property restitution, including through the establishment of national procedures, institutions, mechanisms and legal frameworks'.

Proponents of the 'pragmatic' approach will argue that peace necessitates compromises. Hence, refugees must be willing to give up their rights in return for peace and the establishment of a State of Palestine. Certainly, compromises are necessary to achieve peace. The question is, what sort of compromises and on what issues? Who determines what is 'politically feasible' and what isn't? The answers to these questions lie outside the scope of our analysis. However, one need only look at the balance sheet of thirty years of Israeli–Palestinian negotiations to determine whether the Oslo Peace Process approach to conflict resolution has succeeded. The OPP's 'political pragmatism' brought about another Intifada (uprising), the Separation Wall, a matrix of checkpoints and settlements in the occupied West Bank, the strangulation of the Gaza Strip leading up to a genocidal war, economic impoverishment in the OPTs, the rise of religious extremism on both sides of the divide and no end in sight to the refugees' forced exile along with the real risk of future forcible transfers of Palestinians in Gaza and the West Bank.[195] If these results are not enough to persuade the international community and the various stakeholders that the OPP's so-called 'pragmatic' approach has failed, there will be little hope for peace and justice between Palestinians and Israelis. A change of course is necessary, one that reinforces the need for accountability and respect for fundamental rights, while reframing the Palestinian question as a struggle for freedom and liberation from apartheid, military occupation and settler-colonialism and the legal and political orders that have sustained them.

Conclusion

This book set out to examine the right to reparation of Palestinian refugees under international law. The focus was on reparation for loss of or damage to property belonging to 1948 Palestinian refugees. The aim was also to provide negotiators, policymakers and refugees alike with a comprehensive legal analysis of the Palestinian refugees' right to reparation, starting with the circumstances giving rise to Palestinian refugee property claims and ending with how these claims were addressed in bilateral Israeli–Palestinian negotiations.

Chapter 1 began by providing a brief overview of the laws regulating land ownership in Palestine, both before and after the creation of the State of Israel in 1948, with the dual aim of providing a rounded source of information for researchers on this issue and demonstrating how land laws were used to dispossess Palestinian refugees. Israel continues to manipulate land laws to this day to expropriate property belonging to Palestinian citizens of Israel[1] and Palestinians residing in the Occupied West Bank and East Jerusalem.[2] Having outlined the process by which Palestinian refugees were dispossessed of their property, Chapter 2 examined the legal grounds for the Palestinian refugees' right to reparation. This chapter demonstrated that the measures taken by Israel against Palestinian refugee property constituted an internationally wrongful act and Israel has an obligation to provide reparations to Palestinian refugees for the destruction and confiscation of their property. Chapter 3 discussed the different legal avenues which can be used by Palestinian refugees to invoke their right to reparation. The chapter outlined the main advantages and drawbacks of a variety of fora and mechanisms which can be used, or have been used in the past, to invoke a right to reparation. It was argued that mass claims tribunals offer the best venue for the resolution of Palestinian refugees' property claims. Chapter 4 outlined the two main forms of reparation for property losses: restitution and compensation. It demonstrated that restitution is the preferred form of reparation under international law. This chapter also identified some of the legal obstacles to the implementation of Palestinian refugee property rights. It was argued that these legal obstacles are not insurmountable. On the other hand, the political and ideological obstacles to a return-based restitution of refugee property are much harder to overcome, particularly as Israel's settler ideology continues to be one of territorial expansion and transfer.[3]

The last chapter examined how Palestinian refugee property claims were addressed in Israeli–Palestinian negotiations. As has been shown, instead of searching for a comprehensive solution to the Israeli–Palestinian conflict – one which would promote respect for international law, the protection of human rights and the reversal of the ethnic cleansing of Palestinians from their homeland – the OPP endorsed an approach based on 'bilateralism', 'incrementalism' and 'pragmatism'. The PLO was isolated in bilateral negotiations. Meanwhile, the UN was excluded from the negotiations process and given an insignificant role as a member of the Middle East Peace Quartet. The conflict was also fragmented into separate issues, which were to be resolved in a piecemeal fashion. As a result, the refugee issue was relegated to final status negotiations, in which the individual rights of refugees were pitted against the collective right of self-determination of the Palestinian people. Palestinian refugee rights were thus reduced to political bargaining chips in the negotiations process. In addition, the law-based, or rights-based, approach to the refugee issue was dismissed in official negotiations and in peace initiatives as 'unrealistic'. With the exception of the Palestinian proposal at Taba, which was the most comprehensive and detailed proposal on the refugee issue to date, none of the other peace initiatives addressed the issue of Palestinian refugee property claims.

To conclude, hardly anything positive can be said about the OPP's approach to the refugee issue, or in fact to the resolution of the conflict altogether. The OPP is an endless process of phased negotiations and interim agreements which leave the core issues unresolved, all while Israel unilaterally changes the facts on the ground to the detriment of the Palestinians and blocks any attempt to hold it accountable as being 'counterproductive' and 'an obstacle to peace'. Thirty years later, it has become all but irrelevant.

The creation of the State of Israel as a settler colonial project began with the displacement and dispossession of the indigenous people of Palestine from their ancestral homes more than seventy-five years ago and was sustained through successive waves of forcible transfer and dispossession, of which the genocide in Gaza is the latest and most extreme manifestation. This is the ongoing Nakba. It is therefore hard to conceive of any permanent resolution of this struggle for decolonization that wouldn't take into account the root cause of it – the theft of a nation. It is only by addressing the rights of refugees and resolving their property claims that we can reverse the historical injustice that was the Nakba and move towards a future of reconciliation, coexistence and equality.[4] The comparative success of other peace agreements, which have included provisions for the return of refugees and displaced persons,[5] suggests that the protection of refugee rights and the resolution of their property claims can contribute to peacemaking. These precedents should encourage the adoption of a law-based approach to the resolution of the refugee issue and embed it within a broader political movement of decolonization in order to halt and reverse the ongoing Nakba.[6] In the meantime, the question of Palestinian refugees and their struggle for justice will persist, and Israel's transfer policies will continue to squeeze Palestinians out of their homeland, with Israel's full knowledge that it would not be called upon to provide reparation to those it has wronged. It is therefore incumbent on us not to allow it to evade accountability and to deploy the law and leverage it in our quest for justice and freedom. We owe it to the survivors of the Nakba, past and present.

Notes

Introduction

1 For more on the siege of Beirut and the Sabra and Shatila massacre, see R. Fisk, *Pity the Nation*, 3rd edn (Oxford: Oxford University Press, 2001).

2 See *inter alia* Canadian Broadcast Center (CBC), Leaked Document Fuels Concern Israel Plans to Push Palestinians from Gaza into Egypt | CBC News, 1 November 2023 (accessed 12 April 2024); Office of the High Commissioner for Human Rights (OHCHR), Israel Working to Expel Civilian Population of Gaza, UN Expert Warns | OHCHR, 22 December 2023 (accessed 12 April 2024), Middle East Eye (MEE), War on Gaza: Israel 'in Talks with Rwanda and Chad' to Exile Palestinians | Middle East Eye, 5 January 2024 (accessed 12 April 2024).

3 UNGA Res.181(II), *Future Government of Palestine*, 29 November 1947.

4 For more on the so-called Partition Plan, see, *inter alia*, H. Cattan, *Palestine and International Law: The Legal Aspects of the Arab-Israeli Conflict* (Bristol: Longman, 1973), pp. 27–82 and J. Quigley, *The Case for Palestine: An International Law Perspective* (Durham, NC: Duke University Press, 2005), pp. 32–40.

5 For more on the Arab–Israeli war, see L. Rogan and A. Shlaim, *The War for Palestine: Rewriting the History of 1948* (Cambridge: Cambridge University Press, 2001).

6 S. H. Abu-Sitta, *The Palestinian Nakba: 1948: The Register of Depopulated Localities in Palestine* (London: The Palestinian Return Centre, 1998), p. 8. According to Abu-Sitta, 414,000 fled from their homes between November 1947 and May 1948. Meron Benvenisti cites a lower figure of 380,000 refugees, which is still more than half the total number of Palestinian refugees accounted for at the end of the war (M. Benvenisti, *Sacred Landscape: The Buried History of the Holy Land since 1948* (London: University of California Press, 2000), p. 124).

7 L. Takkenberg, *The Status of Palestinian Refugees in International Law* (Oxford: Oxford University Press, 1998), p. 19.

8 See fact sheets of the United Nations Relief and Works Agency for Palestine Refugees (UNRWA) available at www.unrwa.org. According to Badil, there are additionally some 1.6 million 1948 Palestinian refugees and their descendants who have not registered with UNRWA, although they are entitled to do so. (See Badil Resource Center for Palestinian Residency and Refugee Rights, *Closing Protection Gaps: Handbook on Protection of Palestinian Refugees in States Signatories to the*

1951 Refugee Convention (Ramallah: al-Ayyam Press, 2005), p. 9 [Hereinafter Badil Handbook on Protection].)

9 UNHCR, Global Trends | UNHCR, June 2023 (accessed 14 April 2024).

10 For more on the causes of the Palestinian refugees' displacement in 1948, see, *inter alia*, N. Masalha, *Expulsion of the Palestinians: The Concept of 'Transfer' in Zionist Political Thought, 1882–1948* (Washington, DC: Institute of Palestine Studies, 1992); N. Masalha, *The Politics of Denial: Israel and the Palestinian Refugee Problem* (London: Pluto Press, 2003); B. Morris, *The Birth of the Palestinian Refugee Problem Revisited* (Cambridge: Cambridge University Press, 2004); I. Pappe, *The Ethnic Cleansing of Palestine* (Oxford: Oneworld, 2006).

11 These estimates exclude any losses in the Occupied West Bank and Gaza Strip. See A. Kubursi, 'Valuing Palestinian Losses in Today's Dollars', in N. Aruri (ed.), *Palestinian Refugees: The Right of Return* (London: Pluto Press, 2001), pp. 217–51. According to Professor Atif Kubursi, estimates of Palestinian material losses total $22.5 billion US dollars in 2000 figures (adjusting for inflation between 1948 and 2000). See also M. Fischbach, *Records of Dispossession: Palestinian Refugee Property and the Arab Israeli Conflict* (New York: Columbia University Press, 2003), pp. 114–30 for the United Nations Conciliation Commission for Palestine (UNCCP)'s valuation of refugee property losses in Palestinian Pounds; and T. J. Senechal and L. Hilal, 'The Value of 1948 Palestinian Refugee Material Damages: An Estimate Based on International Standards', in R. Brynen and R. El-Rifai (eds), *Compensation to Palestinian Refugees and the Search for Palestinian-Israeli Peace* (London: Pluto Press, 2013), pp. 132–58, p. 132.

12 UNRWA, *Palestine Refugees*, www.unrwa.org.

13 According to Badil, there are some 780,000 Palestinians falling under this category (see Badil Handbook on Protection, supra note 8 at p. 9).

14 Fischbach (2003), supra note 11 at p. 3. According to Fischbach, the 'war also triggered the exodus of 30,000 Syrians, Lebanese, Egyptian, Jordanian, and Iraqi Arabs living in Palestine'.

15 For more on internally displaced Palestinians of 1948, see H. Abu Hussein and F. McKay, *Access Denied: Palestinian Land Rights in Israel* (London: Zed Books, 2003).

16 For more on internally displaced Palestinians in the OPTs, see the Joint Pilot Study by Badil, the Norwegian Refugee Council and the Internal Displacement Monitoring Centre, *Displaced by the Wall: Forced Displacement as a Result of the West Bank Wall and Its Associated Regime*, September 2006, available at www.badil. org. See OHCHR, supra note 2 for figures on the displacement in Gaza.

17 See B. H. Khasawneh, 'An appraisal of the right of return and compensation of Jordanian nationals of Palestinian refugee origin and Jordan's right, under International Law, to bring claims relating thereto, on their behalf to and against Israel and to seek compensation as a host state in light of the conclusion of the

Jordan-Israel peace treaty of 1994', doctoral thesis, University of London, London School of Economics, London, 2007.

18 K. Lawand, 'The Right to Return of Palestinians under International Law', *International Journal Refugee Law*, 8 (1996): 532–68; 533. According to Lawand, the bilateral agreements between Israel and Jordan of 1993 and 1994 were the first Arab–Israeli agreements to make reference to the resolution of the refugee problem in accordance with international law. Chapter 5 will examine how property claims were addressed in Israeli–Palestinian negotiations.

19 For a critical analysis of the interplay of law and politics with regard to the question of Palestine, see N. Erakat, *Justice for Some: Law and the Question of Palestine* (Stanford, CA: Stanford University Press, 2019). See also R. Wilde, 'Using the Master's Tools to Dismantle the Master's House: International Law and Palestinian Liberation', *Palestinian Yearbook of International Law 22* (2019–20): 3–74.

20 Erakat, *Justice for Some*, p. 4.

21 See, *inter alia*, L. T. Lee, 'The Right to Compensation: Refugees and Countries of Asylum', *American Journal of International Law*, 80 (1986): 532–67 and L. T. Lee, 'The Preventive Approach to the Refugee Problem', *Willamette Law Review*, 28 (1992): 821–32 for views on how compensation can be used to deter states from creating refugee flows. See also *The Cairo Declaration of Principles of International Law on Compensation to Refugees* adopted by the International Law Association (Cairo, 1992), reprinted in *American Journal of Internationl Law* 87: 157–9. For an alternative view, see G. S.Goodwin-Gill, *The Refugee in International Law*, 2nd edn (Oxford: Oxford University Press, 1998), p. 269. According to Goodwin-Gill, '[A]lthough the principle of compensating the victims of violations of human rights has much to commend it, introducing a financial substitute for State and community obligations risks lending respectability to ethnic, religious and ideological cleansing'.

22 See *inter alia*, Bishara, S, Adalah's Position Paper on 'Prawer II' – Adalah, *Adalah*, 23 February 2017; UN Press Release, Committee on the Exercise of the Inalienable Rights of the Palestinian People, Amid International Inaction, Israel's Systematic 'Demographic Engineering' Thwarting Palestinians' Ability to Pursue Justice, Speakers Tell International Conference | UN Press, GA/PAL/1439, 1 July 2021 and B. White, Israel's Ethnic Cleansing of Palestinians in the West Bank (arabcenterdc. org), *Arab Center*, 12 August 2022.

23 See *inter alia*, OHCHR, UN expert warns of new instance of mass ethnic cleansing of Palestinians, calls for immediate ceasefire | OHCHR, 14 October 2023 and J. Egeland, Gaza Is Being Made Unlivable | TIME, *Time*, 20 December 2023.

24 For economic, historical and political research on Palestinian refugee property claims or reparations, see *inter alia*, S. Samy, *Reparations to Palestinian Refugees: A Comparative Perspective* (London: Routledge, 2010); Kubursi, supra note 11, S.

Hadawi, *Palestinian Rights & Losses in 1948* (London: Saqi Books, 1988); Fischbach, supra note 11, S. Tamari, 'Palestinian Refugee Property Claims: Compensation and Restitution', in A. M. Lesch and I. S. Lustick (eds), *Exile and Return: Predicaments of Palestinians and Jews* (Philadelphia: University of Pennsylvania Press, 2005), pp. 246–60.

25 M. Kagan, 'Restitution as a Remedy for Refugee Property Claims in the Israeli-Palestinian Conflict', *Florida Journal of International Law* 19 (2007): 421–90. See also G. J. Boling, '"Absentees' Property" Laws and Israel's Confiscation of Palestinian Property: A Violation of U.N. General Assembly Resolution 194 and International Law', *Palestinian Yearbook of International Law* 11 (2000–1): 73–130, which does not directly discuss the right to restitution but does provide some analysis of Palestinian property claims.

26 See, *inter alia*, Lawand, supra note 18, J. Quigley, 'Displaced Palestinians and a Right of Return', *Harvard International Law Journal* 39 (1998): 171–229, G. J. Boling, 'The 1948 Palestinian Refugees and the Individual Right of Return: *An International Law Analysis*', Badil Resource Center (January 2001) www.badil.org and R. Lapidoth, 'The Right of Return in International Law, with Special Reference to the Palestinian Refugees', *Israel Yearbook on Human Rights* 16 (1986): 103–25.

27 See discussion in Chapter 4.

28 See, *inter alia*, R. Brynen and R. El-Rifai, *Compensation to Palestinian Refugees and the Search for Palestinian-Israeli Peace* (London: Pluto Press, 2013); M. Lynk, 'Compensation for Palestinian Refugees: An International Law Perspective', *Palestinian Yearbook of International Law* 11 (2000–1): 155–83; E. Benvenisti and E. Zamir, 'Private Claims to Property Rights in the Future Israeli-Palestinian Settlement', *American Journal of International Law* 89 (1995): 295–340.

29 M. Fischbach, *The Peace Process and Palestinian Refugee Claims: Addressing Claims for Property Compensation and Restitution* (Washington, DC: United States Institute of Peace, 2006), pp. 68–70.

Chapter 1

1 T. Herzl, *The Jewish State: An Attempt at a Modern Solution of the Jewish Question (Der Judenstaat)*, 3rd edn (London: Central Office of the Zionist Organization, 1936).

2 The JNF was registered in England in 1907. In its original Memorandum of Association, the primary objective of the JNF was to 'purchase, take on lease or in exchange, or otherwise acquire any lands, forests, rights of possession and other rights … in [Palestine, Syria, Sinai, Turkey] … for the purpose of settling Jews on such lands', cited in Palestine Land Society, *Financing Racism and Apartheid: Jewish*

National Fund's Violation of International and Domestic Law (London, 2005), p. 3. Land acquired by the JNF was to be held on behalf of 'the Jewish People in perpetuity', ibid., p. 4. For more on the JNF's structure and objectives, see also U. Davis and W. Lehn, 'And the Fund Still Lives: The Role of the Jewish National Fund in the Determination of Israel's Land Policies', *Journal of Palestine Studies* 7, no. 4 (1978): 3–33.

3 For a detailed study of land rights in Israel, see H. Abu Hussein and F. McKay, *Access Denied: Palestinian Land Rights in Israel* (London: Zed Books, 2003). See also R. Shehadeh, *The Law of the Land* (Jerusalem: Palestinian Academic Society for the Study of International Affairs (PASSIA), 1993) available at www.passia.org (accessed 12 April 2024) for a study of land rights in the Occupied Palestinian Territory.

4 As will be discussed in this chapter, though Israel enacted a law in 1969 to abolish Ottoman as well as Mandate land laws governing private rights in land, according to Abu Hussein and McKay, '[t]he old Ottoman categories of land tenure still remain relevant for determining rights in land which has not undergone the process of settlement of title, which in 2000 still amounted to over 1 million dunams of land, most of it in the Naqab' (see Abu Hussein and McKay, *Access Denied*, p. 117).

5 Shehadeh argues that the Israeli government has falsified the definition of the different categories of land that existed under Ottoman law (and are still being used in the West Bank) to expropriate land belonging to Palestinians under the presumption that it is state owned. R. Shehadeh, 'The Land Law of Palestine: An Analysis of the Definition of State Lands', *Journal of Palestine Studies* 11, no. 2 (1982): 82–99 at p. 82. It is therefore important to provide an overview of Ottoman land law in this section in order to argue that Israel expropriated privately owned land.

6 Shehadeh (1993), supra note 3 at pp. 11–12.

7 Art.1 of the Ottoman Land Code (OLC) of 7 Ramazan 1274 (21 April 1858). A translation of the OLC can be found in S. Fisher, *Ottoman Land Laws – Containing the Ottoman Land Code and Later Legislation Affecting Law with Notes* (London: Oxford University Press, 1919) and F. Ongley, *The Ottoman Land Code* (London: William Clowes, 1892).

8 Syed Amir Aly, *Student's Handbook of Mohammedan Law*, cited in Goadby and Doukhan, infra note 13 at p. 69.

9 S. Hadawi, *Palestinian Rights & Losses in 1948* (London: Saqi Books, 1988), p. 37.

10 Ibid.

11 A. Kedar, 'The Legal Transformation of Ethnic Geography: Israeli Law and the Palestinian Landholder 1948–1967', *NYU Journal of International Law and Politics* 33 (2001): 923–1000 at pp. 932–3.

12 A. Granott, *The Land System in Palestine: History and Structure* (London: Eyre & Spottiswoode, 1952), p. 88.

13 Goadby and M. J. Doukhan, *The Land Law of Palestine* (Tel-Aviv: Shoshany's Printing, 1935), pp. 6–7.

14 Ibid.

15 Ibid.

16 See OLC, Art. 36–53 for more on the alienation and inheritance of *miri* land.

17 Goadby and Doukhan (1935), supra note 13 at p. 7.

18 Granott (1952) supra note 12 at p. 89.

19 Ibid.

20 Ibid.

21 Goadby and Doukhan (1935), supra note 13 at p. 36.

22 Hadawi (1988), supra note 9 p. 41.

23 See Fisher's translation of the OLC, supra note 7.

24 Abu Hussein and McKay (2003), supra note 3 at p. 107.

25 See Fisher's translation of the OLC, supra note 7.

26 Hadawi (1988), supra note 9 at p. 42.

27 According to Article 2 of the Palestine Order-in-Council, 1922, ' "Public Lands" ' means all lands in Palestine which are subject to the control of the Government of Palestine by virtue of Treaty, convention, agreement or succession, and all lands which are or shall be acquired for the public service or otherwise.' The Palestine Order-in-Council, 10 August 1922 is reprinted in N. Bentwich, *Legislation of Palestine, 1918–1925*, Vol. 1 (Alexandria, Printed for the Government of Palestine by Whitehead Morris, 1926).

28 Shehadeh (1993), supra note 3 at p. 25.

29 Kedar (2001), supra note 11 at pp. 927–8.

30 Shehadeh (1982), supra note 5 at p. 82.

31 Goadby and Doukhan (1935), supra note 13 at p. 298.

32 K. W. Stein, *The Land Question in Palestine, 1917–1939* (Chapel Hill: University of North Carolina Press, 1984), p. 20: 'In order to increase agricultural production and, therefore, tax revenues, the Tabu (Turkish, *Tapu*) Law of 1858 attempted to define land holdings precisely. Title deeds became obligatory for all lands.'

33 Hadawi (1988), supra note 9 at p. 40. According to Stein, 'in 1925 three-quarters of all land in Palestine was held by unregistered title.' (Stein, *The Land Question in Palestine, 1917–1939*, p. 21).

34 Stein, *The Land Question in Palestine, 1917–1939*, p. 24. According to Stein: 'The fellah […] remained on land he had cultivated by prescriptive right and tradition, but his ownership of such land passed to others more economically solvent, financially stronger, and administratively in league with local governmental officials.'

35 Kedar (2001), supra note 11 at p. 933.

36 Stein (1984), supra note 32 at p. 21.

37 Ibid., p. 22.

38 Goadby and Doukhan (1935), supra note 13 at p. 18.

39 Granott (1952), supra note 12 at p. 77.

40 Goadby and Doukhan (1935), supra note 13 at p. 299.

41 See, *inter alia*, Kedar (2001), supra note 11 at p. 933 and Abu Hussein and McKay (2003), supra note 3 at pp. 107–10.

42 The Palestine Order-in-Council, 10 August 1922 is reprinted in Bentwich, supra note 27.

43 According to Stein, the British authorities chose not to revamp the land regime because 'any abrupt reorganization of the land regime would have been construed by the Arabs of Palestine as an overt attempt to turn the country over to the Zionists at once.' See Stein (1984), supra note 32 at p. 31.

44 For an overview of some of these Ordinances, see *inter alia*, S. Dajani, 'Ruling Palestine: A History of the Legally Sanctioned Jewish-Israeli Seizure of Land and Housing in Palestine', Centre on Housing Rights and Evictions (COHRE) and BADIL Resource Center for Palestinian Residency & Refugee Rights, 2005, available at www.miftah.org (accessed on 14 April 2024) at p. 23, Goadby and Doukhan (1935), supra note 13 at pp. 304–5 (for more on the 1926 Correction of Land Registers Ordinances), Stein (1984), supra note 32 at pp. 24, 32–3, 43–51 and Hadawi (1988), supra note 9 at pp. 55–60.

45 For more on this ordinance, see Kedar (2001), supra note 11 at pp. 938–9.

46 The ordinances were the Mahlul Land Ordinance of 1 October 1920 and Mewat Land Ordinance of 1921. For an overview of these Ordinances, see *inter alia*, Stein, supra note 32 at p. 13 and Abu Hussein and McKay (2003), supra note 3 at p. 110.

47 See fn 27. See also Goadby and Doukhan (1935), supra note 13 at pp. 60–8 for more on public lands and state domain.

48 A Survey of Palestine (prepared in December 1945 and January 1946 for the information of the Anglo-American Committee of Inquiry), Vol. I, Palestine, The Government Printer, 1946 at p. 234, para. 30. For more on the settlement of title to land, see pp. 233–7.

49 Granott (1952), supra note 12 at p. 206.

50 Ibid.

51 Hadawi (1988), supra note 9 at p. 40.

52 For the full report of the Committee of Inquiry, see Official Records of the Second Session of the General Assembly, Supplement No. 11, United Nations Special Committee on Palestine (UNSCOP), *Report to the General Assembly*, A/364, 3 September 1947 (hereinafter UNSCOP Report). It is worth pointing out that a minority of the members in the UNSCOP proposed a federal binational state with Jerusalem as its capital.

53 UNGA Res.181 (II), 29 November, 1947 (Partition Plan).

54 Abu Hussein and McKay (2003), supra note 3 at p. 109.

55 Kedar (2001), supra note 11 at p. 938.

56 Hadawi (1988), supra note 9 at p. 44. The stated aim of the *Balfour Declaration* was 'the establishment in Palestine of a national home for the Jewish people'. The Declaration was subsequently incorporated in the Preamble of the Mandate for Palestine. Both the Balfour Declaration (2 November 1917) and the Palestine Mandate (24 July 1922) were reprinted in A. Tulin, *Book of Documents Submitted to the General Assembly of the United Nations Relating to the Establishment of the National Home for the Jewish People: Balfour Declaration, Palestine Mandate, American-British Palestine Mandate Covenant, British White Papers, Observations of Permanent Mandates Commission, Pronouncements of Presidents and Resolutions of Congress of the United States, Jewish Agency Statements and Other Relevant Documents 1917–1947* (New York: The Jewish Agency for Palestine, 1947).

57 Kedar (2001), supra note 11 at p. 939.

58 Ibid.

59 See Dajani, S. (2005), supra note 44 at pp. 23–5. See also Hadawi (1988), supra note 9 at pp. 69–75 for an overview of the Commissions' findings on land and Jewish immigration and Stein (1984), supra note 32 at pp. 88–129 for an analysis of the 1929 Shaw Commission's Report, the 1930 Hope Simpson Report and the 1930 Passfield White Paper, and pp. 163–72 for more on the Lewis French Mission.

60 [Emphasis added]. Report on Immigration, Land Settlement and Development by Sir John Hope Simpson, C.I.E., Cmd 3686, October 1930, London, H.M. Stationery Office at chapter V, p. 54 (hereinafter *Hope Simpson Report*).

61 Ibid., p. 56.

62 For statistics on the JNF's land acquisition during the Mandate Period, see Palestine Land Society (2005), supra note 2 at pp. 4–5, *A Survey of Palestine*, prepared by the Government of Palestine in December 1945 and January 1946 for the information of the Anglo-American Committee of Inquiry or S. Hadawi, *Village Statistics 1945: A Classification of Land and Area Ownership in Palestine* (Beirut: Palestine Liberation Organization Research Center, 1970).

63 See Adalah (The Legal Center for Arab Minority Rights in Israel) at www.adalah.org for the latest updates on JNF activity. See also Amnesty International, 'Israel's Apartheid Against Palestinians: Cruel System of Domination and Crime Against Humanity', 2022 available at www.amnesty.org (accessed 14 April 2024) and Human Rights Watch, 'A Threshold Crossed: Israeli Authorities and the Crimes of Apartheid and Persecution', 2021 available at www.hrw.org (accessed 14 April 2024).

64 Report presented by the Secretary of State for the Colonies to Parliament by Command of His Majesty, Cmd 5479, July 1937, London, H.M. Stationery Office at chapter XII, pp. 380–93 (hereinafter *Peel Commission Report*).

65 Statement of Policy presented by the Secretary for the Colonies to Parliament by Command of His Majesty, Cmd 6019, May 1939 at para 16 (hereinafter *MacDonald White Paper*).

66 Ibid., para. 8.

67 For a description of the different zones and statistics on land transferred to Jews within each zone, see S. Dajani (2005) supra note 44 at p. 25.

68 Hadawi (1988), supra note 9 at p. 59.

69 Ibid.

70 Kedar (2001), supra note 11 at p. 939.

71 According to Hadawi, the 1940 Land Transfer Regulations were enacted at a time when Jews had already acquired a sizeable portion of the most fertile lands in Palestine. Thus, to the Arabs of Palestine, these regulations proved to be too little too late. Though they requested that a total ban be placed on the sale of land by Arabs to Jews over the entire country, Hadawi notes that the British administration failed to act. (See Hadawi (1988), supra note 9 at p. 59.)

72 According to Granott, former head of the Jewish National Fund (JNF), on the date of the declaration of the State of Israel in May 1948, the maximum Jewish land holdings, including property owned by the JNF, stood at only 1.7 million dunums, or 6.5 per cent of the total area of Palestine (see A. Granott, *Agrarian Reform and the Record of Israel* (London: Eyre and Spottiswoode, 1956), p. 28). Palestinian land expert, Sami Hadawi, puts the maximum Jewish land holding on the date of the creation of the State of Israel at 1,492,000 dunums or 5.67 per cent of the total area. See Hadawi (1988), supra note 9 at p. 9. The total land area of Mandate Palestine is 26.3 million dunums (see Stein (1984), supra note 32 at p. 3).

73 The United Nations Partition Plan for Palestine was a proposal by the UN to partition Mandatory Palestine into a Jewish and an Arab state at the end of the British Mandate. In the twenty months period between the date of the adoption of the Partition Plan in November 1947 in UN General Assembly Resolution 181 and the signing of the last Arab–Israeli armistice agreement in July 1949, an estimated 711,000 to 774,000 Palestinians either fled in fear or were forcibly expelled from their homes by Jewish militant groups. (F. P. Albanese and L. Takkenberg, *Palestinian Refugees in International Law* (Oxford: Oxford University Press, 2020), p. 36.)

74 For more on the causes of the 1948 Palestinian exodus, see *inter alia* W. Khalidi, 'Plan Dalet: Master Plan for the Conquest of Palestine', *Journal of Palestine Studies* 18, no. 1 (1988): 4–33; N. Masalha, *Expulsion of the Palestinians: The Concept of 'Transfer' in Zionist Political Thought, 1882–1948* (Washington, DC: Institute of Palestine Studies, 1992); B. Morris, 'Revisiting the Palestinian Exodus of 1948', in L. Rogan and A. Shlaim (eds), *The War for Palestine: Rewriting the History of 1948* 37–59 (Cambridge: Cambridge University Press, 2001); B. Morris, *The Birth of the*

Palestinian Refugee Problem Revisited (Cambridge: Cambridge University Press, 2004) and I. Pappe, *The Ethnic Cleansing of Palestine* (Oxford: Oneworld, 2006).

75 N. Masalha, *The Politics of Denial: Israel and the Palestinian Refugee Problem* (London: Pluto Press, 2003), p. 7.

76 For more on land rights in Israel, see Abu Hussein and McKay (2003), supra note 3. The State of Israel resorted mainly to Emergency Regulations to prevent internally displaced Palestinians from accessing their land and expropriating it under the guise of 'public security'. For a summary of the different Emergency Regulations, see Dajani, S. (2005) supra note 44 at p. 40 and Abu Hussein and McKay (2003), supra note 3 at pp. 80–6. See also H. Dib Nakkara, 'Israeli Land Seizure under Various Defense and Emergency Regulations', *Journal of Palestine Studies* 14, no. 2 (1985): 13–34, and Amnesty International (2022), supra note 63 at pp. 113–63. The latter includes an overview of how these laws were also used to discriminate against or expropriate property belonging to Palestinians in the Occupied Palestinian Territory, including East Jerusalem.

77 For more on the land settlement of title scheme, see earlier discussion at section 1.3.

78 See note 72.

79 Palestine Land Society, supra note 2 at p. 5.

80 Palestine Government, *Village Statistics*, cited in Abu Hussein and McKay (2003), supra note 3 at p. 115. Writing in 1952, Abraham Granott admitted that, though there are no reliable figures on the extent of State lands in Palestine, 'there were in the hands of the State only a few properties registered in its own name which were suitable for agricultural exploitation, empty of cultivators settled on them and free from all kinds of claims, so that the Government should be at liberty to do with them what it pleased and to transfer them to other hands' (Granott (1952), supra note 12 at p. 97). It is important to note that this statement was made by Granott, a former head of the Board of Directors of the Jewish National Fund, who considered any land, including *miri*, *mewat* and *metruke* land, the ownership of which could not be proved either by title or by cultivation as State land. As such, his estimates of State land are probably inflated.

81 Morris (2004), supra note 74 at p. 360.

82 M. Fischbach, *Records of Dispossession: Palestinian Refugee Property and the Arab Israeli Conflict* (New York: Columbia University Press, 2003) at pp. 8–9.

83 The *Haganah* (Hebrew: 'Defense') was a Jewish paramilitary organization in Palestine during the British mandate of Palestine from 1920 to 1948. The *Haganah* later became the modern Israel Defense Forces (IDF) – Israel's army. The ranks of *Haganah* included Israel's first Prime Minister Ben Gurion as well as former Prime Minister Ariel Sharon and Yitzhak Rabin.

84 S. Jiryis, 'The Legal Structure for the Expropriation and Absorption of Arab Lands in Israel', *Journal of Palestine Studies* 2, no. 4 (1973): 82–104 at p. 83.

85 See Fischbach (2003), supra note 82 at p. 15 for more on these ad hoc committees.

86 Morris (2004), supra note 74 at p. 326.

87 Ibid., pp. 348–60.

88 Ibid., p. 395: 'In April 1949, Yoseftal reported that of '190,000' *olim* who had arrived since the establishment of the State, 110,000 had been settled in abandoned Arab houses.' See also Fischbach (2003), supra note 82 at pp. 10–11.

89 Morris (2004), supra note 74 at pp. 361–6 and Fischbach (2003), supra note 82 at pp. 12–13.

90 See Section 4.3.2.

91 Fischbach (2003), supra note 82 at p. 18.

92 Absentees' Property Law, 5710–1950, 14 March 1950 (hereinafter Absentees' Property Law).

93 Emergency Regulations on Property of Absentees ('Absentee Property Act'), 5709/1948, 2 December 1948.

94 Section 1 of the Absentee Property Act.

95 As early as July 1948, the Israeli Cabinet voted to ban the Palestinian refugees return to their homes, thus denying them access to their land (Morris (2004), supra note 74 at pp. 309–40). Two subsequent laws were enacted to regulate the right of admission into Israel: the Law of Return of 1950 and the Nationality Law of 1952 (see Law of Return, 5710–1950, 5 July 1950 and Nationality Law, 5712–1952, 1 April 1952). The provisions of the Law of Return cannot be used by Palestinian refugees to return to their homes and access their property inside Israel (see Sections 1 and 4 of the Law of Return). Similarly, the Nationality Law of 1952 was used to deny Palestinian refugees Israeli citizenship and entry to Israel (for more on Israeli citizenship and the Nationality Law, see U. Davis, *Citizenship and the State: A Comparative Study of Citizenship Legislation in Israel, Jordan, Palestine, Syria and Lebanon* (Reading: Ithaca Press, 1997), p. 83 at pp. 43–6. See also G. S. Goodwin-Gill, *The Refugee in International Law*, 2nd edn (Oxford: Oxford University Press, 1998), pp. 241–3 and V. Kattan, 'The Nationality of Denationalized Palestinians', *Nordic Journal of International Law* 74 (2005): 67–102 for more on the denationalization of Palestinian refugees by the State of Israel).

96 For more on the status of 'present absentees' and evolving Israeli policies towards the internally displaced (1948–2003), see Masalha (2003), supra note 75 at pp. 142–77. See also Abu Hussein and McKay (2003), supra note 3 for a comprehensive legal study of Palestinian land rights within Israel.

97 Section 28(a) of the Absentee Property Act. This section became section 27 of the Absentees' Property Law of 1950.

98 The perverse use of the definition of 'absentee' to mask discriminatory practices aimed at permanently alienating property from its non-Jewish owners will be explored in more depth in Chapter 2.

99 Section 5(a) of the Absentee Property Act.

100 Section 19(a) of the Absentee Property Act.

101 UNGA Res.194 at para. 11.

102 Fischbach (2003), supra note 82 at p. 23.

103 Morris (2004), supra note 74 at p. 360.

104 Palestine Land Society (2005), supra note 2 at p. 7. According to Forman and Kedar 'the sale agreement [with the JNF] included a clause by which the government agreed to "take upon itself all necessary legislative arrangements to ensure the JNF's full and legal ownership of all the land according to Israeli law."' (G. Forman and A. Kedar (S), 'From Arab land to "Israel Lands": The Legal Dispossession of the Palestinians Displaced by Israel in the Wake of 1948', *Environment and Planning D: Society and Space* 22 (2004): 809–30 at p. 815).

105 Section 1(b), Absentees' Property Law.

106 Section 19, Absentees' Property Law.

107 Development Authority (Transfer of Property) Law, 5710–1950, 31 July 1950 [hereinafter DA Law].

108 Article 1 of the 1960 Basic Law: Israel Lands, 19 July 1960. In the absence of a Constitution for the State of Israel, the Knesset legislated so-called Basic Laws on various subjects. These Basic Laws will form the blueprint of an eventual constitution of the State of Israel.

109 The ILA was created by virtue of the Israel Lands Administration Law, 5710–1960, 25 July 1960. On 18 July 2007, a racist bill entitled the Jewish National Fund Law was passed by the Knesset. This bill added a new provision to the ILA Law related to the management of JNF lands. According to this provision, notwithstanding anything to the contrary in any law, the leasing of JNF lands for the purpose of the settlement of Jews on these lands will not be considered discriminatory (see Adalah, 'Land Controlled by Jewish National Funds for Jews Only', 29 July 2007).

110 I. S. Lustick, *The Arabs in the Jewish State* (Austin: University of Texas Press, 1980), p. 99.

111 According to Adalah, the JNF owns 13 per cent of the total lands in Israel, which is equivalent to 12 per cent of Israel Lands (Adalah, 'Land Controlled by Jewish National Fund for Jews Only', 29 July 2007, www.adalah.org (accessed 14 April 2024). As discussed earlier, JNF-owned lands are held in perpetuity for the benefit of the 'Jewish people'. They are beyond the control of the government and are off limits to the Palestinians, both refugees and citizens of Israel. As Fischbach noted, maintaining land out of the reach of Palestinians was the driving force behind the JNF's purchase agreements with the government. According to Fischbach, the JNF feared that 'if captured refugee land remained in the hands of the state, the state might be forced to allocate land for development on an equitable basis between its

Jewish and Palestinian citizens instead of reserving it exclusively for Jewish usage.' (Fischbach (2003), supra note 82 at p. 59.)

112 Adalah, 'New Israel Land Reform Law Passed by Knesset', 3 August 2009, www.adalah.org (accessed 14 April 2024).

113 Abu Hussein and McKay (2003), supra note 3 at p. 72.

114 See Fischbach (2003), supra note 82 at pp. 32–3 for more on how net profits reaped by the Custodian from the refugee property were used for the settlement of new immigrants instead of being set aside for the original owners.

115 As will be discussed in Chapter 4, restitution is the preferred form of reparation under international law. Compensation is only prescribed if the claimant voluntarily chooses it or if restitution is 'factually impossible'.

Chapter 2

1 L. Takkenberg, *The Status of Palestinian Refugees in International Law* (Oxford: Oxford University Press, 1998), p. 19.

2 B. Morris, *The Birth of the Palestinian Refugee Problem Revisited* (Cambridge: Cambridge University Press, 2004), p. 395.

3 See M. Lynk, 'Compensation for Palestinian Refugees: An International Law Perspective', *Palestine Yearbook of International Law* 11 (2000): 155–83 at pp. 167–8 for historical treaties recognizing displaced peoples' claims for the restitution and/or compensation of their property.

4 S. Haasdijk, 'The Lack of Uniformity in the Terminology of the International Law of Remedies', Leiden Journal of International Law 5 (1992): 245–63.

5 See, for instance, Barkan's use of the terms 'restitution', 'reparation' and 'apology' in E. Barkan, *The Guilt of Nations: Restitution and Negotiating Historical Injustices* (New York: W.W. Norton, 2000), p. XIX, which does not coincide with the legal definition of these concepts.

6 The ILC Articles were adopted by the ILC at its fifty-third session (2001). In United Nations General Assembly (UNGA) Resolution 56/83, the Assembly took note of these Articles and commended them 'to the attention of Governments without prejudice to the question of their future adoption or other appropriate action'. (UNGA Res.56/83, 12 December 2001. See also UNGA Res.59/35, 2 December 2004 and UNGA Res.62/61, 6 December 2007). As for the UN Guidelines on Reparation, they were first adopted by the Commission on Human Rights in its Resolution 2005/35 of 19 April 2005, then by the Economic and Social Council in its Resolution 2005/30 of 25 July 2005 and, finally, by the UNGA in Resolution 60/147 on 16 December 2005. It is important to note that these Guidelines, 'do not entail new international or domestic legal obligations but identify mechanisms,

modalities, procedures and methods for the implementation of *existing legal obligations* under international human rights law and international humanitarian law which are complementary though different as to their norms' [Emphasis added] (See Preamble to the UN Guidelines on Reparation).

7 D. Shelton, *Remedies in International Human Rights Law*, 2nd edn (Oxford: Oxford University Press, 2005), p. 7.

8 See Articles 35–37 of the ILC Articles and Principles 19, 20 and 22 of the Guidelines on Reparation for a definition of these three terms. Moreover, Chapter 4 will discuss in detail the right to restitution and compensation as they are the two main forms of reparation used in cases of property expropriation.

9 [Emphasis added]. G. Echeverria, *Reparation: A Sourcebook for Victims of Torture and Other Violations of Human Rights and International Humanitarian Law* (London: The Redress Trust, 2003), p. 8.

10 Emphasis added.

11 Ibid.

12 *Island of Palmas Case (United States v. the Netherlands),1928, R.I.A.A.*, Vol. II, p. 829 at p. 845. For more on this rule, see T. O. Elias, 'The Doctrine of Intertemporal Law', *American Journal of International Law* 74 (1980): 285–307.

13 J. Crawford, *The International Law Commission's Articles on State Responsibility: Introduction, Text and Commentaries* (Cambridge: Cambridge University Press, 2002), p. 77. The PCIJ applied this principle in the following cases: *Phosphates in Morocco, Preliminary Objections, 1938, P.C.I.J., Series A/B, No.74*, 10, at p. 28; *S.S.'Wimbledon', 1923, P.C.I.J., Series A, No.1*, p. 15, at p. 30; *Factory at Chorzów, Jurisdiction, 1927, P.C.I.J., Series A, No.9*, p. 21; *Factory at Chorzów, Merits, 1928, P.C.I.J., Series A, No.17*, p. 29.

14 Crawford, *The International Law Commission's Articles on State Responsibility*, p. 81. See also *Phosphates in Morocco, Preliminary Objections, 1938, P.C.I.J., Series A/B, No.74*, 10, at p. 28.

15 As discussed in Chapter 1, Israel destroyed entire villages as part of a deliberate policy aimed at preventing the refugees' return (see Morris (2004), supra note 2 at pp. 348–60). It also settled Jewish immigrants in abandoned refugee property (Morris (2004), *The Birth of the Palestinian Refugee Problem Revisited*, p. 395) before adopting laws – namely, the 1950 Absentees' Property Law and the 1950 DA Law – to effectively dispossess Palestinian refugees of their property.

16 According to Tomuschat, 'rights arising from an internationally wrongful act are secondary rights, deriving from a substantive right that has been breached. Hence, if there is no primary right there can be no secondary right.' (C. Tomuschat, 'Individual Reparation Claims in Instances of Grave Human Rights Violations: The Position under General International Law', in A. Randelzhofer and C. Tomuschat (eds), *State Responsibility and the Individual: Reparation in Instances of Grave*

Violations of Human Rights (The Hague: Martinus Nijhoff, 1999), p. 7. See also Crawford (2002), supra note 13 at pp. 14–16).

17 Crawford (2002), supra note 13 at pp. 83–4.

18 Ibid.

19 *Convention (II) with Respect to the Laws and Customs of War on Land and its Annex: Regulations Concerning the Laws and Customs of War on Land*, The Hague, 29 July 1899 (hereinafter *1899 Convention*). *Convention (IV) Respecting the Laws and Customs of War on Land and its Annex: Regulations Concerning the Laws and Customs of War on Land*, The Hague, 18 October 1907 (hereinafter *1907 Hague Convention/Regulations*).

20 Article 4 of the 1907 Hague Convention.

21 Judicial Decisions: International Military Tribunal (Nuremberg), Judgment and Decisions (1947), *American Journal of International Law* 41 (1947): 172–333 at pp. 248–9.

22 D. Kretzmer, *The Occupation of Justice* (Albany: State University of New York Press, 2002), pp. 31–40.

23 In the case of *In re Fiebig*, the Special Court of Cassation of Holland held that 'Section II remained in operation so long as there was still active war between the invading forces and the forces of the invaded country, a period which ends with a capitulation or an armistice […]. After such a capitulation or armistice, while the war may continue elsewhere, it is Section III and no longer Section II which regulates the rights and obligations of the invader as Occupant.' (*In re Fiebig (Special Court of Cassation - Holland)*, *9 December 1950*, Annual Digest and Reports of Public International Law Cases, 1949, Vol. 16, 487 at p. 489.)

24 *Convention (III) relative to the Opening of Hostilities*, The Hague, 18 October 1907.

25 Morris (2004), supra note 2 at pp. 342–60.

26 See *inter alia*, M. Benvenisti, *Sacred Landscape: The Buried History of the Holy Land since 1948* (London: University of California Press, 2000), pp. 108–9. According to Benvenisti, the destruction of villages by the *Haganah* was part of a *defensive* military strategy, also known as Plan D.

27 See *inter alia*, W. Khalidi, 'Plan Dalet: Master Plan for the Conquest of Palestine', *Journal of Palestine Studies* 18, no. 1 (1988): 4–33; I. Pappe, *The Ethnic Cleansing of Palestine* (Oxford: Oneworld, 2006), pp. 86–126; N. Masalha, *Expulsion of the Palestinians: The Concept of 'Transfer' in Zionist Political Thought, 1882–1948* (Washington, DC: Institute of Palestine Studies, 1992), pp. 177–81. Khalidi, Pappe and Masalha rebut the argument that Plan D was a defensive military strategy. See also Morris (2004), supra note 2 at pp. 348–60. Though Morris believes that villages were initially destroyed for military reasons, as the war progressed, the 'destruction of the villages became a major political enterprise. […] The thrust of this enterprise was to prevent a return' (p. 348). It bears noting that this has been and continues

to be Israel's policy, as evidenced in its latest military aggression on the Gaza Strip and the forced displacement of the majority of its population. The aim is to render the Strip uninhabitable and prevent the return of refugees and displaced persons to their homes. Israel's 'transfer policies' throughout the decades have been aimed at controlling as much land as possible with as few Palestinians as possible.

28 *In re Von Lewinski (called von Manstein) (British Military Court at Hamburg - Germany), 19 Dec. 1949,* Annual Digest and Reports of Public International Law Cases, 1949, Vol. 16, 509 at p. 512.

29 See *inter alia*, Morris (2004), supra note 2 at pp. 220–1, 254–7 and M. Fischbach, *Records of Dispossession: Palestinian Refugee Property and the Arab Israeli Conflict* (New York: Columbia University Press, 2003), pp. 8–10.

30 Count Folke Bernadotte was assassinated on 17 September 1948 by three members of LEHI, an underground Zionist group, also known as the Stern Gang.

31 [Emphasis added]. Progress Report of the United Nations Mediator on Palestine Submitted to the Secretary-General for Transmission to the Members of the United Nations, A/648, 16 September 1948, Part V, para. 7 (hereinafter Bernadotte's Progress Report).

32 L. Oppenheim, *International Law: A Treatise*, Vol. II (London: Longmans, Green, 1912), p. 320.

33 Ibid. According to Oppenheim, 'the responsibility of a State for internationally illegal acts on the part of members of its armed forces is, provided the acts have not been committed by the State's command or authorization, only a vicarious responsibility, but nevertheless the State concerned must [...] pay damages for these acts when required.' For more on a State's vicarious responsibility for acts committed by its officials and armed forces, see L. Oppenheim, *International Law: A Treatise*, Vol. I (London: Longmans, Green, 1912), pp. 218–21. See also *Jean-Baptiste Caire Case (France and Mexico: Mixed Claims Commission), 7 June 1929*, Annual Digest and Reports of Public International Law Cases, 1929–30, Vol. 5, 146. In this case, recalling the doctrine of *'responsabilité objective'*, the President stated that 'international responsibility might be incurred by a State notwithstanding the absence of any fault on its side, seeing that a State was responsible for all acts committed by its officers or organs and constituting delinquencies from the point of view of the law of nations, regardless of whether the officers or organs in question have acted within the limits of their competence or have exceeded it.' (*Jean-Baptiste Caire Case*, p. 147).

34 According to the Special Court of Cassation of Holland, in the case of *In re Fiebig*, as soon as an armistice agreement is signed, as was the case in 1949 when Israel signed a series of armistice agreements with neighbouring Arab countries, 'it is Section III and no longer Section II which regulates the rights and obligations of the invader as

Occupant.' (*In re Fiebig* (*Special Court of Cassation - Holland*), *9 Dec. 1950*, Annual Digest and Reports of Public International Law Cases, 1949, Vol. 16, 487 at p. 489.

35 *Legal Consequences of the Construction of a Wall in the Occupied Palestinian Territory*, ICJ Advisory Opinion, 9 July 2004, ICJ Rep. 2004, 136 at para. 124.

36 The Partition Plan adopted in UN Resolution 181 divided the territory of Mandate Palestine into two states: a Jewish state on over 56.47 per cent of the territory, an Arab state on over 42.88 per cent and an International Zone of Jerusalem on about 0.65 per cent. At the end of the 1948 war, Israel was in control of 78 per cent of the territory of Mandate Palestine, thus encroaching on almost half the territory designated for the Arab state in the Partition Plan. The remaining 22 per cent (i.e. the West Bank and Gaza Strip) fell under the control of Jordan and Egypt, respectively, until they were occupied by Israel in the 1967 war. United Nations Security Council Resolution 242, which was adopted in the aftermath of the 1967 war, called on the Israeli armed forces to withdraw 'from territories occupied in the recent conflict', which included the West Bank and Gaza Strip (see UNSC Res.242, 22 November 1967 at para. 1(i)).

37 For a discussion of the legality of the Partition Plan and the establishment of the State of Israel, see H. Cattan, *Palestine and International Law: The Legal Aspects of the Arab-Israeli Conflict* (Bristol: Longman Group Ltd, 1973). See also N. Erakat (2019), *Justice for Some* (Stanford, CA: Stanford University Press), pp. 44–54.

38 In the Declaration of Principles signed between the Israeli Government and the PLO on 13 September 1993, Israel and the PLO agreed to base 'permanent status' negotiations on UNSC Resolution 242, thus implicitly recognizing the pre-1967 borders of Israel and agreeing to establish a Palestinian State in the West Bank and Gaza Strip only. The 2002 Arab Peace Initiative, which was adopted by the Arab League, lent further support to the two-state solution and the establishment of a Palestinian state in the West Bank and Gaza Strip in return for the Arab States' normalization of relations with Israel and recognition of that State within its pre-1967 borders. The Road Map to Peace in the Middle East, which was presented to Palestinian and Israeli leaders by Quartet mediators (the United States, the United Nations, the European Union and Russia) in April 2003 constitutes an additional endorsement of a settlement to the Israeli–Palestinian conflict based on a two-state solution and UNSC Resolution 242.

39 This author has not found evidence of any case law supporting the application of Section III outside the context of occupation. See, *inter alia, City of Pärnu v. Pärnu Loan Society* (*Special Court of Cassation - Estonia*), *28 Feb. 1921*, Annual Digest and Reports of Public International Law Cases, 1935–7, Vol. 8, 503; *In re Krauch and Others (I.G. Farben Trial) (United States Military Tribunal at Nuremberg), 29 July 1948*, Annual Digest and Reports of Public International Law Cases, 1948, Vol. 15, 668; *Public Trustee v. Chartered Bank of India, Australia and China (Original*

Civil Jurisdiction – Singapore), 21 Feb. 1956, Annual Digest and Reports of Public International Law Cases, 1956, Vol. 23, 687.

40 Emphasis added. *In re Krauch and Others (I.G. Farben Trial) (United States Military Tribunal at Nuremberg), 29 July 1948*, Annual Digest and Reports of Public International Law Cases, 1948, Vol. 15, 668 at p. 672.

41 UNCCP, *Compensation to Refugees for Loss of or Damage to Property to be Made Good under Principles of International Law or in Equity*, W/30, 31 October 1949 at para.13.

42 M. Kagan, 'Destructive Ambiguity: Enemy Nationals and the Legal Enabling of Ethnic Conflict in the Middle East', Columbia Human Rights Law Review 38 (2007): 263–319 at p. 269.

43 Oppenheim (Vol. II, 1912), supra note 32 at p. 179.

44 Ibid.

45 Kagan ('Destructive Ambiguity', 2007), supra note 42 at p. 273.

46 Ibid.

47 L. Mc.Nair and A. D. Watts, *The Legal Effects of War* (Cambridge: Cambridge University Press, 1966), p. 332. See also, Oppenheim (Vol. II, 1912), supra note 32 at p. 179. According to Oppenheim, should an invading belligerent 'confiscate and sell private land or buildings, the buyer would acquire no right whatever to the property.'

48 In the First World War, Britain enacted the 1914 British Enemy (Amendment) Act, which established the first custodian of enemy property in order to collect revenues on German property. (See, *inter alia*, Mc Nair and Watts, *The Legal Effects of War*, p. 332, L. Oppenheim, *International Law: A Treatise*, Vol. II (London: Longmans, Green, 1935) at pp. 227–8 and M. Kagan, 'Restitution as a Remedy for Refugee Property Claims in the Israeli-Palestinian Conflict', *Florida Journal of International Law* 19 (2007): 422–89 at p. 451.)

49 For more on this law, see McNair and Watts (1966), supra note 47 at pp. 332–5.

50 Fischbach (2003), supra note 29 at p. 22. See also G. Forman and A. (S) Kedar, 'From Arab land to "Israel Lands": The Legal Dispossession of the Palestinians Displaced by Israel in the Wake of 1948', *Environment and Planning D.: Society and Space* 22 (2004): 809–30 at p. 815.

51 Forman and Kedar, 'From Arab land to "Israel Lands"', at pp. 816–17.

52 Ibid., pp. 816–17.

53 Ibid. For a discussion of the 1950 Absentees' Property Law and the 1950 DA Law, see Chapter 1, Section 1.4.

54 Oppenheim (Vol. II, 1935), supra note 48 at p. 222. Kagan also comments on the differences in British and US policies vis-à-vis enemy aliens and their property; see Kagan ('Destructive Ambiguity', 2007), supra note 42 at pp. 272–90.

55 *Convention (V) respecting the Rights and Duties of Neutral Powers and Persons in Case of War on Land*, The Hague, 18 October 1907. According to Article 16 of this Convention, '[t]he nationals of a State which is not taking part in the war are considered as neutrals.'

56 Oppenheim (Vol. II, 1935), supra note 48 at pp. 222–3.

57 *Trading with the Enemy Act*, 1939 (chapter 89), defines 'enemy' at section 2 (b) as 'any individual resident in enemy territory'.

58 Oppenheim (Vol. II, 1935), supra note 48 at p. 226.

59 Section 1(b) of the Absentees' Property Law.

60 Forman and Kedar (2004), supra note 50 at p. 812. See also, M. Kagan ('Restitution', 2007), supra note 48 at pp. 453–4.

61 To Tsizling, the land's settlement and development had to be permanent: '[i]f the law must be a fiction, the development must not be.' (cited in Forman and Kedar (2004), supra note 50 at p. 814).

62 See discussion in Chapter 1, Section 1.4.

63 Forman and Kedar (2004), supra note 50 at p. 815.

64 For more on the JNF's objectives and activities, see Palestine Land Society, *Financing Racism and Apartheid: Jewish National Fund's Violation of International and Domestic Law* (London, 2005).

65 See discussion in Chapter 1 on Regulation 28(a) of the 1948 Emergency Regulations on Property of Absentees, Section 1.4. See also, Forman and Kedar (2004), supra note 50 at p. 815 and Fischbach (2003), supra note 29 at p. 25.

66 Forman and Kedar (2004), supra note 50 at p. 817.

67 Kagan ('Destructive Ambiguity', 2007), supra note 42 at p. 297.

68 Emphasis added. UNGA Res.181, 29 Nov. 1947, Chapter 2 at para. 8.

69 The Declaration of the Establishment of the State of Israel, 14 May 1948.

70 United Nations Committee on the Exercise of the Inalienable Rights of the Palestinian People (CEIRPP), *The Right of Return of the Palestinian People*, ST/SG/SER.F/2, 1 November 1978 at chapter IV.

71 United Nations Palestine Commission, *Legislative Power: the Question of the Continuity of Laws*, A/AC.21/W.27, 19 February 1948 at para. IV.

72 UNSC Res., S/Res/46, 17 April 1948, S/723 at para.1(d). See also Kagan ('Restitution', 2007), supra note 48 at pp. 449–50.

73 Khalidi, W. (1988), supra note 27 at p. 29. The Haganah High Command adopted Plan D (*Tochnit Dalet*) on 10 March 1948. Plan D outlined the Haganah's main mission which was to 'gain control of the areas of the Hebrew state and defend its borders. [The Plan] also aims at gaining control of the areas of Jewish settlement and concentration which are located outside the borders [of the Hebrew state] against regular, semi-regular, and small forces operating from bases outside or

inside the state.' An English translation of the full text of Plan D is cited in ibid., pp. 24–33.

74 See Bernadotte's Progress Report, supra note 31.

75 For arguments in favour of a right to return based on Resolution 194, see *inter alia*, J. Quigley, 'Displaced Palestinians and a Right of Return', *Harvard International Law Journal* 39 (1998): 171–229 and G. J. Boling, 'The 1948 Palestinian Refugees and the Individual Right of Return: *An International Law Analysis*', Badil Resource Center, 2001 www.badil.org (accessed 14 April 2024). For arguments against the right of return, see R. Lapidoth, 'The Right of Return in International Law, with Special Reference to the Palestinian Refugees', *Israel Yearbook on Human Rights* 16 (1986): 103–25.

76 [Emphasis added]. UNCCP, Analysis of paragraph 11 of the General Assembly's Resolution of 11 December 1948, W/45, 15 May 1950 at p. 1 (hereinafter UNCCP, W/45).

77 Ibid., pp. 1–2.

78 Emphasis added. Ibid., p. 2.

79 Ibid., p. 3.

80 Ibid.

81 UNCCP, *Letter and Memorandum dated 22 November 1949, Concerning Compensation, received by the Chairman of the Conciliation Commission from Mr. Gordon Clapp, Chairman, United Nations Economic Survey Mission for the Middle East*, W/32, 19 January 1950 at pp. 12–13 (hereinafter UNCCP, W/32).

82 See P. Contini, *Legal Aspects of the Problem of Compensation to Palestine Refugees* (dated 22 November 1949), attached to ibid., p. 13. According to Contini, 'restitution could be applicable to property of returning refugees and personal property – especially blocked accounts – of non-returning refugees'. As Fischbach has shown, the UNCCP eventually facilitated the release of blocked accounts and assets (bonds, safe deposit boxes) belonging to some 20,000–30,000 refugees, in addition to other assets. For details on the UNCCP's efforts to unblock refugee bank accounts and other assets, see Fischbach (2003), supra note 29 at pp. 195–209.

83 Lapidoth (1986), supra note 75 at p. 116.

84 UNCCP, W/45, supra note 76 at p. 5.

85 Morris (2004), supra note 2 at p. 86.

86 M. Benvenisti (2000), supra note 26 at p. 106 for more on the non-aggression pact signed between Jaffa and Tel Aviv in the interest of preserving the citrus industry. See also Morris, *The Birth of the Palestinian Refugee Problem Revisited*, pp. 114–15.

87 Morris (2004), supra note 2 at p. 91.

88 UNCCP, W/45, supra note 76 at p. 5.

89 Quigley ('Displaced Palestinians', 1998), supra note 75 at p. 189.

90 Bernadotte's Progress Report, supra note 31 at Part I, Section VIII, para. 4(i). In another quote in Section VIII, para. 3(e), Bernadotte states that '[T]he right of innocent people, uprooted from their homes by the present terror and ravages of war, to return to their homes, should be affirmed and made effective, with assurance of adequate compensation for the property of those who may choose not to return'.

91 See *inter alia*, UNGA Res.3236, 22 November 1974, para. 2 in which the General Assembly '[r]eaffirms also the inalienable right of the Palestinians to return to their homes and property from which they have been displaced and uprooted, and calls for their return'.

92 UNCCP, W/45, supra note 76 at p. 5.

93 See Lapidoth (1986), supra note 75 at p. 116 and Eban's declarations to the General Assembly during debates on Israel's application for admission to membership in the UN, UNGA, *Application of Israel for admission to membership in the United Nations (A/818)*, A/AC.24/SR.45, 5 May 1949.

94 Guatemala's version of Resolution 194 states that the General Assembly 'Resolves that the Arab refugees wishing to return to their homes and live at peace with their neighbours should be permitted to do so at the earliest *possible date after the proclamation of peace between the contending parties in Palestine, including the Arab states* [...]'. See UNCCP, W/45, supra note 76 at p. 12.

95 Ibid., p. 6.

96 Ibid.

97 Ibid., p. 7.

98 Ibid., p. 1.

99 Emphasis added. UNCCP, W/32, supra note 81 at p. 13.

100 In his memorandum to the UNCCP, Contini states that 'A refusal to accept the principle of compensation to non-returning refugees for all their property vested in the Custodian would be equivalent to a confiscation of private property. Such action would appear to be contrary to a legal principle which is generally recognized both under the domestic law of most countries and under international law. See Contini's letter, ibid., p. 7.

101 UNCCP, W/30, supra note 41 at para. 12.

102 Ibid., para. 13. See also discussion in Section 2.3.1 of this chapter.

103 Ibid., para. 8.

104 See UNCCP, W/45, supra note 76 at pp. 11–12 for the draft resolutions submitted by the US, Columbia and Guatemala.

105 UNCCP, W/30, supra note 41 at para. 9.

106 UNCCP, *Returning Refugees and the Question of Compensation*, W/36, 7 February 1950 at p. 4.

107 UNCCP, W/30, supra note 41 at para. 14.

108 UNCCP, W/32, supra note 81 at p. 2.

109 Ibid., p. 7.

110 In 1965, Frank Jarvis, head of the UNCCP's Technical Office, estimated that 43.6 per cent of Palestinian refugees were landowners (see Fischbach (2003), supra note 29 at p. 277).

111 See discussion above on the use of the term 'refugees' in paragraph 11. According to the drafting history of Resolution 194, paragraph 11, the word 'Arab' preceded the word 'refugees' in the first two texts of the United Kingdom's draft resolution. It was, however, omitted in the final text which was approved by the Assembly on 11 December 1948. See UNCCP, W/45, supra note 76 at p. 1.

112 See UNGA Res.181, Chapter 2 at para. 8.

113 Bernadotte's Progress Report, supra note 31 at Part I, Section VIII, para. 3(e), in which Bernadotte states that '[T]he right of innocent people, uprooted from their homes by the present terror and ravages of war, to return to their homes, should be affirmed and made effective, with assurance of adequate compensation for the property of those who may choose not to return.'

114 See UNCCP, W/45, supra note 76 at pp. 11–12 for the draft resolutions submitted by the United States, Columbia and Guatemala.

115 Bernadotte's Progress Report, supra note 31 at Part I, Section VIII, para. 3(e), in which Bernadotte states that '[T]he right of innocent people, uprooted from their homes by the present terror and ravages of war, to return to their homes, should be affirmed and made effective, with assurance of adequate compensation for the property of those who may choose not to return.'

116 L. T. Lee, 'The Preventive Approach to the Refugee Problem', *Willamette Law Review* 28 (1992): 821–32 at pp. 829–30. International law expert Gail Boling offered an alternative interpretation of the General Assembly's reference to 'international law and equity'. According to Boling, this reference 'was inserted at precisely this point in Paragraph 11(1) of Resolution 194 enumerating the right to compensation (and, most significantly, was not *deemed necessary at any point in Resolution 194*), to guarantee that the *returning refugees*' right to compensation would be protected at the internationally guaranteed levels, in the event that Israel's domestic compensation laws failed to accord with international standards.' See Boling (2001), supra note 75 at fn. 23.

117 See Lee, 'The Preventive Approach to the Refugee Problem', p. 829 and S. A. Bleicher, 'The Legal Significance of Re-Citation of General Assembly Resolutions', *American Journal of International Law* 63 (1969): 444–78. According to Michael Lynk, Resolution 194 has been reaffirmed or referred to, by an overwhelming majority, at least 130 times since its adoption in 1948 (Lynk (2000), supra note 3 at p. 169.)

118 Lee, supra note 117 at p. 829.

119 CEIRPP (1978), supra note 70 at chapter VII.

120 Ibid. See also UNGA Res.273 (III), 11 May 1949. The Provisional Government of Israel had previously submitted an application for UN membership in November 1948. The application was, however, rejected by the UN Security Council in December of that year. The main objection to Israel's admission at that time came from the UK. The UK's position was that 'residual problems of the war, especially the question of the status of the city of Jerusalem and the Arab refugees, should be clarified before admission was recommended.' (Cited in UNGA *Application of Israel for admission to membership in the United Nations report of the Ad Hoc Political Committee* (A/855), A/PV.207, 11 May 1949). See also J. Quigley, *The Case for Palestine: An International Law Perspective* (Durham, NC: Duke University Press, 2005), pp. 87–90. Israel reapplied for admission in March 1949 and, upon the recommendation of the Security Council, the General Assembly admitted Israel to the UN in May of that year.

121 For a full text of Israel's declarations, see UNGA *Application of Israel for admission to membership in the United Nations report of the Ad Hoc Political Committee* (A/855), A/PV.207, 11 May 1949.

122 Ibid.

123 Ibid.

124 Ibid.

125 UNSC Res.237, 14 June 1967.

126 UNGA Res.2452 (XXIII) (A–C), 19 December 1968.

127 UNSC Res.242, 22 November 1967 and UNSC Res.338, 22 October 1973.

128 See, *inter alia*, UNGA Res.36/146 C of 16 December 1981, which '*Requests the Secretary-General to take all appropriate steps, in consultation with the United Nations Conciliation Commission for Palestine, for the protection and administration of Arab property, assets and property rights in Israel, and to establish a fund for the receipt of income derived therefrom, on behalf of their rightful owners* [...]', UNGA Res.51/129, 13 December 1996; UNGA Res.55/128, 8 December 2000, UNGA Res.61/407, 14 December 2006 and UNGA Res. 78/75, 7 December 2023.

129 UNGA Res 78/75, 7 December 2023.

130 Ibid.

131 The International Convention on the Elimination of Racial Discrimination (CERD) was adopted and opened for signature and ratification by GA Resolution 2106 (XX), 21 December 1965. It entered into force on 4 January 1969.

132 S. Leckie, 'New Directions in Housing and Property Restitution' in S. Leckie, *Returning Home: Housing and Property Restitution Rights of Refugees and Displaced Persons* (New York: Transnational, 2003), p. 4.

133 UNGA Res.217A(III), 10 December 1948.

134 When the Declaration was adopted in a UNGA resolution, it was not considered a source of binding obligations under international law. However, it is possible that the Declaration, or at least parts of it (like the prohibition of torture) has become binding as a new rule of customary international law. See P. Malanczuk, *Akehurst's Modern Introduction to International Law*, 7th edn (London: Routledge, 1997), pp. 212–13.

135 See, *inter alia*, K. Lawand, 'The Right to Return of Palestinians under International Law', *International Journal of Refugee Law* 8 (1996): 532–68 at pp. 547–58 and Boling, supra note 75 at pp. 36–42 for a detailed analysis of the application of Art. 12(4) to Palestinian refugees. See also CEIRPP (1978), supra note 70 at chapter II and Lynk (2000), supra note 3 at pp. 171–2.

136 The International Covenant on Civil and Political Rights (ICCPR) was adopted and opened for signature, ratification and accession by GA Resolution 2200A (XXI), 16 December 1966. It entered into force on 23 March 1976.

137 UN Committee on the Elimination of Racial Discrimination, Consideration of Reports Submitted by States Parties under Article 9 of the Convention: Concluding Observations of the Committee on the Elimination of Racial Discrimination, Seventieth Session, CERD/C/ISR/CO/13, 14 June 2007 at para.18.

138 Amnesty International (2022), 'Israel's Apartheid Against Palestinians: Cruel System of Domination and Crime Against Humanity', available at www.amnesty. org (accessed 14 April 2024) at p. 93.

139 Human Rights Watch, 'Human Rights Watch Policy on the Right to Return', Right to Return – Human Rights Watch Policy Page (hrw.org) (accessed 14 April 2024).

140 *The Factory at Chorzow, Jurisdiction, 1927*, supra note 13 at p. 21.

141 Article 33(1), ILC Articles.

142 Crawford (2002), supra note 13 at p. 209.

143 Article 33(2), ILC Articles.

144 For an example of such a practice, see *inter alia*, E. Klein, 'Individual Reparation Claims under the International Covenant on Civil and Political Rights: The Practice of the Human Rights Committee', in A. Randelzhofer and C. Tomuschat (eds), *State Responsibility and the Individual: Reparation in Instances of Grave Violations of Human Rights* (The Hague: Martinus Nijhoff, 1999); Echeverria (2003), supra note 9, I. Bottigliero, *Redress for Victims of Crimes Under International Law* (Leiden: Martinus Nijhoff, 2004).

145 E. B. Weiss, 'Invoking State Responsibility in the Twenty-First Century', *American Journal of International Law* 96 (2002): 798–816 at p. 816.

146 Economic and Social Council, Commission on Human Rights, Sixty-First Session, Basic Principles and Guidelines on the Right to a Remedy and Reparation for Victims of Gross Violations of International Human Rights Law and Serious

Violations of International Humanitarian Law, E/CN.4/2005/L.10/Add.11, 19
April 2005.

147 For an overview of the drafting history of the Guidelines on Reparation, see G.
Echeverria, 'Codifying the Rights of Victims in International Law: Remedies and
Reparation', in The International Bureau of the Permanent Court of Arbitration,
*Redressing Injustices through Mass Claims Processes: Innovative Responses to Unique
Challenges* (Oxford: Oxford University Press, 2006), pp. 287–92.

148 See ibid., p. 291 for similarities and differences between the ILC Articles and the
Guidelines on Reparation.

149 Principle 15 of the Guidelines on Reparation. According to this Principle,
'[…]a State shall provide reparation to victims for acts or omissions which
can be attributed to the State and constitute gross violations of international
humanitarian law'.

Chapter 3

1 For more on the structure, composition and jurisdiction of these tribunals, see
inter alia, P. Sands, R. Mackenzie and Y. Shany, *Manual on International Courts
and Tribunals* (London: Butterworths, 1999), pp. 273–300 (hereinafter *Manual on
ICT*); C. Bassiouni, 'Former Yugoslavia: Investigating Violations of International
Humanitarian Law and Establishing an International Criminal Tribunal', *Security
Dialogues* 25, no. 4 (1994): 409–23 and J. Karhilo, 'The Establishment of the
International Tribunal for Rwanda', *Nordic Journal of International Law* 64
(1995): 681–711.

2 For more on the court, see *inter alia*, Sands, Mackenzie and Shany, *Manual on
International Courts and Tribunals*, pp. 255–286; M. Rita Saulle, 'The International
Criminal Court', *UC Davis Journal of International Law and Policy* 5 (1999): 119–
31; R. S. Lee, *The International Criminal Court: Elements of Crimes and Rules of
Procedure and Evidence* (Ardsley: Transnational, 2001).

3 See, *inter alia*, the extradition case brought against Chilean dictator Augusto
Pinochet in UK courts (*R v Bow Street Metropolitan Stipendiary Magistrate ex
parte Pinochet Ugarte (No.3)* [2000] 1 AC 147 (HL); earlier phases of the case are
reported at *ex parte Pinochet Ugarte (No.2)* [2000] 1 AC 119 and *ex parte Pinochet
Ugarte (No.1)* [2000] 1 AC 61.) See also Special Dossier, *The 'Sabra and Shatila'
Case in Belgium, Palestine Yearbook of International Law*, 12 (2002): 183–289 for
documents pertaining to the case filed in Belgian courts against former Israeli
Prime Minister, Ariel Sharon, for his alleged involvement in the 1982 Sabra and
Shatila massacre of Palestinian refugees.

4 See, *inter alia*, P. Van Der Auweraert, 'Holocaust Reparation Claims Fifty
   Years After: The Swiss Banks Litigation, *Nordic Journal of International Law*
   71 (2002): 557–83; M. J. Bazyler and A. L. Fitzgerald, 'Trading with the
   Enemy: Holocaust Restitution, the United States Government, and American
   Industry', *Brooklyn Journal of International Law* 28 (2003): 683–810 and M.
   J. Bazyler, *Holocaust Justice: The Battle for Restitution in America's Courts*
   (New York: New York University Press, 2003).

5 See, *inter alia*, D. Minami, 'Japanese-American Redress', *African-American Law
   & Policy Report* 1 6 (2004): 27–34 and R. L. Brooks, 'Japanese American Redress
   and the American Political Process', in R. L. Brooks (eds), *When Sorry Isn't
   Enough: The Controversy over Apologies and Reparations for Human Injustice*
   (New York: New York University Press, 1999).

6 See, *inter alia*, R. Robinson, *The Debt: What America Owes to Blacks*
   (New York: Plume, 2001); R. Robinson, 'What America Owes to Blacks and
   What Blacks Owe to Each Other', *African-American Law & Policy Report* 1
   6 (2004): 1–13 and J. Levitt, 'Black African Reparations: Making a Claim for
   Enslavement and Systematic De Jure Segregation and Racial Discrimination
   under American and International Law', *Southern University Law Review*
   (1997): 1–42.

7 See, *inter alia*, E. Barkan, *The Guilt of Nations: Restitution and Negotiating Historical
   Injustices* (New York: W.W. Norton, 2000), pp. 112–56 and J. J. Renzulli, 'Claims
   of U.S. Nationals under the Restitution of Laws of Czechoslovakia', *Boston College
   International and Comparative Law Review* 15 (1992): 165–88.

8 See, *inter alia*, N. Jessup Newton, 'Indian Claims for Reparations, Compensation,
   and Restitution in the United States Legal System' in R. L. Brooks (eds), *When Sorry
   Isn't Enough: The Controversy over Apologies and Reparations for Human Injustice*
   (New York: New York University Press, 1999) and Barkan (2000), *The Guilt of
   Nations*, pp. 169–282.

9 See Chapter 5 for a discussion of Palestinian refugee property claims in Israeli–
   Palestinian negotiations.

10 The *Weisshaus* v. *Union Bank of Switzerland*, No. 96 CV 4849 (EDNY) was filed in
   the United States District Court for the Eastern District of New York on 03 October
   1996. For a chronology of the litigation against Swiss banks, and links to the original
   copies of the filed complaints, see the archives of the official website of the *Swiss
   Banks Settlement: In re Holocaust Victim Assets Litigation*: http://www.swissbankcla
   ims.com (accessed 14 April 2024).

11 For an analysis of the litigation process against Swiss banks, see, *inter alia*, Van
   Der Auweraert, supra note 4 at pp. 567–70, Bazyler (*Holocaust Justice*, 2003),
   supra note 4 at pp. 22–5 and M. I. Weiss, 'A Litigator's Postscript to the Swiss
   Banks and Holocaust Litigation Settlements: How Justice Was Served', in M. J.

Bazyler and R. P. Alford (eds), *Holocaust Restitution: Perspectives on the Litigation* (New York: New York University Press, 2006).

12 Bazyler and Fitzgerald supra note 4 at p. 690.

13 S. D. Murphy, 'Contemporary Practice of the US relating to International Law', *American Journal of International Law* 94 (2000): 102–39 at pp. 107–12 on Nazi-Era claims against German companies; B. Neuborne, 'A Tale of Two Cities: Administering the Holocaust Settlements in Brooklyn and Berlin', in M. J. Bazyler and R. P. Alford (eds), *Holocaust Restitution: Perspectives on the Litigation* (New York: New York University Press, 2006); L. Ulsamer, 'German Economy and the Foundation Initiative: An Act of Solidarity for Victims of National Socialism', in M. J. Bazyler and R. P. Alford (eds), *Holocaust Restitution: Perspectives on the Litigation* (New York: New York University Press, 2006) and R. M. Witten, 'How Swiss Banks and German Companies Came to Terms with the Wrenching Legacies of the Holocaust and World War II: A Defense Perspective', in M. J. Bazyler and R. P. Alford (eds), *Holocaust Restitution: Perspectives on the Litigation* (New York: New York University Press, 2006).

14 See *Agreement between the Government of the Federal Republic of Germany and the Government of the United States of America concerning the Foundation 'Remembrance, Responsibility and the Future'*, signed on 17 July 2000 at pp. 2–3, Articles 2 and 3 and para. 4 of Annex B [hereinafter US-German Agreement]. According to Article 3(4) of this Agreement, '[t]he United States shall take appropriate steps to oppose any challenge to the sovereign immunity of the Federal Republic of Germany with respect to any claim that may be asserted against the Federal Republic of Germany concerning the consequences of the National Socialist era and World War II.'

15 In the US–German Agreement, the signatory parties noted that 'by means of the Foundation Initiative, its member companies wish to respond to the moral responsibility of German business arising from the use of forced laborers and from damage to property caused by persecution, and from all other wrongs suffered during the National Socialist era and World War II'.

16 See Preamble to the Law on the Creation of a Foundation 'Remembrance, Responsibility and Future', 17 July 2000 in which German enterprises acknowledge their historical, political and moral responsibility but not any legal responsibility.

17 H. Lessing and F. Azizi, 'Austria Confronts Her Past', in M. J. Bazyler and R. P. Alford (eds), *Holocaust Restitution: Perspectives on the Litigation* (New York: New York University Press, 2006).

18 The Austrian Federal Law Concerning the Fund for Voluntary Payments by the Republic of Austria to Former Slave Laborers and Forced Laborers of the National Socialist Regime (Reconciliation Fund Law) was promulgated on August 8, 2000, in Federal Law Gazette No. 74/2000 and came into force on 27 November 2000, as

announced by the Federal government on 1 December 2000, in Federal Law Gazette
No. 122/2000. Section 1 of the law states that the purpose of the Reconciliation
Fund was to provide 'payments to former slave laborers and forced laborers of the
Nazi regime on the territory of present-day Austria.' These payments were to be
understood as 'a voluntary gesture' because no claim could be brought against the
Republic under international law.

19 See M. Ratner and C. Becker, 'The Legacy of Holocaust Class Action Suits: Have
They Broken Ground for Other Cases of Historical Wrongs' in M. J. Bazyler
and R. P. Alford (eds), *Holocaust Restitution: Perspectives on the Litigation*
(New York: New York University Press, 2006) and Bazyler (*Holocaust Justice*, 2003),
supra note 4 at pp. 307–334, for more on how the Holocaust restitution movement
encouraged victims of other historical injustices to file claims in the US against
private companies (e.g. claims were filed against Japanese companies for their use of
slave labour during the Second World War).

20 N. G. Finkelstein, 'Lessons of Holocaust Compensation', in N. Aruri (eds),
Palestinian Refugees: The Right of Return (London: Pluto Press, 2001) and G. Karmi,
'The Question of Compensation and Reparations', in G. Karmi and E. Cotran, *The
Palestinian Exodus 1948–1998* (Reading: Ithaca Press, 1999).

21 M. Fischbach, *Records of Dispossession: Palestinian Refugee Property and the Arab
Israeli Conflict* (New York: Columbia University Press, 2003), p. 340.

22 See, *inter alia*, M. J. Bazyler, 'Litigating the Holocaust', *University of Richmond
Law Review* 33 (1999): 5–283; M. J. Bazyler, 'Nuremberg in America: Litigating
the Holocaust in American Courts', *University of Richmond Law Review* 34
(2000): 1–283; M. J. Bazyler, 'The Holocaust Restitution Movement in Comparative
Perspective', *Berkeley Journal of International Law* 20 (2002): 11–44; Bazyler and
Fitzgerald, supra note 4 and Bazyler (*Holocaust Justice*, 2003), supra note 4.

23 Bazyler (*Holocaust Justice*, 2003),.preface at pp. xii–xiii.

24 On 15 May 1997 Swiss banks responded to plaintiffs' complaints by filing several
motions to dismiss or, in the alternative, to stay the lawsuits in the Eastern District
of New York.

25 Four separate claims were filed against German companies Degussa and Siemens
and were consolidated under the caption *Burger-Fischer* v. *Degussa AG*, 65
F.Supp. 2d 248 (D.N.J. 1999) (hereinafter *Burger-Fischer* case). All four claims were
dismissed by Judge Debevoise. See also *Iwanowa* v. *Ford Motor Co.*, 67 F.Supp. 2d
424 (D.N.J. 1999) (hereinafter the *Iwanowa* case).

26 Bazyler (*Holocaust Justice*, 2003) supra note 4 at p. 75.

27 See *Iwanowa* case, supra note 25 at para. 33, 59–66. See also the conclusion in the
Burger-Fischer case, supra note 25 at pp. 281–5.

28 Bazyler (*Holocaust Justice*, 2003) supra note 4 at p. 77. See also Neuborne, supra
note 13 at pp. 73–7 for more on Judge Korman's role in the success of the litigation

against Swiss banks. According to Neuborne, 'with the important exception of Judge Korman and his colleagues in the Brooklyn federal courthouse, the Holocaust settlements were attained despite American judges, not because of them' (p. 74).

29 See also Barkan, supra note 7 at pp. 88–111.

30 See also R. J. Bettauer, 'The Role of the United States Government in Recent Holocaust Claims Resolution', *American Society of International Law Proceedings* 95 (2001): 37–41.

31 Ratner and Becker, supra note 19 at pp. 345–351.

32 See, *inter alia*, N. Chomsky, *The Fateful Triangle: The United States, Israel and the Palestinians* (Boston, MA: South End Press, 1999) and H. Friel and R. Falk, *Israel-Palestine on Record: How the New York Times Misreports Conflict in the Middle East* (New York: Verso, 2007).

33 In October and December 2023, the US vetoed two Security Council resolutions calling for a ceasefire, which would have halted Israel's disproportionate military aggression on Palestinians in Gaza.

34 Visit the Center for Constitutional Rights (ccrjustice.org) (accessed 14 April 2024) for updates.

35 For more on the threat of financial sanctions, see Bazyler (*Holocaust Justice*, 2003), supra note 4 at pp. 21–25.

36 Bazyler (*Holocaust Justice*, 2003), supra note 4 at pp. 24–5.

37 See *Crosby* v. *National Foreign Trade Council*, 530 US 363, 147 L.Ed. 2d 352 (2000). This case involved a law passed by Massachusetts in June 1996 to bar state entities from buying goods or services from companies doing business with Burma. Three months later, Congress imposed mandatory and conditional sanctions on Burma. The case reached the US Supreme Court, which eventually ruled that the law infringed on the federal government's exclusive power over foreign affairs.

38 R. L. Brooks, *Atonement and Forgiveness: A New Model for Black Reparations* (Berkeley: University of California Press, 2004), p. 99. See also Neuborne, supra note 13 at p. 74. According to Neuborne, '[t]he Holocaust cases are not legal launching pads for other efforts to right historical wrongs precisely because there is no legal platform from which to launch.'

39 *Burger-Fischer* case, supra note 25 at pp. 265–85 and *Iwanowa* case, supra note 25 at pp. 447–61. In these cases, the judges ruled that wartime claims and reparations had to be pursued only through government-to-government negotiations.

40 R. Dolzer, 'The Settlement of War-Related Claims: Does International Law Recognize A Victim's Private Right of Action? Lessons After 1945', *Berkeley Journal of International Law* 20 (2002): 296–341 at p. 338.

41 Taba Negotiations: The Moratinos Non-Paper, January 2001, para. 3.7.

42 *Trendex Trading Corp. Ltd* v *Central Bank of Nigeria* [1977] 1 Q.B. 529, at p. 552.

43 For more on the evolution of the doctrine of state immunity, including its codification in UK and US legislation, see H. Fox, *The Law of State Immunity*, 3rd edn (Oxford: Oxford University Press, 2008) and R. K. Gardiner, *International Law* (London: Pearson Education Limited, 2003), pp. 339–44 and pp. 365–87. See also, the *European Convention on State Immunity* (16 May 1972), the US *Foreign Sovereign Immunities Act* (1976) and the UK's *State Immunity Act* (20 July 1978).

44 UNGA Res.59/38, 16 December 2004.

45 According to the UN Convention on JISP (Part III, Articles 10–17), no state can invoke state immunity as a defence against commercial transactions, contracts of employment or some cases pertaining to damage, ownership, possession and use of property, including intellectual and industrial property.

46 The issue of state immunity was discussed in cases in UK courts involving acts of torture allegedly committed by a State and its agents. Arguments were made by the victims' representatives that a state cannot raise the defence of state immunity when it is accused of violating peremptory norms of international law, such as the prohibition of torture. In the case of *Al Adsani* v. *the United Kingdom*, this argument was rejected by UK courts and eventually by the European Court of Human Rights by a slim majority of 9 to 8 judges. The majority ruled that 'Notwithstanding the special character of the prohibition of torture in international law, the Court is unable to discern in the international instruments, judicial authorities or other materials before it any firm basis for concluding that, as a matter of international law, a State no longer enjoys immunity from civil suit in the courts of another State where acts of torture are alleged.' (See *Al Adsani* v. *the United Kingdom*, [2002] 34 E.H.R.R. 11 at para. 61.) The issue of whether a peremptory norm of international law supersedes the norm on state immunity was brought up again in the *Jones* v. *Ministry of the Interior of the Kingdom of Saudi Arabia*. Both the Court of Appeal and the House of Lords upheld the claims to state immunity made on behalf of the Kingdom of Saudi Arabia and other defendants (see *Jones* v. *Ministry of the Interior of the Kingdom of Saudi Arabia (Secretary of State for Constitutional Affairs intervening)* [2005] Q.B. 699 (Court of Appeal) and the House of Lord's decision [2006] UKHL 26). Even if the courts had accepted the plaintiffs' argument, Palestinian refugee claimants would not be able to resort to it. As discussed in Chapter 2, Israel's actions would still have to be evaluated according to the law which existed at the time they took place. Since the norm of *jus cogens* is a relatively new development in international law, it can hardly be argued that Israeli expropriations of property in the late 40s and early 50s violated peremptory norms of international law. Victims of current violations of international law in the Occupied Palestinian Territory could, however, benefit from developments in the law on state immunity, particularly if domestic courts were to allow claims against states accused of violating peremptory norms of international law.

47 See, for instance, *Corrie v. Caterpillar*, 503 F.3d 974 (C.A.9. 2007), which is a federal lawsuit filed against Illinois-based Caterpillar, Inc. on behalf of the parents of Rachel Corrie, an American peace activist who was run over and killed by a Caterpillar bulldozer in Gaza on 16 March 2003, and on behalf of Palestinian families whose family members were killed or injured when bulldozers demolished their homes on top of them. The case was filed by the Center for Constitutional Rights. It was dismissed by the US Court of Appeal in 2007, which found that the court did not have jurisdiction to decide the case because Caterpillar's bulldozers were ultimately paid for by the US Government and a decision by the court would impermissibly intrude upon the executive branch's foreign policy decisions. In its decision, the Court did not rule on the question of whether Caterpillar aided and abetted Israeli war crimes.

48 See, *inter alia, Ryuichi Shimoda et Al. v. The State (District Court of Tokyo - Japan), 07 Dec. 1963,* International Law Reports, 1966, Vol. 32, 626 at pp. 636–40. In this case, Japanese nationals, residents either of Hiroshima or of Nagasaki, filed claims for damages against the United States for injury they suffered through the dropping of atomic bombs. The District Court of Tokyo ruled that 'there is in general no way open to an individual who suffers injuries from an act of hostilities contrary to international law to claim damages on the level of international law […]' (p. 638). The court further ruled that the doctrine of state immunity would prevent claimants from seeking compensation before the municipal courts of either the US or Japan (p. 638–40). See also *Goldstar (Panama) SA v. United States (United States Court of Appeals, Fourth Circuit), 16 June 1992,* International Law Reports, 1994, Vol. 96, 55 at pp. 58–59 in which the court ruled that Article 3 of the 1907 Hague Convention does not explicitly provide for a privately enforceable cause of action (p. 58).

49 Chapter 2, Section 2.4.

50 A statute of limitations will vary according to the nature of the claim and the jurisdiction in which it is filed. The slave-labour claim brought against Ford Motors in the late 1990s is an example, among many others, of a time-barred claim (*Iwanowa* case, supra note 25 at para. 34–43 and 55–9).

51 Brooks (*Atonement and Forgiveness*, 2004) supra note 38 pp. 119–38.

52 See, for instance, the ruling in *Cato v. United States* (70 F.3rd 1103 (C.A.9, 1995)). One of the grounds for the dismissal of this case was the claimants' lack of standing to pursue such claims, since they themselves were never slaves. According to the court, '[A] plaintiff must allege personal injury fairly traceable to the defendant's allegedly unlawful conduct and likely to be redressed by the requested relief. No plaintiff has standing 'to complain simply that their Government is violating the law.' Neither does Cato have standing to litigate claims based on the stigmatizing injury to all African Americans caused by racial discrimination'. (pp. 1109–10).

53 For more on these laws, see Renzulli, supra note 7 at pp. 177–81. The two main laws that govern restitution in the Czech Republic are known as the Small Restitution Law of 2 October 1990 and the Large Restitution Law of 21 February 1991. (The author has not been able to find English translations of these laws.)

54 R. Hochstein, 'Jewish Property Restitution in the Czech Republic', *Boston College International and Comparative Law Review* 19 (1996): 423–47 at p. 423.

55 Ibid., p. 424.

56 Ibid. According to Hochstein, a subsequent amendment to the Large Restitution Law allowed for the restitution of property confiscated by the Nazis and belonging to the Jewish community of Czechoslovakia (Hochstein, 'Jewish Property Restitution in the Czech Republic', p. 442). For a discussion of Sudeten German property claims, see, *inter alia*, P. Macklem, 'Rybna 9, Praha 1: Restitution and Memory in International Human Rights Law', *European Journal of International Law* 16 (2005): 1–23; A. Gattini, 'A Trojan Horse for Sudeten Claims? On Some Implications of the *Prince of Liechtenstein* v. *Germany*', *European Journal of International Law* 13 (2002): 513–44; European Parliament, Directorate-General for Research (Working Paper), 'Legal Opinion on the Benes-Decrees and the accession of the Czech Republic to the EU' (October 2002).

57 Civil Liberties Act (*Restitution for World War II Internment of Japanese-Americans and Aleuts*), 50 App.U.S.C.A §1989b et seq.

58 Minami, supra note 5 at p. 33.

59 For more on the passage of this Act, see L. T. Hatamiya, 'Institutions and Interest Groups: Understanding the Passage of the Japanese American Redress Bill', in R. L. Brooks (ed.), *When Sorry Isn't Enough: The Controversy over Apologies and Reparations for Human Injustice* (New York: New York University Press, 1999).

60 On 5 January 1993, Black Congressman John Conyers introduced a bill before Congress to

acknowledge the fundamental injustice, cruelty, brutality, and inhumanity of slavery in the United States and the 13 American colonies between 1619 and 1865 and to establish a commission to examine the institution of slavery, subsequent *de jure* and *de facto* racial and economic discrimination against African Americans, and the impact of these forces on living African Americans, to make recommendations to the Congress on appropriate remedies, and for other purposes.' (Cited in Robinson (2001), supra note 6 at p. 201)

According to Robinson, the 'bill, which did not ask for reparations for the descendants of slaves but merely a commission to study the effects of slavery, won from the 435-member U.S. House of Representatives only 28 cosponsors, 18 of whom were black'. See Robinson, supra note 6 at pp. 201–34 for more on Blacks' efforts to gain restitution in the US.

61 Dispossessed Palestinians in Israel and in the 1967 Occupied Territories have resorted to Israeli courts and the special military objection committees to demand a remedy to their dispossession. These fora, however, are only accessible to those dispossessed Palestinians who remain within the borders of their historic homeland and are out of reach for Palestinian refugees. See, *inter alia*, T. Rempell, 'Housing and Property Restitution: The Palestinian Refugee Case', in S. Leckie, *Returning Home: Housing and Property Restitution Rights of Refugees and Displaced Persons* (New York: Transnational, 2003), p. 299 and H. Abu Hussein and F. McKay, *Access Denied: Palestinian Land Rights in Israel* (London: Zed Books, 2003).

62 As of December 2023, there were over 5.9 million Palestinian refugees registered with UNRWA (source: www.unrwa.org). Arguably, the majority of refugees, peasants, city dwellers and landowners, must have possessed some sort of property, whether it was a small house or several orange groves.

63 For a more in-depth analysis of these three models of reparations, see N. Roht-Arriaza, 'Reparations in the Aftermath of Repression and Mass Violence', in E. Stover and H. M. Weinstein (eds), *My Neighbor, My Enemy: Justice and Community in the Aftermath of Mass Atrocity* (Cambridge: Cambridge University Press, 2004), pp. 129–36.

64 Ibid., p. 127.

65 P. De Greiff, 'Justice and Reparations', in De Greiff, P. (ed.), *The Handbook of Reparations* (Oxford: Oxford University Press, 2006) at p. 458. According to De Greiff, 'the difference in the awards may send a message that the violation of the rights of some people is worse than the violation of the same rights of others, thereby undermining an important egalitarian concern and resulting in a hierarchy of victims.'

66 N. Roht-Arriaza, 'Reparations Decisions and Dilemmas', *Hastings International and Comparative Law Review* 27 (2004): 157–219 at p. 169.

67 Fischbach, supra note 21 at p. 137.

68 Brooks (*Atonement and Forgiveness*, 2004) supra note 38 at pp. 138–40.

69 For a criticism of the fees charged by the lawyers in the Holocaust Restitution Movement and the token amounts of money received by survivors from the billion-dollar awards, see N. G. Finkelstein, *The Holocaust Industry*, 2nd edn (London: Verso, 2003), pp. 106–7, pp. 151–69 and pp. 245–52. See also J. Authers, 'Making Good Again: German Compensation for Forced and Slave Laborers', in P. De Greiff (ed.), *The Handbook of Reparations* (Oxford: Oxford University Press at p. 441. According to John Authers, 'the single best-paid lawyer [in a case brought against German corporations in the US] received a fee of US$ 7.5 million (a figure three orders of magnitude higher than the highest compensation paid to one of his victim-clients).

70 Authers, 'Making Good Again', pp. 431–2.

71 Ibid., pp. 429–32.

72 E. Coleman Jordan, 'The Non-Monetary Value of Reparations Rhetoric', *African-American Law & Policy Report 1* 6(2004): 21–5.

73 Referring to the US lawsuits against German corporations, Authers notes that 'there was agreement on all sides that the sum [of the negotiated settlement] would have been far lower without the lawsuits.' Authers, supra note 69 at p. 440.

74 Supra note 14.

75 For more on the JCC, see, *inter alia*, R. W. Zweig, *German Reparations and the Jewish World: A History of the Claims Conference*, 2nd edn (London: Frank Cass, 2001); N. Robinson, *Spoliation and Remedial Action: the Material Damage Suffered by Jews under Persecution, Reparations, Restitution and Compensation* (New York: New York Institute of Jewish Affairs, 1962); A. Colonomos and A. Armstrong, 'German Reparations to the Jews after World War II: A Turning Point in the History of Reparations', in P. De Greiff (ed.), *The Handbook of Reparations* (Oxford: Oxford University Press, 2006).

76 A. Armstrong, 'The Role of Civil Society Actors in Reparations Legislation' in The International Bureau of the Permanent Court of Arbitration', *Redressing Injustices through Mass Claims Processes: Innovative Responses to Unique Challenges* (Oxford: Oxford University Press, 2006), p. 248.

77 See, *inter alia*, the ICJP's written notice of intention to prosecute UK government officials for aiding and abetting war crimes in Gaza issued in October 2023 (www.icjpalestine.com, accessed on 14 April 2024). See also Al-Haq, Al Mezan and the Palestinian Center for Human Rights (PCHR)'s submission to the Office of the Prosecutor of the International Criminal Court (ICC) providing a detailed description and analysis of the war crimes and crimes against humanity committed during the May 2021 Israeli military offensive against Palestinian civilians in the Gaza Strip and again in November 2023 (www.alhaq.org, accessed 14 April 2024). Adalah regularly files cases in Israeli courts to challenge and object to discriminatory legislation impacting Arab minority rights in Israel (www.adalah.org, accessed 14 April 2024). These include several cases related to discriminatory land laws and the expropriation of property.

78 Visit www.stopthejnf.ca (accessed on 14 April 2024) to learn more about the campaign to revoke JNF Canada's charitable status and expose, challenge and stop the JNF's discriminatory and harmful activities. See also Adalah's ongoing cases against JNF available on its site.

79 Individual petitions can be submitted before the Inter-American Commission on Human Rights (IACHR) alleging a violation of the American Convention on Human Rights by a state party. For more on the IACHR's jurisdiction and composition, see *Manual on ICT*, supra note 1 at pp. 216–32 and G. Echeverria, *Reparation: A Sourcebook for Victims of Torture and Other Violations of Human*

Rights and International Humanitarian Law (London: The Redress Trust, 2003), pp. 35–37 (hereinafter *REDRESS sourcebook*). The African Commission on Human and Peoples' Rights (ACHR) is an expert body empowered to ensure compliance with the African Charter on Human and Peoples' Rights. The commission can consider individual complaints at the request of the majority of its members. For more on the ACHR, see *Manual on ICT* at pp. 233–46 and *REDRESS sourcebook* at pp. 33–5. The European Court of Human Rights (ECHR) can also hear individual complaints against a state party to the European Convention of Human Rights. For more on the ECHR, see *Manual on ICT* at pp. 199–215 and *REDRESS sourcebook* at pp. 37–9.

80 *Loizidou* v. *Turkey* (Merits) (*Application no. 15318/89*), 18 December 1996 [hereinafter *Loizidou* case].

81 See *inter alia*, Kagan, M. (2005), 'Do Israeli Rights Conflict with the Palestinian Right of Return?', Working Paper No.10, BADIL Resource Center for Palestinian Residency & Refugee Rights (Badil), www.badil.org at p. 18 and Akram, S.M., 'Fora Available for Palestinian Refugee Restitution, Compensation and Related Claims', Badil Information and Discussion Brief, Issue No. 2, February 2000, www.badil.org (accessed 14 April 2024), and F. P. Albanese and L. Takkenberg, *Palestinian Refugees in International Law*, 2nd edn (Oxford: Oxford University Press, 2020), pp. 371–372.

82 *Loizidou* v. *Turkey* (Preliminary Objections) *(Application no. 15318/89)*, 23 March 1995 at para. 99–105.

83 *Loizidou* case, supra note 80 at para. 39–47.

84 Ibid., para. 42–45.

85 Ibid., para. 39–47.

86 On 28 July 1998, a Grand Chamber of the ECtHR ordered Turkey to pay Ms. Loizidou damages pursuant to the 1996 judgement. According to the court, Turkey had to pay Ms. Loizidou pecuniary and nonpecuniary damages as well as costs and expenses (*Loizidou* v. *Turkey* (Article 50) (40/1993/435/514), 28 July 1998). On 2 December 2003, Turkey executed the 1998 judgement by paying Ms. Loizidou the sum she was awarded. Ms. Loizidou thus became the first individual to receive a payment of damages from Turkey. (See P. Staible, K. Edison and L. Rosenblum, 'Updates from the Regional Human Rights Systems', *Hum. Rts. Brief 27* 11, no. 2 (2004): 27–30 at pp. 28–29.)

87 *Loizidou* case, supra note 80 at para. 64.

88 Immovable Property Commission official website: Immovable Property Commission > HOMEPAGE (ct.tr) (accessed 14 April 2024).

89 T. Cleaver and E. Halil, 'Turkey, TRNC pleased with COE's Loizidou case decision', 1 October 2022, PressReader.com – Digital Newspaper & Magazine Subscriptions (accessed 14 April 2024).

90 For a list of the cases and advisory opinions delivered by the ICJ, visit www. icj-cij.org.

91 J. G. Merrills, *International Dispute Settlement*, 3rd edn (Cambridge: Cambridge University Press, 1998), p. 169.

92 *Legal Consequences of the Construction of a Wall in the Occupied Palestinian Territory*, ICJ Advisory Opinion, 9 July 2004, ICJ Rep. 2004, 136 [hereinafter Wall Advisory Opinion].

93 The Republic of South Africa institutes proceedings against the State of Israel and requests the Court to indicate provisional measures (icj-cij.org) (dated 29 December 2023).

94 Request for Advisory Opinion on *Legal Consequences arising from the Policies and Practices of Israel in the Occupied Palestinian Territory, including East Jerusalem,* filing of written comments on 14 November 2023 (www.icj-cij.org).

95 M. Kagan, 'Destructive Ambiguity: Enemy Nationals and the Legal Enabling of Ethnic Conflict in the Middle East', *Columbia Human Rights Law Review* 38 (2007): 263–319 at p. 318. For arguments on the politicization of international law, see the written statements of the Governments of Israel, the UK and the US on the ICJ's jurisdiction and propriety of giving an advisory opinion on the Wall (statements available online at www.icj-cij.org.

96 See, *inter alia*, S. Rosenne, *The World Court: What It Is and How It Works*, 5th edn (London: Nijhoff, 1995); S. Rosenne and Y. Ronen, *The Law and Practice of the International Court of Justice: 1920–2005*, 4th edn (Leiden: Martinus Nijhoff, 2006) and *Manual on ICT*, supra note 1 at pp. 4–22.

97 The Charter of the United Nations, 26 June 1945, XV UNCIO 335 (hereinafter 'UN Charter').

98 Statute of the International Court of Justice, 26 June 1945, Annex to UN Charter, XV UNCIO 355 (hereinafter 'ICJ Statute').

99 ICJ Statute, Article 34(1).

100 ICJ Statute, Article 35(1).

101 A state can consent to the Court's jurisdiction in a number of ways. It can grant its consent before the dispute arises by means of a compromissory clause in a treaty or a declaration made under Article 36(2) of the ICJ Statute (the so-called 'Optional Clause').

102 Israel has repeatedly demonstrated its aversion to the ICJ having jurisdiction over disputes. For instance, in Article 15 of the 1993 Declaration of Principles on Interim Self-Government Arrangements, both Israel and the PLO favoured conciliation and arbitration, over submissions to the ICJ, for the resolution of any disputes arising from the application or interpretation of the agreement. An additional indication of Israel's indisposition towards the ICJ is its steadfast opposition to the court's jurisdiction to grant even an advisory opinion on the

Wall in the Occupied Territories (see Request for an Advisory Opinion from the tenth Emergency Special Session of the United Nations General Assembly on 'the legal consequences arising from the construction of the wall being built by Israel', Written Statement of the Government of Israel on Jurisdiction and Propriety, 30 January 2004 at pp. 55–88). It has also expressed 'disgust' at South Africa's submission in December 2023 to the ICJ against what it called Israel's genocidal acts in Gaza.

103 S. Akram, 'Palestinian Refugee Rights Part Three: Strategies for Change', Center for Policy Analysis on Palestine, 2000). In its recent complaint to the ICJ, South Africa also relied on that argument to assert the court's jurisdiction by basing it on Article 36, paragraph 1, of the Statute of the Court and on Article IX of the Genocide Convention, to which both South Africa and Israel are parties (The Republic of South Africa institutes proceedings against the State of Israel and requests the Court to indicate provisional measures | INTERNATIONAL COURT OF JUSTICE (icj-cij.org)).

104 States not parties to the Statute to which the Court may be open | INTERNATIONAL COURT OF JUSTICE (icj-cij.org)

105 See discussions in Chapter 2, Section 2.3 on the Hague Conventions.

106 UN Charter, Article 96(1).

107 UN Charter, Article 96(2). See *Manual on ICT*, supra note 1 at p. 11 for a list of organs and agencies authorized to request advisory opinions.

108 UNGA Res. ES-10/14, 8 Dec 2003.

109 *Report of Sub-Committee 2 of the Ad Hoc Committee on the Palestinian Question*, General Assembly Official Records, UN Doc. A/AC.14/32, 11 November, 1947 at para. 8, 21, 34–40.

110 *Report of the Ad Hoc Committee on the Palestinian Question*, General Assembly Official Records, UN Doc. A/516, 25 November 1947 at para. 24.

111 B. H. Khasawneh, *An appraisal of the right of return and compensation of Jordanian nationals of Palestinian refugee origin and Jordan's right, under International Law, to bring claims relating thereto, on their behalf to and against Israel and to seek compensation as a host state in light of the conclusion of the Jordan-Israel peace treaty of 1994*, doctoral thesis, University of London, 2007 (London School of Economics), p. 283.

112 *Report of the Committee on the Exercise of the Inalienable Rights of the Palestinian People*, Official Records of the General Assembly, Thirty-first Session, Supplement No. 35 (A/31/35), 21 July 1976 at para. 18–32 and 66–9.

113 Ibid., para 21–32.

114 Ibid., para 22(d).

115 *The Right of Return of the Palestinian People*, ST/SG/SER.F/2, 1 November 1978, Chapter. VII.

116 Ibid.

117 See UNGA Res.31/20, 24 November 1976 and UNGA Res.32/40, 15
     December 1977.

118 In his separate opinion issued in the Wall Advisory Opinion, Judge Elaraby noted
     the failure to resort to the ICJ to clarify complex legal issues in the Palestine–Israel
     conflict, despite the UN's 'special responsibility' towards the question of Palestine.
     As a result, '[D]ecisions with far-reaching consequences were taken on the basis
     of political expediency, without due regard for the legal requirements.' See Wall
     Advisory Opinion, supra note 92, Separate Opinion of Judge Elaraby, at para.1.

119 Wall Advisory Opinion, *Legal Consequences of the Construction of a Wall in
     the Occupied Palestinian Territory*, ICJ Advisory Opinion, 9 July 2004, ICJ
     Rep. 2004, 136.

120 S. Akram and M. Lynk, 'The Wall and the Law: A Tale of Two Judgements',
     Netherlands Quarterly of Human Rights 24, no. 1 (2006): 61–106 at pp. 83–84.

121 Wall Advisory Opinion, supra note 92 at para. 152–3.

122 Ibid., para. 90–101.

123 Article 49, *Convention (IV) relative to the Protection of Civilian Persons in Time of
     War*, Geneva, 12 August 1949.

124 Wall Advisory Opinion, supra note 92 at para. 89–114.

125 Akram and Lynk, supra note 120 at pp. 83–84.

126 UNGA Res. 77/247, 30 December 2022.

127 Article 18 of the UN Charter lists the questions requiring a two-thirds majority
     vote in the General Assembly. None of these questions include decisions on
     requests for ICJ advisory opinions, thus suggesting that a simple majority of votes
     in the General Assembly would be sufficient. Nevertheless, Khasawneh argues that
     it would be preferable to obtain a two-thirds majority vote for political reasons,
     even though it is not a legal requirement. See Khasawneh, supra note 111 at
     pp. 282–283.

128 Ibid., p. 284. See also *Report of the Committee on the Exercise of the Inalienable
     Rights of the Palestinian People* (A/31/35), supra note 112 at para. 29 for more
     examples of legal questions which could be clarified through an advisory opinion
     of the ICJ.

129 C. Tomuschat, 'Individual Reparation Claims in Instances of Grave Human Rights
     Violations: The Position under General International Law', in A. Randelzhofer and
     C. Tomuschat (eds), *State Responsibility and the Individual: Reparation in Instances
     of Grave Violations of Human Rights* (The Hague: Martinus Nijhoff, 1999), p. 23.

130 H. Das, 'The Concept of Mass Claims and the Specificity of Mass Claims
     Resolution' in The International Bureau of the Permanent Court of Arbitration,
     *Redressing Injustices through Mass Claims Processes: Innovative Responses to Unique
     Challenges* (Oxford: Oxford University Press, 2006), pp. 9–10.

131 T. Rempel, 'The Ottawa Process: Workshop on Compensation and Palestinian Refugees', *Journal of Palestine Studies*, 29, no. 1 (1999): 36–49 at p. 45.

132 H. M. Holtzmann and E. Kristjansdottir, *International Mass Claims Processes: Legal and Practical Perspectives* (Oxford: Oxford University Press, 2007), pp. 17–18.

133 See analysis of the mixed claims commissions established between Bulgaria and Greece, Turkey and Bulgaria and Turkey and Greece in S. Ladas, *The Exchange of Minorities: Bulgaria, Greece and Turkey* (New York: Macmillan, 1932).

134 *Declaration of the Government of the Democratic and Popular Republic of Algeria concerning the Settlement of Claims by the Government of the United States of America and the Government of the Islamic Republic of Iran*, 19 January 1981.

135 *General Framework Agreement for Peace in Bosnia and Herzegovina*, initialed in Dayton, 21 Nov. 1995, signed in Paris, 14 December 1995, Annex 7 [hereinafter Dayton Agreement].

136 UNSC Res.687, 3 April 1991, Section E.

137 UNMIK Regulation 1999/23, 15 November 1999.

138 Holtzmann and Kristjansdottir, supra note 132 at p. 20.

139 See the UNCC's official website at https://uncc.ch for more statistics on the claims.

140 J. R. Crook, 'Mass Claims Processes: Lessons Learned over Twenty-Five Years' in The International Bureau of the Permanent Court of Arbitration, *Redressing Injustices through Mass Claims Processes: Innovative Responses to Unique Challenges* (Oxford: Oxford University Press, 2006), p. 44.

141 Ibid.

142 D. J. Bederman and R. B. Lillich, 'Jurisprudence of the Foreign Claims Settlement Commission: Iran Claims', *Am. J. Int'l L.* 91 (1997): 436–65 at pp. 436–7. Pursuant to the 1990 Settlement Agreement, a lump sum amount of $105 million was disbursed in return for the 'full, final and definitive settlement' of these small claims.

143 The Tribunal was established following the 1979 Iran–US hostage crisis which arose out of the detention of US nationals at the US Embassy in Tehran and the subsequent freeze of Iranian assets by the United States of America. The government of Algeria conducted extensive negotiations with both parties until it was able to extract commitments from both sides on ways to resolve the crisis amicably. The negotiations resulted in the adoption of two Declarations on 19 January 1981: the 'General Declaration' and the 'Claims Settlement Declaration', known as the Algiers Accord. The General Declaration records the central commitments of the parties while the Claims Settlement Declaration establishes the Tribunal and gives it jurisdiction to decide certain claims arising out of the 1979 hostage crisis. For more on the jurisdiction and composition of the tribunal, visit the tribunal's website at http://www.iusct.org/index-english.html.

144 C. N. Brower, 'The Lessons of the Iran-United States Claims Tribunal: How May They Be Applied in the Case of Iraq?', *Virginia Journal of International Law* 32 (1992): 421–30 at p. 422. According to Brower, the need to preserve equality between the two parties 'virtually insured that the Tribunal could not be operated with as high a degree of administrative rationality as one would have liked'.

145 Ibid., p. 422.

146 For more on the refugee crisis in Kosovo, see, *inter alia*, UNHCR Standing Committee., 'The Kosovo Refugee Crisis: An Independent Evaluation of UNHCR's Emergency Preparedness and Response', February 2000, EC/50/SC/CRP.12, www. unhcr.org (accessed 14 April 2024).

147 In March 2006, by virtue of UNMIK Regulation 2006/10, the HDP was subsumed into the Kosovo Property Agency, which is an independent body established to resolve claims resulting from the 1998–9 armed conflict in Kosovo pertaining to private immovable property.

148 During its eight years of operation, the CRPC issued over 300,000 decisions pertaining to individual property rights (see Holtzmann and Kristjansdottir, supra note 132 at pp. 23–4.)

149 P. Prettitore, 'The Right to Housing and Property Restitution in Bosnia and Herzegovina', BADIL Resource Center for Palestinian Residency & Refugee Rights, 2003, www.badil.org at p. 5.

150 The *Dayton Peace Accords* (or Dayton Agreement) formally ended three and a half years of war in Bosnia. The agreement was initiated at Wright-Patterson Air Force Base in Dayton, Ohio, on 21 November 1995 and signed in Paris on 14 December 1995.

151 Dayton Agreement, Annex 7, Article XI.

152 Holtzmann and Kristjansdottir, supra note 132 at p. 23.

153 Ibid., p. 24.

154 Crook (2006), supra note 140 at p. 46.

155 Report of the Secretary-General of 2 May 1991, U.N. Doc. S/225559, para. 20, cited in Holtzmann and Kristjansdottir, supra note 123 at p. 22.

156 Crook (2006), supra note 140 at pp. 47–8.

157 For a discussion of whether this type of representation constitutes diplomatic protection, see *inter alia*, C. Alzamora, 'The UN Compensation Commission: An Overview', in B. Lillich, *The United Nations Compensation Commission (Thirteenth Sokol Colloquium)* (Irvington: Transnational, 1995), pp. 8–9 and A. Gattini, 'The UN Compensation Commission: Old Rules, New Procedures on War Reparations', *European Journal of International Law* 13 (2002): 161–81 at pp. 170–1.

158 Claims for stateless Palestinians were eventually submitted to the UNCC by UNRWA, the UN Development Program (UNDP), the Office of the UN High Commissioner for Refugees (UNHCR) and the International Committee for the

Red Cross (ICRC). For more on this issue see, Alzamora, 'The UN Compensation Commission', p. 7 and D. J. Bederman, 'Historic Analogues of the UN Compensation Commission' in B. Lillich (ed.), *The United Nations Compensation Commission (Thirteenth Sokol Colloquium)* (Irvington, New York: Transnational, 1995), pp. 302–3.

159 J. R. Crook, 'The United Nations Compensation Commission – A New Structure to Enforce State Responsibility', *American Journal of International Law* 87 (1993): 144–57 at p. 150. Bederman notes how this procedure may have had its origins in earlier claims tribunals. Bederman also contrasts the UNCC's novel procedure to the Iran–US CT's rejection of claims of stateless individuals. See Bederman (*Historic Analogues*, 1995), p. 303, fn. 237.

160 See Gattini, supra note 157 at pp. 170-1 for more details on the disbursement of claims.

161 All information and statistical data about the different categories of claims used in this section are taken from the UNCC's official website, supra note 139.

162 Ibid.

163 D. D. Caron and B. Morris, 'The UN Compensation Commission: Practical Justice, not Retribution', *European Journal of International Law* 13 (2002): 183–99 at p. 188.

164 UNCC's official website, supra note 139.

165 Ibid.

166 Caron and Morris, supra note 163 at p. 188.

167 UNSC Res. 2621, 22 February 2022.

168 See Final Report of the Governing Council on the work of the Compensation Commission (S/2022/104) to the Security Council, 22 February 2022 for a summary of compensation awards by submitting entity and claims category.

169 Caron and Morris, supra note 163 at p. 188.

170 Brower, supra note 144 at p. 422-3.

171 D. J. Bederman, 'The United Nations Compensation Commission and the Tradition of International Claims Settlement', *NYU Journal of International Law and Politics* 27 (1996): 1–42 at p. 14.

172 Ibid., pp. 14–15.

173 Ibid., p. 15.

174 I. Bottigliero, *Redress for Victims of Crimes Under International Law* (Leiden: Martinus Nijhoff, 2004) at p. 95.

175 Bederman (*Historic Analogues*, 1995), supra note 158 at p. 308.

176 UNGA Res.194, para. 11, sub-para. 2. See also Fischbach, supra note 21 for more on the UNCCP. The UNCCP's conciliation efforts will be briefly discussed in Chapter 4.

177 Chapter 4 will outline the various mechanisms which have hitherto been suggested in peace proposals and Israeli–Palestinian negotiations.

178 See Chapter 2, Section 2.3.3.

179 Dayton Agreement, Annex 7, Article XI.

180 Annex 7, Article XIV(1). See also E. Rosand, 'The Right to Compensation in Bosnia: An Unfulfilled Promise and a Challenge to International Law', *Cornell International Law Journal* 33 (2000): 113–57.

181 Crook (2006) supra note 140 at p. 56.

Chapter 4

1 C. Dolan, 'Repatriation from South Africa to Mozambique – Undermining Durable Solutions?' in R. Black and K. Koser (eds), *The End of the Refugee Cycle?* (Oxford: Berghahn Books, 1999).

2 M. Eastmond and J. Ojendal, 'Revisiting a "Repatriation Success": The Case of Cambodia', in R. Black and K. Koser (eds), *The End of the Refugee Cycle?* (Oxford: Berghahn Books, 1999).

3 P. Marsden, 'Repatriation and Reconstruction: The Case of Afghanistan', in R. Black and K. Koser (eds), *The End of the Refugee Cycle?* (Oxford: Berghahn Books, 1999).

4 See, *inter alia*, E. Rosand, 'The Right to Return under International Law Following Mass Dislocation: the Bosnia Precedent?', *Mich. J. Int'l L.* 19 (1998): 1091–139; N. Barbara Delaney and J. Fischel de Andrade, 'Minority Return to South-Eastern Bosnia and Herzegovina: A Review of the 2000 Return Season', *Journal of Refugee Studies* 14, no. 3 (2001): 315–30.

5 R. Black and K. Koser, *The End of the Refugee Cycle?* (Oxford: Berghahn Books, 1999), p. 3.

6 P. Weiss Fagen, 'UNHCR and repatriation', in M. Dumper (ed.), *Palestinian Refugee Repatriation: Global Perspectives* (Abingdon: Routledge, 2006), p. 47. Refugee return was incorporated in the UN negotiated peace agreements in Namibia (1989), Cambodia (1991), El Salvador (1991) and Mozambique (1992).

7 See Chapter 5 for a discussion of the refugee issue in the context of Israeli–Palestinian negotiations.

8 Cited in N. Masalha, *The Politics of Denial: Israel and the Palestinian Refugee Problem* (London: Pluto Press, 2003), p. 228. Israel's rejection of the right of return was so categorical that the Knesset eventually passed a law in 2001 precluding negotiators from even discussing the right of return of the Palestinian refugees. (See *The Law to Deny the Right of Return – 2001*, Israel's Law to Deny the Right of Return – 2001, reprinted in *Palestine Yearbook of International Law* 11 (2000–1) at pp. 315–16.)

9 See *inter alia*, Masalha, *The Politics of Denial*, and I. Pappe, *The Ethnic Cleansing of Palestine* (Oxford: Oneworld Publications, 2006), pp. 235–47.

10 For a discussion of the feasibility of the Palestinian refugees' return see, *inter alia*, S. H. Abu-Sitta, 'The Right of Return: Sacred, Legal and Possible', in N. Aruri (ed.), *Palestinian Refugees: The Right of Return* (London: Pluto Press, 2001), p. 195, and S. H. Abu-Sitta, *The Return Journey: A Guide to the Depopulated and Present Palestinian Towns, Villages and Holy Sites* (London: Palestine Land Society, 2007). See also C. Beyani, 'Political and Legal Analysis of the Problem of the Return of Forcibly Transferred Populations', *Refugee Survey Quarterly* 16, no. 3 (1997): 1–25 for a more general discussion of the political and legal problems which obstruct the return of populations to territories from which they were forcibly displaced – or transferred – on grounds of ethnicity.

11 For an example of some of these legal arguments, see *inter alia* M. Medved, 'Palestinian Claims of 'Right of Return' Block All Possible Negotiations', *Nexus* 8 (2003): 17–30, and M. Kagan, 'Do Israeli Rights Conflict with the Palestinian Right of Return?', Working Paper No. 10, BADIL Resource Center for Palestinian Residency & Refugee Rights, 2005, www.badil.org (accessed 14 April 2024).

12 *The Factory at Chorzow* (Jurisdiction), *1927*, P.C.I.J., *Series A, No.9* at p. 21.

13 *The Factory at Chorzow* (Merits), *1928*, P.C.I.J., *Series A, No.17* at p. 47.

14 See Chapter 2 for a more detailed discussion of UNGA Resolution 194.

15 *Island of Palmas Case (United States v. the Netherlands),1928*, R.I.A.A., Vol. II, p. 829 at p. 845. For more on this rule, see T. O. Elias, 'The Doctrine of Intertemporal Law', *American Journal of International Law* 74 (1980): 285–307.

16 Ibid. See also R. Higgins, 'Time and the Law: International Perspectives on an Old Problem', *International & Comparative Law Quarterly* 46 (1997): 501–20 at pp. 515–19 for a discussion of the relationship between these two passages of the Island of Palmas case.

17 See, *inter alia*, *Legal Consequences for States of the Continued Presence of South Africa in Namibia (South West Africa) Notwithstanding Security Council Resolution 276 (1970)*, ICJ Advisory Opinion, 21 June 1971 at para.53 in which the International Court held that an 'international instrument must be interpreted and applied within the framework of the juridical system in force at the time of the interpretation'. Similarly, an acquired right, such as the right to restitution or compensation, must be interpreted according to subsequent legal developments affecting the definition of that right. See also, *Aegean Sea Continental Shelf Case (Greece v. Turkey)*, ICJ Judgment, 19 December 1978 at para. 77.

18 See discussion in Chapter 2, Section 2.4.

19 UN Sub-Commission on the Promotion and Protection of Human Rights, 'Principles on Housing and Property Restitution for Refugees and Displaced Persons', E/CN.4/Sub.2/2005/17, 11 August 2005 (hereinafter 'Pinheiro Principles').

20 UN Sub-Commission on the Promotion and Protection of Human Rights
    Resolution 1998/26, *Housing and Property Restitution in the Context of the Return of
    Rights for Refugees and Internally Displaced Persons*, 26 August 1998.

21 UN Sub-Commission on the Promotion and Protection of Human Rights
    Resolution 2002/7, *Housing and Property Restitution in the Context of Refugees and
    Other Displaced Persons*, 14 August 2002.

22 Joint Publication by OCHA/IDD, UN Habitat, UNHCR, FAO, OHCHR, the
    Norwegian Refugee Council (NRC) and the Internal Displacement Monitoring
    Centre (IDMC), *Handbook on Housing and Property Restitution for Refugees and
    Displaced Persons: Implementing the Pinheiro Principles*, March 2007, available
    at www.internal-displacement.org (accessed 14 April 2024) at p. 19 (hereinafter
    Handbook on the Pinheiro Principles).

23 Ibid., p. 11.

24 Principle 1 of the Pinheiro Principles.

25 Papamichalopoulos and Others v. Greece *(Application no. 14556/89)*, 31 October
    1995 (hereinafter *Papamichalopoulos* case).

26 *Loizidou* v. *Turkey* (Merits) *(Application no. 15318/89)*, 18 December 1996
    (hereinafter *Loizidou* case).

27 *Papamichalopoulos case*, supra note 25 at para. 34, 38–9.

28 *Loizidou* case (Merits), supra note 26 at para. 39–47.

29 *Loizidou* v. *Turkey* (Article 50) (40/1993/435/514), 28 July 1998 at para. 31 and 39.

30 *Legal Consequences of the Construction of a Wall in the Occupied Palestinian
    Territory*, ICJ Advisory Opinion, 9 July 2004 at para. 152–3.

31 Ibid.

32 M. Dumper, *The Future for Palestinian Refugees: Toward Equity and Peace*
    (London: Lynne Rienner, 2007), p. 140.

33 S. Leckie, 'New Directions in Housing and Property Restitution', in S. Leckie (ed.),
    *Returning Home: Housing and Property Restitution Rights of Refugees and Displaced
    Persons* (New York: Transnational, 2003), pp. 13–14.

34 UNHCR EXCOM, *Conclusion on Legal Safety Issues in the Context of Voluntary
    Repatriation of Refugees*, No.101 (LV), 8 October 2004 at para. (c) and (h).

35 UNHCR EXCOM, *General Conclusions on International Protection*, No. 68 (XLIII),
    9 October 1992. at para.(s).

36 UNCCP, *Analysis of paragraph 11 of the General Assembly's Resolution of 11 Dec.
    1948*, W/45, 15 May 1950 at p. 3.

37 See, Contini, P., *Legal Aspects of the Problem of Compensation to Palestine Refugees*
    (dated 22 November 1949), attached to United Nations Conciliation Commission
    for Palestine, *Letter and Memorandum dated 22 November 1949, Concerning
    Compensation, received by the Chairman of the Conciliation Commission from Mr.
    Gordon Clapp, Chairman, United Nations Economic Survey Mission for the Middle*

East, W/32, 19 January 1950 at p. 13. According to Contini, 'restitution could be applicable to property of returning refugees and personal property – especially blocked accounts – of non-returning refugees.'

38 Restitution in international law is typically defined as the reestablishment of the status quo before the violation of international law occurred (see Principle 19 of the Guidelines on Reparation and Article 35 of the ILC Articles for a general definition of restitution under international law). As such, return is a form of restitution for displacement and has been identified as the 'preferred remedy for displacement' under Principle 2.2 of the Pinheiro Principles.

39 For an analysis of the right of return under international law, see *inter alia* K. Lawand, 'The Right of Return of Palestinians under International Law', *International Journal of Refugee Law* 8 (1996): 532–68 and G. J. Boling, 'The 1948 Palestinian Refugees and the Individual Right of Return: *An International Law Analysis*', Badil Resource Center, 2001, www.badil.org (accessed 14 April 2024).

40 See the *Protocol on the Treatment of Palestinians in Arab States* (also known as the *Casablanca Protocol*) which was adopted by the Arab League in 1965 and called upon Arab host countries to treat Palestinians residing on their territory as if they were nationals, 'while keeping their Palestinian nationality.' For more on the status of Palestinian refugees in the Arab world see *inter alia*, A. Shiblak, 'Residency Status and Civil Rights of Palestinian Refugees in Arab Countries', *Journal of Palestine Studies*, 25, no. 3 (1996): 36–45 and F. P. Albanese and L. Takkenberg, *Palestinian Refugees in International Law*, 2nd edn (Oxford: Oxford University Press, 2020), pp. 183–269.

41 See also Principle 10.3 of the Pinheiro Principles which stipulates in part that 'Refugees and displaced persons should be able to effectively pursue durable solutions to displacement other than return, if they so wish, without prejudicing their right to the restitution of their housing, land and property'.

42 For an overview of the status of Palestinian refugees in Jordan, see Albanese and Takkenberg (2020), supra note 40 at pp. 198–208.

43 Handbook on the Pinheiro Principles, supra note 22 at p. 27.

44 Ibid., pp. 27–8.

45 Estimates of the number of depopulated and destroyed villages during the Nakba vary from about 400, according to Israeli historian Benny Morris, to 531 villages, according to Palestinian land expert Salman Abu Sitta. (For more on destroyed villages see *inter alia* B. Morris, *The Birth of the Palestinian Refugee Problem Revisited* (Cambridge: Cambridge University Press, 2004), pp. 342–60, W. Khalidi, *All That Remains: the Palestinian Villages Occupied and Depopulated by Israel in 1948* (Washington, DC: Institute for Palestine Studies, 1992) and S. H. Abu-Sitta, *The Palestinian Nakba: 1948: The Register of Depopulated Localities in Palestine* (London: The Palestinian Return Centre, 1998)).

46 See, for example, *The Factory at Chorzow* (Merits), supra note 13 at p. 47, Article 35 of the ILC Articles, Article 19 of the Guidelines on Reparation and Principle 2.1 of the Pinheiro Principles.

47 Handbook on the Pinheiro Principles, supra note 22 at p. 94.

48 According to research conducted by Salman Abu Sitta, the majority of the land in Israel on which Palestinian villages formerly stood is largely uninhabited. See Abu-Sitta (2001), supra note 10 at pp. 198–200.

49 See commentary on Principle 2 in the Handbook on the Pinheiro Principles, supra note 22 at p. 25.

50 Article 35 of the ILC Articles.

51 See Kagan (2005), supra note 11 at pp. 23–8.

52 See Chapter 2, Section 2.3.3 for a more detailed analysis of Resolution 194.

53 For cases involving property losses in which compensation was awarded for loss of enjoyment and other non-material damages, see *inter alia*, the *Papamichalopoulos* case, supra note 25 at para. 34, 38–9 and the *Loizidou* case (Article 50), supra note 29 at para. 31 and 39. The UNCC also awarded compensation for non-pecuniary damages such as death, mental pain or serious personal injury. In addition, Principle 20 of the Guidelines on Reparation stipulates that compensation should be provided for economically assessable damage such as physical or mental harm, lost opportunities or moral damage.

54 For more on compensation, see R. Brynen and R. El-Rifai, *Compensation to Palestinian Refugees and the Search for Palestinian Israeli Peace* (London: Pluto Press, 2013).

55 J. Crisp, 'No Solutions in Sight: The Problem of Protracted Refugee Situations in Africa', *Refugee Survey Quarterly* 22, no. 4 (2003): 114–50 at p. 114.

56 This book is being written as Palestinian refugees in Gaza are being forcibly displaced from their homes, while Israeli officials are openly calling for a 'Second Nakba' and their expulsion to the Egyptian Sinai or their resettlement in third countries. See, *inter alia*, 'Leaked document fuels concern Israel plans to push Palestinians from Gaza into Egypt' | CBC News and 'Israel right-wing ministers' comments add fuel to Palestinian fears' (cbc.ca/news).

57 Abu-Sitta (2001), supra note 10 at p. 195. According to Abu Sitta, '86 per cent of the refugees live in historical Palestine and within a 100 mile-radius around it'.

58 See Chapter 1, Section 1.4.

59 Medved (2003), supra note 11. See also Kagan (2005), supra note 11.

60 See, *inter alia*, P. Prettitore, 'The Right to Housing and Property Restitution in Bosnia and Herzegovina', BADIL Resource Center for Palestinian Residency & Refugee Rights, 2003, www.badil.org at p. 6, C. Philpott, 'Though the Dog Is Dead, the Pig Must Be Killed: Finishing with Property Restitution to Bosnia-Herzegovina's IDPs and Refugees', *Journal of Refugee Studies* 18, no. 1 (2005): 1–24 at p. 3 and

H. Das, 'Restoring Property Rights in the Aftermath of War', *International & Comparative Law Quarterly* 53 (2004): 429–44 at pp. 431–2.

61 Ibid. See also, M. Cox and M. Garlick, 'Musical Chairs: Property Repossession and Return Strategies in Bosnia & Herzegovina', in S. Leckie, *Returning Home: Housing and Property Restitution Rights of Refugees and Displaced Persons* (New York: Transnational, 2003), pp. 67–9. According to Cox and Garlick, laws were used in Bosnia to declare owned property as abandoned and to strip refugees and displaced persons of their occupancy rights.

62 Ibid., p. 68.

63 Ibid.

64 See Chapter 1, Section 1.4.

65 Article 1(3) of Annex 7 of the Dayton Agreement.

66 Rosand (1998), supra note 4 at p. 1103.

67 Ibid., pp. 1104–5. See also Philpott (2005), supra note 61 at pp. 3–4 and C. Philpott, 'From the Right to Return to the Return of Rights: Completing Post-War Property Restitution in Bosnia Herzegovina', *International Journal of Refugee Law* 18 (2006): 30–80 at pp. 39–42 for more details on the 'property laws' or 'laws on cessation' which were adopted to repeal discriminatory wartime and post-war legislation. The laws adopted in the Federation were entitled *Law on Cessation of the Application of the Law on Temporarily Abandoned Real Property Owned by Citizens*, FBiH Official Gazette, No. 11/98 and *Law on the Cessation of the Application of the Law on Abandoned Apartments*, FBiH Official Gazette, No. 11/98. The *Law on the Cessation of the Application of the Law on the Use of Abandoned Property*, RS Official Gazette, No. 38/98 was adopted in the RS. Bosnian laws on property are reprinted in S. Leckie, *Housing, Land, and Property Restitution Rights of Refugees and Displaced Persons: Laws, Cases and Materials* (Cambridge: Cambridge University Press, 2007), pp. 198–288.

68 Rosand (1998), supra note 4 at p. 1105.

69 The Office of the High Representative (OHR) is an ad hoc international institution responsible for overseeing the implementation of civilian aspects of the Dayton Agreement. The position of High Representative was created under Annex 10 of the Dayton Agreement. The High Representative is also an EU Special Representative (EUSR) in Bosnia and Herzegovina.

70 Cox and Garlick (2003), supra note 62 at p. 75.

71 Philpott (2005), supra note 61 at p. 4.

72 The international community has also played a significant role in the reversal of various housing and property laws which were used to discriminate against ethnic Albanians in Kosovo. See UNMIK Regulation 1999/10 on the *Repeal of Discriminatory Legislation Affecting Housing and Rights in Property*, 13 October 1999.

73 In addition to denying Palestinian refugees access to their land, these laws continue to affect the property rights of internally displaced Palestinians living inside Israel. See H. Abu Hussein and F McKay, *Access Denied: Palestinian Land Rights in Israel* (London: Zed Books, 2003).

74 Large-scale secondary occupation has hindered return efforts in Azerbaijan, Rwanda, Bosnia-Herzegovina, Croatia, Kosovo and elsewhere. (See Leckie (2003) supra note 33 at p. 47.)

75 Kagan (2005), supra note 11 at p. 24.

76 Handbook on the Pinheiro Principles, supra note 22 at p. 81.

77 See Chapter 5 for a discussion of the so-called 'pragmatic' solutions to the refugee issue.

78 Abu-Sitta (2001) supra note 10 at pp. 197–9.

79 Kagan (2005), supra note 11 at pp. 26–7.

80 See also M. Kagan, 'Restitution as a Remedy for Refugee Property Claims in the Israeli-Palestinian Conflict', *Florida Journal of International Law* 19 (2007): 421–90 at p. 468.

81 Dayton Agreement, Annex 7, Article XI.

82 Ibid., Article XIV(1).

83 E. Rosand, 'The Right to Compensation in Bosnia: An Unfulfilled Promise and a Challenge to International Law', *Cornell International Law Journal* 33 (2000): 113–58 at p. 117.

84 Cox and Garlick (2003), supra note 62 at p. 76.

85 Ibid.

86 Ibid., p. 77. In March 2003, implementation of property law had reached 78 per cent throughout Bosnia and Herzegovina (see *Housing and Property Restitution in the Context of the Return of Refugees and IDPs* – Preliminary Report of the Special Rapporteur, Paulo Sergio Pinheiro, UN Doc. E/CN.4/Sub2/2003/11 at para. 29).

87 UNSC Res.1244, 10 June 1999. This Resolution did not provide specific guidelines governing property rights.

88 UNMIK Regulation No. 2000/60, 31 October 2000.

89 It must be noted that restitution alone was not sufficient to reverse ethnic cleansing in Bosnia. According to Charles Philpott, '[a]ccess to property was not the only or, in many cases, the main barrier to return. Security and discrimination concerns, lack of education opportunities and employment prospects, and the elapse of time (and attendant diminishing of ties with the pre-war locale) have all negatively impacted upon the willingness of IDPs and refugees to return'. (Philpott (2005), supra note 61 at p. 17).

    The restitution programme in Kosovo also suffered some setbacks. Several factors contributed to the shortcomings of the programme, such as inadequate levels of funding from the international community and a lack of strong leadership among the local population. For more on this issue, see A. Dodson and V. Heiskanen, 'Housing and Property Restitution in Kosovo' in S. Leckie (ed.), *Returning Home: Housing and Property Restitution Rights of Refugees and Displaced Persons* (New York: Transnational, 2003).

90 Norwegian Refugee Council, 'Ensuring Durable Solutions for Rwanda's Displaced People: A Chapter Closed Too Early', 8 July 1995, at pp. 5–8 available at www.internal-displacement.org (accessed 14 April 2024). See also L. Jones, 'Giving and Taking Away: The Difference Between Theory and Practice Regarding Property in Rwanda' in S. Leckie(ed.), *Returning Home: Housing and Property Restitution Rights of Refugees and Displaced Persons* (New York: Transnational, 2003), pp. 200–1.

91 Ibid.

92 *Protocol of Agreement between the Government of the Republic of Rwanda and the Rwandese Patriotic Front on the Repatriation of Rwandese Refugees and the Settlement of Displaced Persons*, signed at Arusha, 9 June 1993.

93 Jones (2003), supra note 91 at pp. 203–4.

94 *Housing and Property Restitution in the Context of the Return of Refugees and IDPs* – Preliminary Report of the Special Rapporteur, Paulo Sergio Pinheiro, UN Doc. E/CN.4/Sub2/2003/11 at para. 31.

95 Jones (2003), supra note 91 at p. 207. Jones, however, notes that the government 'appears to be reconsidering restitution of property to the Tutsi returnees, or at least allowing such claims to be made' (p. 223).

96 UNHCR, 'The Problem of Access to Land and Ownership in Repatriation Operations', Inspection and Evaluation Service, Eval/03/98, May 1998, www.unhcr.org (accessed 14 April 2024) at para. 49–50.

97 E. Bourdeaux Smith, 'South Africa's Land Reform Policy and International Human Rights Law', *Wisconsin International Law Journal* 19 (2001): 267–88 at pp. 268–9.

98 Ibid.

99 According to Dr. Roodt, '[b]y the early 1900s the process of European land conquest was all but complete, with the majority of the original inhabitants, constituting approximately 80 per cent of the population, confined to reserves that made up 7 per cent of the land surface of the country. In 1936 these reserves were extended to 13 per cent of the total land.' (M. J. Roodt, 'Land Restitution in South Africa', in S. Leckie (ed.), *Returning Home: Housing and Property Restitution Rights of Refugees and Displaced Persons* (New York: Transnational, 2003), p. 243).

100 See Section 2 of the *Restitution of Land Rights Act 22* (South Africa), 25 November 1994 and Section 25(7) of the *South Africa Constitution No.108*, 18 December 1996 (reprinted in Leckie (2007), supra note 68 at pp. 355–6).

101 Ibid.

102 Bourdeaux Smith (2001), supra note 98 at p. 285.

103 See *inter alia*, O. L. Zirker, 'This Land Is My Land: The Evolution of Property Rights and Land Reform in South Africa', *Connecticut Journal of International Law* 18 (2002): 621–41 at p. 641 and Roodt (2003), supra note 100 at pp. 270–1.

104 J. Du Plessis, 'Land Restitution in South Africa: Overview and Lessons Learned', Working Paper No. 6, 2004, Bethlehem: Badil Resource Center at p. 8 (available in print).

105 Article 4 of the *Protocol of Agreement between the Government of the Republic of Rwanda and the Rwandese Patriotic Front on the Repatriation of Rwandese Refugees and the Settlement of Displaced Persons*, signed at Arusha, 9 June 1993.

106 See UNRWA's website at www.unrwa.org.

107 See UNHCR, Handbook on Procedures and Criteria for Determining Refugee Status under the 1951 Convention and the 1967 Protocol relating to the Status of Refugees, HCR/IP/4Eng/Rev.4, 1979, Reissued in 1992 and 2019, Geneva, (hereinafter Handbook on RSD) at para.184 which states that 'If the head of a family meets the criteria of the definition, [for refugee status] his dependants are normally granted refugee status according to the principle of family unity.'

108 For more on the loss of refugee status under general principles of refugee law, see Handbook on RSD, UNHCR, Handbook on Procedures and Criteria for Determining Refugee Status under the 1951 Convention and the 1967 Protocol relating to the Status of Refugees, HCR/IP/4Eng/Rev.4, 1979, Reissued in 1992 and 2019, Geneva,, para. 111–39 and G. S. Goodwin-Gill, *The Refugee in International Law*, 2nd edn (Oxford: Oxford University Press, 1998), pp. 80–7.

109 Handbook on the Pinheiro Principles, supra note 22 at p. 86.

110 CRPC Book of Regulations on the Conditions and Decision Making Procedure for Claims for Return of Real Property of Displaced Persons and Refugees (Consolidated Version), Articles 10 and 32.

111 UNMIK Regulation No. 2000/60, 31 October 2000 at para. 7.2.

112 Section 2(1) of the *Restitution of Land Rights Act 22* (South Africa), 25 November 1994, reprinted in Leckie (2007), supra note 68 at p. 355.

113 Handbook on the Pinheiro Principles, supra note 22 at p. 25.

114 See Leckie (2007), supra note 68 at pp. 45–56 for examples of voluntary repatriation agreements signed in the 1990s between the UNHCR and various countries in which the right of refugees to return to the homes from which they were initially displaced is reaffirmed. See also Article 1 of Annex 7 of the Dayton Agreement and UNMIK Regulation No. 2000/60, 31 October 2000 at Sections 2.2 and 2.5.

115 Handbook on the Pinheiro Principles, supra note 22 at p. 10.

116 Cox and Garlick (2003), supra note 62 at p. 66. See also, Philpott (2005), supra note 61 at p. 17 and Philpott (2006), supra note 68.

117 Kagan (2005), supra note 11 at pp. 5, 29–32.

Chapter 5

1 For a comparative study of the role that international law and human rights played in negotiated peace agreements, see C. Bell, *Peace Agreements and Human Rights* (Oxford: Oxford University Press, 2000), and C. Bell, 'Negotiating Justice? Human Rights and Peace Agreements' (Geneva: International Council on Human Rights Policy, 2006).

2 See, *inter alia*, P. De Greiff, 'Justice and Reparations', in P. De Greiff (ed.), *The Handbook of Reparations* (Oxford: Oxford University Press, 2006) and R. Falk, 'Reparations, International Law, and Global Justice: A New Frontier', in P. De Greiff (ed.), *The Handbook of Reparations*, International Center for Transitional Justice (New York: Oxford University Press, 2006). See also, P. Allan and A. Keller, 'The Concept of a Just Peace, or Achieving Peace through Recognition, Renouncement, and Rule' in P. Allan and A. Keller (eds), *What Is a Just Peace?* (New York: Oxford University Press, 2006); E. W. Said, 'A Method for Thinking about Just Peace', in P. Allan and A. Keller (eds), *What Is a Just Peace?* (New York: Oxford University Press, 2006) and Y. Beilin, 'Just Peace: A Dangerous Objective', in P. Allan and A. Keller (eds), *What Is a Just Peace?* (New York: Oxford University Press, 2006).

3 The Palestinian NGO, BADIL Resource Center for Palestinian Residency & Refugee Rights, is perhaps the most vocal proponent of the rights-based (or law-based) approach to the refugee issue. According to its website, Badil 'believes that the only feasible and durable solution is one that is based on rights and justice; derived from international human rights, humanitarian and refugee law, the principles of justice, and the best practices of states' (www.badil.org). See also, J. Quigley, 'The Role of Law in a Palestinian-Israeli Accommodation', *Case Western Reserve Journal of International Law* 31 (1999): 351–81; S. Howlett, 'Palestinian Private Property Rights in Israel and the Occupied Territories', *Vanderbilt Journal of Transnational Law* 34 (2001): 117–67; T. Rempel, 'Housing and Property Restitution: The Palestinian Refugee Case', in S. Leckie (ed.), *Returning Home: Housing and Property Restitution Rights of Refugees and Displaced Persons* (New York: Transnational, 2003) and R. Falk, 'International Law and the Peace Process', *Hastings International and Comparative Law Review* 28 (2005): 331–48.

4 See, *inter alia*, International Crisis Group, 'Palestinian Refugees and the Politics of Peacemaking', ICG Middle East Report No. 22, 5 February 2004, www.crisisgroup.org; E. Benvenisti and E. Zamir, 'Private Claims to Property Rights in the Future Israeli-Palestinian Settlement', *American Journal of International Law* 89 (1995): 295–340; A. C. Helton, 'End of Exile: Practical Solutions to the Palestinian Refugee Question', *Fordham International Law Journal* 28 (2005): 1325–60 for some views on the need to abandon a formalist approach to the refugee issue in favour of a more 'pragmatic' one.

5 UNGA Res. 194, para. 11, sub-paragraph 2.

6 M. Fischbach, *Records of Dispossession: Palestinian Refugee Property and the Arab Israeli Conflict* (New York: Columbia University Press, 2003), pp. 91–102,

7 Ibid., pp. 130–4.

8 In UNGA res. 512 (IV), 26 January 1952, the General Assembly noted '*with regret* that [...], the Commission has been unable to fulfil its mandate under the resolutions of the General Assembly'. The General Assembly held the governments concerned primarily responsible 'for reaching a settlement of their outstanding differences in conformity with the resolutions of the General Assembly on Palestine' and considered 'that the Conciliation Commission for Palestine should continue its efforts to secure the implementation of the resolutions of the General Assembly on Palestine and accordingly should be available to the parties to assist them in reaching agreement on outstanding questions'. For more on the UNCCP's valuation efforts, see Fischbach, *Records of Dispossession*, pp. 102–44.

9 UNSC Res. 242, 22 November 1967.

10 UNSC Res. 338, 22 October 1973 at para. 3.

11 UN Division for Palestinian Rights, *The Need for Convening the International Peace Conference on the Middle East (in accordance with General Assembly resolution 38/58 C)*, 1 February 1989 at section I (C) [hereinafter UNDPR Report on International Peace Conference].

12 The conference was, however, followed by an increased interest of the UN in the Palestinian dimension of the conflict and a considerable advancement of the status of the PLO. In 1974, the GA granted the PLO, as the representative of the Palestinian people, the status of observer and invited it to participate in sessions of the GA as well as in any international conference convened under the auspices of the UN or one of its organs. UNGA Res.3237 (XXIX), 22 Nov. 1974. See also UNGA Res.3210 (XXIX), 14 Oct. 1974, in which the GA invited the PLO to participate in its deliberations on the question of Palestine.

13 UNGA Res.3236 (XXIX), 22 November 1974.

14 Ibid.

15 See *inter alia* UNGA Res.35/207, 16 December 1980 and UNGA Res.36/226 A, 17 December 1981.

16 UNGA Res.36/120 C, 10 December 1981.

17 UNDPR Report on International Peace Conference, supra note 11 at section II (B).

18 See UNGA Res.38/58 C, 13 December 1983 for a list of the six guidelines endorsed at the Conference.

19 UNDPR Report on International Peace Conference, supra note 11 at section II (B).

20 Ibid., section III (A).

21 See UNGA Res.39/49 D, 11 December 1984, UNGA Res.40/96 D, 12 December 1985, UNGA Res.41/43 D, 2 December 1986, UNGA Res.42/66 D, 2 December

1987, UNGA Res.43/176, 15 December 1988, UNGA Res.44/42, 6 December 1989, UNGA Res.45/83 A, 13 December 1990 and UNGA Res.46/75, 11 December 1991.

22 See *inter alia* UNGA Res.45/83 A, 13 December 1990.

23 See *inter alia* UNGA Res.43/176, 15 December 1988 and UNGA Res.44/42, 6 December 1989, UNGA Res.46/75, 11 December 1991.

24 This statement by the Secretary General was recited in UNGA Res. 42/66 D, 2 December 1987. See also UNGA Res.40/96 D, 12 December 1985 in which the GA calls upon 'the Governments of Israel and the United States of America to reconsider their positions towards the attainment of peace in the Middle East through the convening of the Conference'.

25 U.S. Letter of Assurances to the Palestinians, 18 October 1001, reprinted in *Palestine Yearbook of International Law, Vol. VI* (1990–1), 281 at pp. 281–2.

26 Quigley ('The Role of Law', 1999) supra note 3 at p. 357.

27 Ibid.

28 In a special document on the Madrid Peace Conference, the *Journal of Palestine Studies* reprinted the main points from the US Letters of Assurances on the Terms of the Peace Conference, as well as invitations and statements made by participants at the conference (see Special Document File on the Madrid Peace Conference, *Journal of Palestine Studies* 21, no. 2 (1992): 117–49).

29 See US–Soviet Letter of Invitation to Peace Talks in Madrid, 18 October 1991, in Special Document File on the Madrid Peace Conference, supra note 28 at pp. 120–1.

30 Ibid., p. 121.

31 UNGA Res.38/58 C, 13 December 1983.

32 Israel refused to participate in the Madrid conference if the PLO was given any official role. In addition, Israel imposed conditions on the composition of the joint Jordanian–Palestinian delegation by demanding that Palestinian participants be residents of the West Bank (excluding East Jerusalem) and the Gaza Strip, have no formal links with the PLO and that the PLO be denied any role in the delegates' selection process. The latter condition was ignored as Palestinian negotiators had been designated by the PLO though they refrained from declaring so publicly. For more on the Palestinian representation in Madrid see *inter alia* Special Document File on the Madrid Peace Conference, supra note 28 at pp. 121–3 and L. Zittrain Eisenberg and N. Caplan, *Negotiating Arab-Israeli Peace: Patterns, Problems, Possibilities* (Bloomington: Indiana University Press, 1998) at pp. 81–2.

33 See, *inter alia*, UNGA Res.3236 (XXIX), 22 November 1974, UNGA Res.35/207, 16 Dec. 1980 and UNGA Res.36/226 A, 17 December 1981.

34 See, *inter alia*, UNGA Res.45/83 A, 13 December 1990.

35 US–Soviet Letter of Invitation to Peace Talks in Madrid, in Special Document File on the Madrid Peace Conference, supra note 28 at p. 121.

36 Quigley ('The Role of Law', 1999), supra note 3 at p. 356.

37 Ibid.

38 See US–Soviet Letter of Invitation to Peace Talks in Madrid, 18 October 1991, cited in Special Document File on the Madrid Peace Conference, supra note 28 at p. 121.

39 See Palestinian Refugee ResearchNet (PRRN) archival documents on the RWG (Research Material >> Documents (mcgill.ca)).

40 R. Brynen et al. (2003), 'The "Ottawa Process": Examination of Canada's Track Two Involvement in the Palestinian Refugee Issue', paper presented at the *Stocktaking Conference on Palestinian Refugee Research* in Ottawa – Canada (available at PRRN, accessed 14 April 2024).

41 Ibid.

42 According to Elia Zureik, '[A]side from statements by the Palestinian and some Arab delegations, the RWG has not dealt with the larger political issues of either the 1948 or 1967 refugees, and the question of return has been touched upon only within the context of discussions on the "humanitarian issue" of family reunification'. See E. Zureik, 'Palestinian Refugees and Peace', *Journal of Palestine Studies* 24, no. 1 (1994): 5–17 at p. 7.

43 Zureik, 'Palestinian Refugees and Peace', pp. 13–14.

44 Ibid., p. 14.

45 Ibid., p. 10.

46 Brynen et al. (2003), supra note 40, p. 3.

47 For more on the Ottawa Process, see Brynen et al. (2003), supra note 40.

48 Ibid., p. 7.

49 Ibid., p. 10.

50 Zittrain Eisenberg and Caplan (1998), supra note 32 at p. 82.

51 The letters of recognition were reprinted in Special Document File on the Peace Process, *Journal of Palestine Studies* 23, no. 1 (1993): 104–24.

52 For more on the DOP and subsequent interim agreements signed between Israel and the PLO, see *inter alia* G. Golan, *Israel and Palestine: Peace Plans from Oslo to Disengagement* (Princeton, NJ: Markus Wiener, 2007) at pp. 9–37 and Bell (2000), supra note 1 at pp. 81–91.

53 UNGA Res.48/58, 14 December 1993.

54 See *inter alia*, S. Ben-Ami, 'The slow, tragic death of the Oslo Accords', 28 September 2023, The Strategist (The slow, tragic death of the Oslo Accords | The Strategist (aspistrategist.org.au); M. Bishara, 'Oslo Is Dead, Long Live the Peace Process', 12 September 2023, *Al Jazeera* (Oslo is dead, long live the peace process | Opinions | Al Jazeera).

55 Proceedings instituted by South Africa against the State of Israel, 29 December 2023, www.icj-cij.org.

56 For a critical analysis of the OPP, see *inter alia* E. W. Said, *Peace and Its Discontents* (New York: Vintage Books, 1996) and M. Bishara, *Palestine/Israel: Peace or*

Apartheid? (London: Zed Books, 2002). For a legal critique of the DOP see, *inter alia*, Bell (2000), supra note 1; E. Benvenisti, 'The Israeli-Palestinian Declaration of Principles: A Framework for Future Settlement', *European Journal of International Law* 4 (1993): 542–54; R. Shihadeh, 'Can the Declaration of Principles Bring about a "Just and Lasting Peace"?', *European Journal of International Law* 4 (1993): 555–63; R. Falk, 'Some International Law Implications of the Oslo/Cairo Framework for the PLO/Israeli Peace Process', *Palestine Yearbook of International Law* 8 (1994): 19–34; J. Quigley, 'The Oslo Accords: More Than Israel Deserves', *American Journal of International Law and Policy* 12 (1997): 285–98 and G. R. Watson, *The Oslo Accords: International Law and the Israeli-Palestinian Peace Agreements* (Oxford: Oxford University Press, 2003).

57 Article I of the DOP.

58 Articles V(1), VI-IX of the DOP. See also Benvenisti (1993), supra note 56 at pp. 546–51.

59 According to Article XVII(1) of the DOP, the Declaration enters into force one month after its signing.

60 Article XII of the DOP.

61 According to Article V(2) of the DOP, permanent status negotiations shall cover the following issues: 'Jerusalem, refugees, settlements, security arrangements, borders, relations and cooperation with other neighbors, and other issues of common interest'.

62 *Report of the Committee on the Exercise of the Inalienable Rights of the Palestinian People*, Official Records of the General Assembly, Thirty-first Session, Supplement No.35 (A/31/35), 21 July 1976 at para 21 [hereinafter Report of the CEIRPP – 1976].

63 Ibid.

64 Ibid., para. 22.

65 Ibid., para. 29.

66 Ibid., para. 22–23.

67 S. Tamari, *Palestinian Refugee Negotiations: From Madrid to Oslo II* (Washington, DC: Institute for Palestine Studies, 1996), p. 38.

68 See earlier discussion on the shortcomings of the RWG talks. See also M. Dumper, *The Future for Palestinian Refugees: Toward Equity and Peace* (London: Lynne Rienner, 2007), p. 118 for more on the UN and UNRWA's involvement in the negotiations. According to Dumper, neither the UN nor UNRWA was initially included in the negotiations. However, 'UNRWA eventually succeeded in being allowed to attend RWG meetings and was able to play an increasingly active role in the multilateral track of the peace process. [...] It continued to be excluded from the Continuing Committee'.

69 See Tamari (1999), supra note 67 at p. 84. According to Tamari, the committee 'met seven or eight times between 1994 and 1997, but could not reach any agreement on numbers or modalities'.

70 A. Ben-Zvi, *Between Lausanne and Geneva: International Conferences and the Arab-Israeli Conflict* (London: Routledge, 1990), pp. 8–22 for arguments on the benefits of an incremental approach to conflict resolution. According to Ben-Zvi, this approach was championed by Henri Kissinger in the 1970s. In 1975, Kissinger stated that 'for 30 years it proved nearly impossible even to begin the process of negotiation. Every attempt to discuss a comprehensive solution failed – from the partition plan, to the Lausanne Conference [1949], to the Rogers Plan and the Four-Power talks of 1969 and 1970, to the UN Security Council deliberations. *To discuss simultaneously issues of such complexity, between countries whose deep mutual mistrust rejected even the concept of compromise was futile until a minimum of confidence had been established'*. (Cited in Ben-Zvi at pp. 12–13). According to Eyal Benvenisti, 'the agreement to postpone negotiations on [Jerusalem, settlements, security and the refugee issue] greatly facilitated the mutual acceptance of the Declaration'. (Benvenisti (1993), supra note 56 at p. 552).

71 For a list of the interim agreements and a summary of their content, see Bell (2000), supra note 1 at pp. 88–91.

72 Bell (2006), supra note 1 at p. 1.

73 Ibid.

74 A. G. E. Sabet, 'The Peace Process and the Politics of Conflict Resolution', *Journal of Palestine Studies* 27, no. 4 (1998): 5–19 at p. 12.

75 Bell (2006), supra note 1 at p. 2.

76 Report of the CEIRPP – 1976, supra note 98 at para. 22–23.

77 K. Lawand, 'The Right of Return of Palestinians under International Law', *International Journal of Refugee Law* 8 (1996): 532–68 at p. 533.

78 Resolution 242 affirmed 'the necessity [f]or achieving a just settlement to the refugee problem', while Resolution 338 simply called on parties to initiate negotiations aimed at achieving a 'just and durable peace in the Middle East' and to implement Resolution 242 in all its parts.

79 The Joint Working Group was a project of the Program on International Conflict Analysis and Resolution based at Harvard University's Weatherhead Center for International Affairs.

80 J. Alpher and K. Shikaki, 'The Palestinian Refugee Problem and the Right of Return' (Cambridge: Weatherhead Center for International Affairs, Harvard University, 1998).

81 Emphasis added. Ibid., p. 19.

82 Emphasis added. Article VII(1) of the Beilin-Abu Mazen Document, 31 October 1995 [hereinafter Beilin-Abu Mazen document].

83 UNCCP, *Stand taken by the Governments of the Arab States and the Government of Israel with regard to the task entrusted to the Conciliation Commission by the General Assembly*, W/1, 1 March 1949 at pp. 1–2.

84 See Sabet (1998), supra note 111 at pp. 10–12 for a critique of the PLO's peace concessions at Oslo and what he terms the 'strategy of defeat'.

85 See earlier discussion on this issue in Section 5.2.

86 Beilin-Abu Mazen Document at Article VII(2).

87 Ibid., Article VII(3).

88 Ibid., Article VII(4)(b).

89 Ibid., Article VII(4)(a).

90 Ibid., Article VII(4)(c) and (d).

91 See discussion in Chapter 4, Section 4.2.1.

92 Beilin-Abu Mazen Document at Article VII(3)(f)(5).

93 Ibid., Article VII(3)(f)(6).

94 See discussion in Chapter 4, Section 4.2.1.

95 Emphasis added. Report of the CEIRPP – 1976, supra note 62 at para. 20.

96 In addition to dismissing the right of return as 'impracticable', the Palestinian side agreed to '*encourage* the rehabilitation and resettlement of Palestinian refugees presently resident in the West Bank and Gaza Strip, within these areas'. Beilin–Abu Mazen Document at Article VII(6).

97 Ibid., Article VII(5).

98 Ibid., Article VII(7). See discussion in Chapter 3, Section 3.2.2.

99 See Article I of the Beilin–Abu Mazen document for more on the creation of the State of Palestine.

100 J. Massad, 'Return or Permanent Exile? Palestinian Refugees and the Ends of Oslo', in J. Massad (ed.), *The Persistence of the Palestinian Question: Essays on Zionism and the Palestinians* (Abingdon: Routledge, 2006) at p. 117.

101 For details on Shimon Peres' time in office, see Enderlin, *Shattered Dreams*, pp. 11–41.

102 For Netanyahu's views on the peace process and activities in office, see Enderlin, *Shattered Dreams*, pp. 42–110.

103 For more on the Wye River Memorandum, see *inter alia* Golan (2007), supra note 52 at pp. 27–33 and Enderlin (2003), supra note 101 at pp. 84–96. This memorandum was preceded by the Protocol Concerning the Redeployment in Hebron signed on 17 January 1997. For a summary of the protocol and the memorandum, see Bell (2000), supra note 1 at p. 90.

104 In his first speech to his supporters following his victory in the elections, Barak stated that '[T]he time for [making] peace has come' and promised to move quickly towards a separation from the Palestinians. Enderlin, *Shattered Dreams*, p. 112.

105 There is no final version of the Stockholm 'non-paper', and the wording of some of the articles is unclear at some points. Excerpts were reprinted in Enderlin, *Shattered Dreams*, pp. 153–8. Article 7 is at p.157. The letters P and I refer to the Palestinian and Israeli comments.

106 As noted earlier, in the Beilin–Abu Mazen document, the Palestinian side acknowledged that the 'right of the Palestinian refugees to return to their homes is enshrined in international law and natural justice', but failed to mention Resolution 194.

107 O. M. Dajani, 'Shadow or Shade? The Roles of International Law in Palestinian-Israeli Peace Talks', *Yale Journal of International Law* 32 (2007): 61–124 at p. 93.

108 Ibid.

109 Emphasis added. Enderlin (2003), supra note 101 at p. 157.

110 Ibid., p. 158.

111 For more on the reasons why the Stockholm talks were terminated, see A. Bregman, *Elusive Peace: How the Holy Land Defeated America* (London: Penguin Books, 2005), p. 69.

112 See *inter alia* C. E. Swisher, *The Truth about Camp David: The Untold Story about the Collapse of the Middle East Peace Process* (New York: Nation Books, 2004); A. Hanieh, 'The Camp David Papers', *Journal of Palestine Studies* 30, no. 2 (2001): 75–97; A. Qurie, *From Oslo to Jerusalem: The Palestinian Story of the Secret Negotiations* (London: I.B. Tauris, 2006); G. Sher, *The Israeli-Palestinian Peace Negotiations, 1999–2001: Within Reach* (London: Routledge, 2006); Enderlin (2003), supra note 101; D. Ross, *The Missing Peace: The Inside Story of the Fight for Middle East Peace* (New York: Farrar, Straus and Giroux, 2004); S. J. Helmick, *Negotiating Outside the Law: Why Camp David Failed?* (London: Pluto Press, 2004); Bregman, *Elusive Peace*; O. Balaban, *Interpreting Conflict: Israeli-Palestinian Negotiations at Camp David II and Beyond* (New York: Peter Lang, 2005) and Golan (2005), supra note 52.

113 Golan, *Israel and Palestine*, p. 38.

114 It is interesting to note that Arafat chose Abu Mazen, along with Nabil Shaath, as the lead negotiators on the refugee issue at Camp David (see Enderlin (2003), supra note 101 at p. 183).

115 Ross (2004), supra note 112 at p. 4.

116 Israeli negotiator Shlomo Ben-Ami suggested that Israel would absorb, over a period of years, between ten thousand to fifteen thousand refugees under the principle of 'family reunification'. The Palestinians rejected this proposal outright for its inadequacy. (Swisher (2004), supra note 112 at p. 208.)

117 According to Gilead Sher, co-chief negotiator for Israel at Camp David II, Clinton mentioned a cap of 10 to 20 billion dollars for the compensation and rehabilitation of refugees (Sher (2006), supra note 112 at p. 103).

118 According to Dennis Ross, the Americans proposed to Israeli and Palestinian negotiators the 'concept of an international mechanism and fund that would finance the rehabilitation, resettlement, and repatriation of Palestinians to Palestine, to third countries, or in limited circumstances to Israel.' (Ross (2004), supra note 112 at p. 655.)

119 Bregman (2005), supra note 111 at p. 88.

120 Balaban (2005), supra note 112 at p. 127.

121 Enderlin (2003), supra note 101 at p. 181.

122 Ibid., p. 191. In another statement, Arafat demonstrated his willingness to address Israel's demographic concerns: 'On the refugee issue, yes, there's Resolution 194, but we have to find a happy medium between the Israelis' demographic worries and our own concerns.' (Swisher (2004), supra note 112 at p. 226.)

123 See Enderlin (2003), supra note 101 at pp. 196–200 for more on the discussions between Israeli and Palestinian negotiators on the issue of refugees.

124 Swisher (2004), supra note 112 at p. 282.

125 According to one of Arafat's senior aides, Muhammad Rashid, Arafat

has practically conceded the Right of Return. All that he needs now is to find a way to save face before the Arab world and his own people. The issue of territory concerns him greatly. If he receives clarifications that the maps do not cut Palestine into little pieces, and that this map can be presented without shame in a Palestinian classroom, he will be satisfied'. (Cited in Sher (2006), supra note 112 at p. 211.)

126 Enderlin (2003), supra note 101 at p. 252. Enderlin notes that, 'in the absence of progress on Jerusalem, Arafat had forbidden Nabil Shaath to discuss the functioning of the international compensation fund for the refugees'.

127 Swisher (2004), supra note 112 at p. 324.

128 M. Fischbach, *The Peace Process and Palestinian Refugee Claims: Addressing Claims for Property Compensation and Restitution* (Washington, DC: United States Institute of Peace, 2006), pp. 92–3.

129 Ibid.

130 Swisher (2004), supra note 112 at p. 324.

131 Golan, supra note 89 at p. 41. According to Akram Hanieh, a member of the Palestinian team to Camp David, 'Israeli proposals made no reference to international legality. Not a single international resolution was mentioned, not even the resolutions that are supposed to constitute the very basis of the peace process'. (Hanieh (2001), supra note 112 at p. 81).

132 This statement was published in the Israeli newspaper *Yediot Aharonot* on 11 July 2000. It was recited in Aruri, *Palestinian Refugees*, pp. 71–2.

133 Balaban (2005), supra note 112 at p. 132.

134 This statement by Barak was cited in Balaban, *Interpreting Conflict*, p. 132.

135 It is commonly held that the Camp David summit failed on account of the Jerusalem issue rather than the refugee problem. See *inter alia* Golan, supra note 89 at p. 45; Enderlin (2003), supra note 101 at p. 264 and Helmick (2004), supra note 112 at p. 183. By contrast, Hanieh refers to the refugee issue as 'the greatest failure of the summit' (Hanieh (2001), supra note 112 at p. 82.).

136 Enderlin, *Shattered Dreams*, pp. 262–7.

137 Ibid., p. 329.

138 The Clinton Parameters are reprinted in Ross (2004), supra note 112 at pp. 801–5.

139 See ibid., pp. 803–4 for Clinton's views on the refugee issue.

140 Sher (2006), supra note 112 at p. 207. For more on Israel's response to the Clinton Parameters, see Bregman (2005), supra note 111 at p. 145.

141 The Palestinian position regarding Clinton's proposals was published in *Le Monde Diplomatique* on 1 January 2001.

142 Ibid.

143 See Golan (2007), supra note 52 at pp. 55–61 and Enderlin (2003), supra note 101 at pp. 339–57 for more on the Taba negotiations.

144 The so-called Moratinos Non-Paper is reprinted in a Special Document File on the Taba Negotiations (2002), *Journal of Palestine Studies* 31, no. 3: 79–89 at pp. 81–9.

145 The joint statement is reprinted in a Special Document File on the Taba Negotiations (2002), *Journal of Palestine Studies* 31, no. 3: 80–1.

146 The proposals were republished in Annex to Badil Occasional Bulletin No.10, 'Principles and Mechanisms for a Durable Solution for Palestinian Refugees: The "Taba Proposals", November 2001, Badil, www.badil.org (accessed 14 April 2024).

147 Badil Occasional Bulletin No. 10, 'Principles and Mechanisms for a Durable Solution for Palestinian refugees, p. 1.

148 Palestinian Proposal on Palestinian Refugees, 22 January 2001, at para. 4.

149 Moratinos Non-Paper at section 3.

150 See para. 5 of the Israeli Private Response to the Palestinian Refugee Proposal, 22 January 2001, which stipulates that the 'wish to return shall be implemented in a manner consistent with the existence of the State of Israel as the homeland for Jewish people, and the establishment of the State of Palestine as the homeland of the Palestinian people'. It is important to note the Israelis' use of the expression '*wish* to return' rather than '*right* of return', which indicates Israel's refusal to recognize that Palestinian refugees have such a right under international law.

151 Moratinos Non-Paper at Section 3.2 and para. 8 of the Israeli Private Response to the Palestinian Refugee Proposal, 22 January 2001.

152 See para. 33 of the Palestinian Proposal on Palestinian refugees which stipulates that '[T]he rights of return and compensation are independent and cumulative. A refugee's exercise of his or her right of return to Israel shall not prejudice

his or her right to receive compensation […], nor shall a refugee's receipt of compensation prejudice his or her right of return […]'.

153 See discussion in Chapter 4, Section 4.2.1.

154 See Israeli Private Response to the Palestinian Refugee Proposal, 22 January 2001.

155 Palestinian Proposal on Palestinian Refugees, 22 January 2001, at para. 7–14.

156 Palestinian Proposal on Palestinian Refugees, 22 January 2001, at para. 42–50. See discussion on the CRPC in Bosnia in Chapter 3, Section 3.4.

157 See discussion in Chapter 3 (Section 3.4) on the lack of funding for the Refugees and Displaced Persons Fund in Bosnia, from which funds would have been used to settle claims for compensation.

158 Palestinian Proposal on Palestinian Refugees, 22 January 2001, at para. 51–58. According to paragraph 57, '[A]ssistance from the Fund shall include *inter alia* support for: return, compensation, repatriation assistance, rehabilitation assistance, transitional costs and related socio-economic assistance. Assistance for compensation shall be disbursed through the Compensation Commission.'

159 Moratinos Non-Paper at Section 3.3. See also Israeli Private Response to the Palestinian Refugee Proposal, 22 January 2001 at para. 10–12.

160 Moratinos Non-Paper at Section 3.3. See also discussion in Chapter 3 (Section 3.5).

161 Moratinos Non-Paper at Section 3.2. See also para. 15 of the Palestinian Proposal on Palestinian Refugees and para. 8(a) and 14 of the Israeli Private Response to the Palestinian Refugee Proposal.

162 See fn 62. Even at the Camp David summit, the Israelis maintained their decades-old insistence to link the claims of Jewish refugees from Arab countries to those of Palestinian refugees (see Fischbach (2006), supra note 128 at p. 93. By contrast, the Israelis at Taba acknowledged that the 'issue of compensation for former Jewish refugees from Arab countries is not part of the bilateral Israeli-Palestinian agreement' (para. 15 of the Israeli Private Response to the Palestinian Refugee Proposal).

163 Moratinos Non-Paper at Section 3.7.

164 Moratinos Non-Paper at Section 3.4. See also para. 29 of the Palestinian Proposal on Palestinian Refugees and para. 13 of the Israeli Private Response to the Palestinian Refugee Proposal.

165 Moratinos Non-Paper at Section 3.1. See also para. 2–3 of the Palestinian Proposal on Palestinian Refugees and para. 2–4 of the Israeli Private Response to the Palestinian Refugee Proposal.

166 Moratinos Non-Paper at Section 3.

167 Badil Occasional Bulletin No. 10, supra note 147 at p. 1.

168 Ibid., p. 2.

169 Golan (2007), supra note 52 at p. 61.

170 The Arab Peace Initiative was published in Documents and Source Material (2002), *Journal of Palestine Studies* 31, no. 4 (2002): 175–98 at p. 182.

171 Para. 2(b) of the Arab Peace Initiative.

172 Golan (2007), supra note 52 at p. 70.

173 The Road Map was published in Special Documents: The Road Map, *Journal of Palestine Studies* 32, no. 4 (2003): 83–99 at pp. 88–94.

174 International Crisis Group, A Middle East Road Map to Where? International Crisis Group (ICG), 2 May 2003, https://www.refworld.org/reference/countryrep/icg/2003/en/33205 (accessed 18 April 2024) at p. 3.

175 A copy of the Nusseibeh–Ayalon Agreement is reprinted in A. Ayalon and S. Nusseibeh, 'Finding Common Ground: The Missing Pieces of Middle East Peace', *Seattle Journal for Social Justice* 2 (2004): 415–46 at pp. 422–3.

176 Fischbach (2006), supra note 128 at p. 98.

177 Article 4 of the Nusseibeh–Ayalon Agreement.

178 A full text of the proposal is posted on the Geneva Initiative's official website at www.geneva-accord.org.

179 GI at Article 7(1).

180 K. Nabulsi, 'The Peace Process and the Palestinians: A Road Map to Mars', *International Affairs* 80 (2004): 221–31 at p. 224.

181 GI at Article 7(4).

182 Ibid., Article 7(5).

183 Ibid., Articles 7(3) and 7(9).

184 Ibid., Articles 7(11)(i)(c)(2) and (3).

185 Ibid., Article 7(11)(v)(b) (i).

186 Ibid., Article 7(11)(v)(b) (ii).

187 Ibid., Article 7(10).

188 Ibid., Article 7(12).

189 Ibid., Article 7(9)(iii).

190 Ibid., Article 7(8).

191 Ibid., Article 7(14).

192 F. P. Albanese and L. Takkenberg, *Palestinian Refugees in International Law* (Oxford: Oxford University Press, 2020), pp. 63–6.

193 See Human Rights Watch (2021), A Threshold Crossed: Israeli Authorities and the Crimes of Apartheid and Persecution | HRW, B'Tselem (2021), Apartheid | B'Tselem (btselem.org), 2021, Al Haq (2022), *Israeli Apartheid: Tool of Zionist Settler Colonialism*, alhaq.org/cached_uploads/download/2022/12/22/israeli-apartheid-web-final-1-page-view-1671712165.pdf, Amnesty International (2022), Israel's apartheid against Palestinians: Cruel system of domination and crime against humanity – Amnesty International and OHCHR (2022), Special Rapporteur on the situation of human rights in the Occupied Palestinian

Territories: Israel has imposed upon Palestine an apartheid reality in a post-apartheid world | OHCHR.

194 See Amnesty International Policy Statement, 'The Right to Return: The Case of the Palestinians', 30 March 2001, Amnesty International (www.amnesty.org). According to paragraph 14 of this policy statement: 'Any peace agreement reached should resolve the issue of the Palestinian diaspora through means that respect and protect individual human rights. Amnesty International recognizes that there are other considerations that must be addressed in the negotiations – the security concerns of both sides, for instance – but these issues must be resolved within a framework that does not sacrifice individual human rights to political expediency'. See also Human Right Watch, 'Human Right Watch Policy on the Right to Return', June 2000, http://www.hrw.org/campaigns/israel/return/, which reaffirms the international community's 'duty to ensure that claims of a right to return are resolved fairly, that individual holders of the right are permitted freely and in an informed manner to choose whether to exercise it, and that returns proceed in a gradual and orderly manner. Governments' legitimate security concerns should be met consistently with these principles and other internationally recognized human rights'.

195 See, *inter alia*, S. Roy, *Failing Peace: Gaza and the Palestinian-Israeli Conflict* (London: Pluto Press, 2006); R. Dolphin, *The West Bank Wall: Unmaking Palestine* (London: Pluto Press, 2006); S. Makdisi, *Palestine Inside Out: An Everyday Occupation* (New York: W.W. Norton, 2008), and N. Masalha, 'The Concept of "Transfer" in Zionist Thinking and Practice: Historical Roorts and Contemporary Challenges', Institute for Palestine Studies, Policy Paper, 2023, Issue No. 007.

Conclusion

1 See, *inter alia*, H. Abu Hussein and F. McKay, *Access Denied: Palestinian Land Rights in Israel* (London: Zed Books, 2003), and A. Kedar, 'The Legal Transformation of Ethnic Geography: Israeli Law and the Palestinian Landholder 1948–1967', NYU Journal of International Law and Politics 33 (2001): 923–1000.

2 See, *inter alia*, R. Shehadeh, 'The Land Law of Palestine: An Analysis of the Definition of State Lands', *Journal of Palestine Studies* 11, no. 2 (1982): 82–99, R. Shehadeh, *The Law of the Land* (Jerusalem: Palestinian Academic Society for the Study of International Affairs (PASSIA), 1993); G. E. Bisharat, 'Land, Law, and Legitimacy in Israel and the Occupied Territories', American University Law Review 43 (1994): 467–561.

3 N. Masalha, 'The Concept of 'Transfer' in Zionist Thinking and Practice: Historical Roorts and Contemporary Challenges', Institute for Palestine Studies, Policy Paper, Issue No. 007, 2023.

4 For some of the proposals for a peaceful resolution, see *inter alia*, A. Abunimah, *One Country: A Bold Proposal to End the Israeli-Palestinian Impasse* (New York: Metropolitan Books, 2006); L. Farsakh, 'Palestine Beyond Partition and the Nation State', Al Shabaka, 2022 (https://al-shabaka.org, accessed 14 April 2024); One Democratic State Initiative (ODSI), https://odsi.co/en; and Land for All, *From Conflict to Reconciliation: A New Vision for Palestinian-Israeli Peace*, booklet-english.pdf (alandforall.org).

5 See, *inter alia*, S. Leckie, *Returning Home: Housing and Property Restitution Rights of Refugees and Displaced Persons* (New York: Transnational, 2003). and C. Bell, 'Negotiating Justice? Human Rights and Peace Agreements', Geneva: International Council on Human Rights Policy, 2006, http://www.ichrp.org/ at pp. 55–74.

6 See N. Erakat, *Justice for Some: Law and the Question of Palestine* (Standford: Stanford University Press, 2019 at pp. 228–34) on the shortfalls of a rights-based approach and the need to embed it within a wider political framework that addresses the settler-colonial nature of the State of Israel.

Bibliography

A Survey of Palestine (prepared in December 1945 and January 1946 for the information of the Anglo-American Committee of Inquiry), Vol. I, Palestine, The Government Printer, 1946.

Absentees' Property Law, 5710–1950, 14 March 1950.

Abu Hussein, H., and McKay, F. (2003), *Access Denied: Palestinian Land Rights in Israel*, London: Zed Books.

Abunimah, A. (2006), *One Country: A Bold Proposal to End the Israeli-Palestinian Impasse*, New York: Metropolitan Books.

Abu-Sitta, S. H. (1998), *The Palestinian Nakba: 1948: The Register of Depopulated Localities in Palestine*, London: The Palestinian Return Centre.

Abu-Sitta, S. H. (2001), 'The Right of Return: Sacred, Legal and Possible', in N. Aruri (ed.), *Palestinian Refugees: The Right of Return*, 195–207. London: Pluto Press.

Abu-Sitta, S. H. (2007), *The Return Journey: A Guide to the Depopulated and Present Palestinian Towns, Villages and Holy Sites*, London: Palestine Land Society.

Adalah, 'Land Controlled by Jewish National Fund for Jews Only', 29 July 2007, www.adalah.org (accessed 14 April 2024).

Adalah, 'New Israel Land Reform Law Passed by Knesset', 3 August 2009, www.adalah.org (accessed 14 April 2024).

Aegean Sea Continental Shelf Case (Greece v. *Turkey)*, ICJ Judgment, 19 December 1978.

Agreement between the Government of the Federal Republic of Germany and the Government of the United States of America Concerning the Foundation 'Remembrance, Responsibility and the Future', signed on 17 July 2000.

Akram, S. M. (2000), 'Fora Available for Palestinian Refugee Restitution, Compensation and Related Claims', *Badil Information and Discussion Brief*, (2), February 2000, www.badil.org (accessed 14 April 2024).

Akram, S., and Lynk, M. (2006), 'The Wall and the Law: A Tale of Two Judgements', *Netherlands Quarterly of Human Rights* 24(1): 61–106.

Albanese, F. P., and Takkenberg, L. (2020), *Palestinian Refugees in International Law*, Oxford: Oxford University Press.

Allan, P., and Keller, A. (2006), 'The Concept of a Just Peace, or Achieving Peace through Recognition, Renouncement, and Rule', in P. Allan and A. Keller (eds), *What Is a Just Peace?*, 195–215. New York: Oxford University Press.

Alpher, J., and Shikaki, K. (1998), *The Palestinian Refugee Problem and the Right of Return*, Cambridge: Weatherhead Center for International Affairs, Harvard University.

Al Shabaka (https://al-shabaka.org, accessed 14 April 2024).

Alzamora, C. (1995), 'The UN Compensation Commission: An Overview', in B. Lillich, *The United Nations Compensation Commission (Thirteenth Sokol Colloquium)*, 3–14. Irvington, NY: Transnational Publishers.

Amnesty International (2022), 'Israel's Apartheid against Palestinians: Cruel System of Domination and Crime against Humanity', available at www.amnesty.org (accessed 14 April 2024).

Arab Peace Initiative, published in Documents and Source Material (2002), *Journal of Palestine Studies*, 31 (4) (2002): 175–98.

Armstrong, A. (2006), 'The Role of Civil Society Actors in Reparations Legislation', in The International Bureau of the Permanent Court of Arbitration, *Redressing Injustices through Mass Claims Processes: Innovative Responses to Unique Challenges*, Oxford: Oxford University Press.

Authers, J. (2006), 'Making Good Again: German Compensation for Forced and Slave Laborers', in P. De Greiff (ed.), *The Handbook of Reparations*, 420–48. Oxford: Oxford University Press.

Ayalon, A. and Nusseibeh, S. (2004), 'Finding Common Ground: The Missing Pieces of Middle East Peace', *Seattle Journal for Social Justice* 2 (2004): 415–46.

Badil Occasional Bulletin No. 10, 'Principles and Mechanisms for a Durable Solution for Palestinian Refugees: The "Taba Proposals"', November 2001, Badil, www.badil.org (accessed 14 April 2024).

Badil Resource Center for Palestinian Residency and Refugee Rights (2005), *Closing Protection Gaps: Handbook on Protection of Palestinian Refugees in States Signatories to the 1951 Refugee Convention*, Ramallah: al-Ayyam Press.

Balaban, O. (2005), *Interpreting Conflict: Israeli-Palestinian Negotiations at Camp David II and Beyond*, New York: Peter Lang.

Barbara Delaney, N. and Fischel de Andrade, J. (2001), 'Minority Return to South-Eastern Bosnia and Herzegovina: A Review of the 2000 Return Season', *Journal of Refugee Studies*, 14, no. 3: 315–30.

Barkan, E. (2000), *The Guilt of Nations: Restitution and Negotiating Historical Injustices*, New York: W.W. Norton.

Basic Law: Israel Lands, 19 July 1960.

Bassiouni, C. (1994), 'Former Yugoslavia: Investigating Violations of International Humanitarian Law and Establishing an International Criminal Tribunal', *Security Dialogues* 25, no. 4: 409–23.

Bazyler, M. J. (1999), 'Litigating the Holocaust', *University of Richmond Law Review* 33: 5–283.

Bazyler, M. J. (2000), 'Nuremberg in America: Litigating the Holocaust in American Courts', *University of Richmond Law Review* 34: 1–283.

Bazyler, M. J. (2002), 'The Holocaust Restitution Movement in Comparative Perspective', *Berkeley Journal of International Law* 20: 11–44.

Bazyler, M. J. (2003), *Holocaust Justice: The Battle for Restitution in America's Courts*, New York: New York University Press.

Bazyler, M. J. and Fitzgerald, A. L. (2003), 'Trading with the Enemy: Holocaust Restitution, the United States Government, and American Industry', *Brooklyn Journal of International Law* 28: 683–810.

Bederman, D. J. (1995), 'Historic Analogues of the UN Compensation Commission' in B. Lillich (ed.), *The United Nations Compensation Commission (Thirteenth Sokol Colloquium)*, Irvington, NY: Transnational.

Bederman, D. J. (1996), 'The United Nations Compensation Commission and the Tradition of International Claims Settlement', *NYU Journal of International Law and Politics* 27: 1–42.

Bederman, D. J. and Lillich, R. B. (1997), 'Jurisprudence of the Foreign Claims Settlement Commission: Iran Claims', *American Journal of International Law* 91: 436–65.

Beilin, Y. (2006), 'Just Peace: A Dangerous Objective', in P. Allan and A. Keller (eds), *What Is a Just Peace?*, 130–48. New York: Oxford University Press.

Bell, C. (2000), *Peace Agreements and Human Rights*, Oxford: Oxford University Press.

Bell, C. (2006), 'Negotiating Justice? Human Rights and Peace Agreements', Geneva: International Council on Human Rights Policy, http://www.ichrp.org/.

Ben-Ami, S., 'The Slow, Tragic Death of the Oslo Accords', 28 September 2023, The Strategist (The slow, tragic death of the Oslo Accords | The Strategist (aspistrategist.org.au).

Ben-Zvi, A. (1990), *Between Lausanne and Geneva: International Conferences and the Arab-Israeli Conflict*, London: Routledge.

Bentwich, N. (1926), *Legislation of Palestine, 1918–1925*, Vol. 1, Alexandria, Printed for the Government of Palestine by Whitehead Morris.

Benvenisti, E. (1993), 'The Israeli-Palestinian Declaration of Principles: A Framework for Future Settlement', *European Journal of International Law* 4, no. 4: 542–54.

Benvenisti, E. and Zamir, E. (1995), 'Private Claims to Property Rights in the Future Israeli-Palestinian Settlement', *American Journal of International Law* 89: 295–340.

Benvenisti, M. (2000), *Sacred Landscape: The Buried History of the Holy Land since 1948*, London: University of California Press.

Bettauer, R. J. (2001), 'The Role of the United States Government in Recent Holocaust Claims Resolution', *American Society of International Law Proceedings* 95: 37–41.

Beyani, C. (1997), 'Political and Legal Analysis of the Problem of the Return of Forcibly Transferred Populations', *Refugee Survey Quarterly* 16, no. 3: 1–25.

Bishara, M. (2002), *Palestine/Israel: Peace or Apartheid?*, London: Zed Books.

Bishara, M., 'Oslo Is Dead, Long Live the Peace Process', 12 September 2023, Al Jazeera (Oslo is dead, long live the peace process | Opinions | Al Jazeera).

Bishara, S., Adalah's Position Paper on 'Prawer II' – Adalah, *Adalah*, 23 February 2017.

Bisharat, G. E. (1994), 'Land, Law, and Legitimacy in Israel and the Occupied Territories', *American University Law Review* 43: 467–561.

Black, R. and Koser, K. (1999), *The End of the Refugee Cycle?*, Oxford: Berghahn Books.

Bleicher, S. A. (1969), 'The Legal Significance of Re-Citation of General Assembly Resolutions', *American Journal of International Law* 63: 444–78.

Boling, G. J. (2000–1), '"Absentees' Property" Laws and Israel's Confiscation of Palestinian Property: A Violation of U.N. General Assembly Resolution 194 and International Law', *Palestine Yearbook of International Law* 11: 73–130.

Boling, G. J. (2001), 'The 1948 Palestinian Refugees and the Individual Right of Return: *An International Law Analysis*', Badil Resource Center, www.badil.org.

Bottigliero, I. (2004), *Redress for Victims of Crimes Under International Law*, Leiden: Martinus Nijhoff.

Bourdeaux Smith, E. (2001), 'South Africa's Land Reform Policy and International Human Rights Law', *Wisconsin International Law Journal* 19: 267–88.

Bregman, A. (2005), *Elusive Peace: How the Holy Land Defeated America*, London: Penguin Books.

Brooks, R. L. (1999), 'Japanese American Redress and the American Political Process', in R. L. Brooks (eds), *When Sorry Isn't Enough: The Controversy over Apologies and Reparations for Human Injustice*, 157–64. New York: New York University Press.

Brooks, R. L. (2004), *Atonement and Forgiveness: A New Model for Black Reparations*, Berkeley: University of California Press.

Brower, C. N. (1992), 'The Lessons of the Iran-United States Claims Tribunal: How May They Be Applied in the Case of Iraq?', *Virginia Journal of International Law* 32: 421–30.

Brynen, R., Eileen Alma, Joel Peters, Roula el-Rifai and Jill Tansley (2003), 'The "Ottawa Process": Examination of Canada's Track Two Involvement in the Palestinian Refugee Issue', paper presented at the *Stocktaking Conference on Palestinian Refugee Research* in Ottawa – Canada available at https://prrn.mcgill.ca (accessed 14 April 2014).

Brynen, R. and El-Rifai, R. (2013), *Compensation to Palestinian Refugees and the Search for Palestinian-Israeli Peace*, London: Pluto Press.

Burger-Fischer v. Degussa AG, 65 F.Supp. 2d 248 (D.N.J. 1999).

The Cairo Declaration of Principles of International Law on Compensation to Refugees adopted by the International Law Association (Cairo, 1992), reprinted in *American Journal of International Law* 87: 157–9.

Canadian Broadcast Center (CBC), Leaked document fuels concern Israel plans to push Palestinians from Gaza into Egypt | CBC News, 1 November 2023 (accessed 12 April 2024).

Caron, D. D. and Morris, B. (2002), 'The UN Compensation Commission: Practical Justice, not Retribution', *European Journal of International Law* 13: 183–99 at p. 188.

Cato v. United States (70 F.3rd 1103 (C.A.9, 1995)).

Cattan, H. (1973), *Palestine and International Law: The Legal Aspects of the Arab-Israeli Conflict*, Bristol: Longman Group Ltd.

Chomsky, N. (1999), *The Fateful Triangle: The United States, Israel and the Palestinians*, Boston, MA: South End Press.

City of Pärnu v. Pärnu Loan Society (*Special Court of Cassation – Estonia*), *28 Feb. 1921*, Annual Digest and Reports of Public International Law Cases, 1935–7, Vol. 8, 503.

Civil Liberties Act (*Restitution for World War II Internment of Japanese-Americans and Aleuts*), 50 App.U.S.C.A §1989b et seq.

Cleaver, T. and Halil, E., 'Turkey, TRNC pleased with COE's Loizidou case decision', 1 October 2022, PressReader.com – Digital Newspaper & Magazine Subscriptions (accessed 14 April 2024).

Coleman Jordan, E. (2004), 'The Non-Monetary Value of Reparations Rhetoric', *African-American Law & Policy Report* 6, no. 1: 21–5.

Colonomos, A. and Armstrong, A. (2006), 'German Reparations to the Jews after World War II: A Turning Point in the History of Reparations', in P. De Greiff (ed.), *The Handbook of Reparations*, 390–419. Oxford: Oxford University Press.

Contini, P., *Legal Aspects of the Problem of Compensation to Palestine Refugees* (dated 22 November 1949), attached to United Nations Conciliation Commission for Palestine, *Letter and Memorandum dated 22 November 1949, Concerning Compensation, Received by the Chairman of the Conciliation Commission from Mr. Gordon Clapp, Chairman, United Nations Economic Survey Mission for the Middle East*, W/32, 19 January 1950.

Convention (II) with Respect to the Laws and Customs of War on Land and Its Annex: Regulations Concerning the Laws and Customs of War on Land, The Hague, 29 July 1899.

Convention (III) relative to the Opening of Hostilities, The Hague, 18 October 1907.

Convention (IV) Respecting the Laws and Customs of War on Land and Its Annex: Regulations Concerning the Laws and Customs of War on Land, The Hague, 18 October 1907.

Convention (V) respecting the Rights and Duties of Neutral Powers and Persons in Case of War on Land, The Hague, 18 October 1907.

Convention (IV) relative to the Protection of Civilian Persons in Time of War, Geneva, 12 August 1949.

Corrie v. *Caterpillar*, 503 F.3d 974 (C.A.9. 2007).

Cox, M. and Garlick, M. (2003), 'Musical Chairs: Property Repossession and Return Strategies in Bosnia & Herzegovina', in S. Leckie, *Returning Home: Housing and Property Restitution Rights of Refugees and Displaced Persons*, New York: Transnational.

Crawford, J. (2002), *International Law Commission's Articles on State Responsibility: Introduction, Text and Commentaries*, Cambridge: Cambridge University Press.

Crisp, J. (2003), 'No Solutions in Sight: The Problem of Protracted Refugee Situations in Africa', *Refugee Survey Quarterly* 22, no. 4: 114–50.

Crook, J. R. (1993), 'The United Nations Compensation Commission – A New Structure to Enforce State Responsibility', *American Journal of International Law* 87: 144–57.

Crook, J. R. (2006), 'Mass Claims Processes: Lessons Learned over Twenty-Five Years', in The International Bureau of the Permanent Court of Arbitration, *Redressing Injustices Through Mass Claims Processes: Innovative Responses to Unique Challenges*, Oxford: Oxford University Press.

CRPC Book of Regulations on the Conditions and Decision Making Procedure for Claims for Return of Real Property of Displaced Persons and Refugees (Consolidated Version).

Crosby v. *National Foreign Trade Council*, 530 US 363, 147 L.Ed. 2d 352 (2000).

Dajani, O. M. (2007), 'Shadow or Shade? The Roles of International Law in Palestinian-Israeli Peace Talks', *Yale Journal of International Law* 32: 61–124.

Dajani, S. (2005), 'Ruling Palestine: A History of the Legally Sanctioned Jewish-Israeli Seizure of Land and Housing in Palestine', Centre on Housing Rights and Evictions (COHRE) and BADIL Resource Center for Palestinian Residency & Refugee Rights available at www.miftah.org (accessed on 14 April 2024).

Das, H. (2004), 'Restoring Property Rights in the Aftermath of War', *International & Comparative Law Quarterly* 53: 429–44.

Das, H. (2006), 'The Concept of Mass Claims and the Specificity of Mass Claims Resolution' in The International Bureau of the Permanent Court of Arbitration, *Redressing Injustices through Mass Claims Processes: Innovative Responses to Unique Challenges*, Oxford: Oxford University Press.

Davis, U. (1997), *Citizenship and the State: A Comparative Study of Citizenship Legislation in Israel, Jordan, Palestine, Syria and Lebanon*, Reading: Ithaca Press.

Davis, U., and Lehn, W. (1978), 'And the Fund Still Lives: The Role of the Jewish National Fund in the Determination of Israel's Land Policies', *Journal of Palestine Studies* 7, no. 4: 3–33.

Declaration of the Establishment of the State of Israel, 14 May 1948.

Declaration of the Government of the Democratic and Popular Republic of Algeria concerning the Settlement of Claims by the Government of the United States of America and the Government of the Islamic Republic of Iran, 19 January 1981.

De Greiff, P. (2006), 'Justice and Reparations', in P. De Greiff (ed.), *The Handbook of Reparations*, Oxford: Oxford University Press.

Development Authority (Transfer of Property) Law, 5710–1950, 31 July 1950.

Dib Nakkara, H. (1985), 'Israeli Land Seizure under Various Defense and Emergency Regulations', *Journal of Palestine Studies* 14, no. 2: 13–34.

Dodson, A. and Heiskanen, V. (2003), 'Housing and Property Restitution in Kosovo', in S. Leckie (ed.), *Returning Home: Housing and Property Restitution Rights of Refugees and Displaced Persons*, New York: Transnational.

Dolan, C. (1999), 'Repatriation from South Africa to Mozambique – Undermining Durable Solutions?', in R. Black and K. Koser (eds), *The End of the Refugee Cycle?*, Oxford: Berghahn Books.

Dolphin, R. (2006), *The West Bank Wall: Unmaking Palestine*, London: Pluto Press.

Dolzer, R. (2002), 'The Settlement of War-Related Claims: Does International Law Recognize a Victim's Private Right of Action? Lessons After 1945', *Berkeley Journal of International Law* 20: 296–341 at p. 338.

Du Plessis, J. (2004), 'Land Restitution in South Africa: Overview and Lessons Learned', Working Paper No. 6, Bethlehem: Badil Resource Center.

Dumper, M. (2007), *The Future for Palestinian Refugees: Toward Equity and Peace*, London: Lynne Rienner.

Eastmond, M. and Ojendal, J. (1999), 'Revisiting a "Repatriation Success": The Case of Cambodia', in R. Black and K. Koser (eds), *The End of the Refugee Cycle?*, Oxford: Berghahn Books.

Echeverria, G. (2003), *Reparation: A Sourcebook for Victims of Torture and Other Violations of Human Rights and International Humanitarian Law*, London: The Redress Trust.

Echeverria, G. (2006), 'Codifying the Rights of Victims in International Law: Remedies and Reparation', in The International Bureau of the Permanent Court of Arbitration, *Redressing Injustices through Mass Claims Processes: Innovative Responses to Unique Challenges*, Oxford: Oxford University Press.

Economic and Social Council, Commission on Human Rights, Sixty-First Session, Basic Principles and Guidelines on the Right to a Remedy and Reparation for Victims of Gross Violations of International Human Rights Law and Serious Violations of International Humanitarian Law, E/CN.4/2005/L.10/Add.11, 19 April 2005.

Egeland, J., Gaza Is Being Made Unlivable | TIME, *Time*, 20 December 2023.

Elias, T. O. (1980), 'The Doctrine of Intertemporal Law', *American Journal of International Law* 74: 285–307.

Emergency Regulations on Property of Absentees ('Absentee Property Act'), 5709/1948, 2 December 1948.

Enderlin, C. (2003), *Shattered Dreams: The Failure of the Peace Process in the Middle East: 1995–2002*, New York: Other Press.

Erakat, N. (2019), *Justice for Some: Law and the Question of Palestine*, Stanford, CA: Stanford University Press.

European Parliament, Directorate-General for Research (Working Paper), 'Legal Opinion on the Benes-Decrees and the accession of the Czech Republic to the EU' (October 2002).

Factory at Chorzów, Jurisdiction, 1927, P.C.I.J., Series A, No.9.

Factory at Chorzów, Merits, 1928, P.C.I.J., Series A, No.17.

Falk, R. (1994), 'Some International Law Implications of the Oslo/Cairo Framework for the PLO/Israeli Peace Process', *Palestine Yearbook of International Law* 8: 19–34.

Falk, R. (2005), 'International Law and the Peace Process', *Hastings International and Comparative Law Review* 28: 331–48.

Falk, R. (2006), 'Reparations, International Law, and Global Justice: A New Frontier', in P. De Greiff (ed.), *The Handbook of Reparations*, International Center for Transitional Justice, New York: Oxford University Press.

Farsakh, L. (2022), 'Palestine Beyond Partition and the Nation State', Al Shabaka
    (https://al-shabaka.org, accessed 14 April 2024).
Final Report of the Governing Council on the work of the Compensation Commission
    (S/2022/104) to the Security Council, 22 February 2022.
Finkelstein, N. G. (2001), 'Lessons of Holocaust Compensation', in N. Aruri (eds),
    Palestinian Refugees: The Right of Return, London: Pluto Press.
Finkelstein, N. G. (2003), *The Holocaust Industry*, 2nd edn, London: Verso.
Fischbach, M. (2003), *Records of Dispossession: Palestinian Refugee Property and the
    Arab Israeli Conflict*, New York: Columbia University Press.
Fischbach, M. (2006), *The Peace Process and Palestinian Refugee Claims: Addressing
    Claims for Property Compensation and Restitution*, Washington, DC: United States
    Institute of Peace.
Fisher, S. (1919), *Ottoman Land Laws – Containing the Ottoman Land Code and Later
    Legislation Affecting Law with Notes*, London: Oxford University Press.
Fisk, R. (2001), *Pity the Nation*, 3rd edn, Oxford: Oxford University Press.
Forman, G. and Kedar, A. (S) (2004), 'From Arab Land to "Israel Lands": The
    Legal Dispossession of the Palestinians Displaced by Israel in the Wake of 1948',
    Environment and Planning D: Society and Space 22: 809–30.
Friel, H. and Falk, R. (2007), *Israel-Palestine on Record: How the New York Times
    Misreports Conflict in the Middle East*, New York: Verso.
Gattini, A. (2002a), 'A Trojan Horse for Sudeten Claims? On Some Implications of
    the *Prince of Liechtenstein* v. *Germany*', *European Journal of International Law*
    13: 513–44.
Gattini, A. (2002b), 'The UN Compensation Commission: Old Rules, New Procedures
    on War Reparations', *European Journal of International Law* 13: 161–81 at pp. 170–1.
General Framework Agreement for Peace in Bosnia and Herzegovina, initialed in Dayton,
    21 November 1995, signed in Paris, 14 December 1995, Annex 7.
Goadby and Doukhan, M. J. (1935), *The Land Law of Palestine*, Tel-Aviv: Shoshany's
    Printing.
Golan, G. (2007), *Israel and Palestine: Peace Plans From Oslo to Disengagement*,
    Princeton, NJ: Markus Wiener Publishers.
Goldstar (Panama) SA v. *United States* (*United States Court of Appeals, Fourth Circuit*),
    16 June 1992, International Law Reports, 1994, Vol. 96, 55.
Goodwin-Gill, G. S. (1998), *The Refugee in International Law*, 2nd edn, Oxford: Oxford
    University Press.
Granott, A. (1952), *The Land System in Palestine: History and Structure*, London: Eyre &
    Spottiswoode.
Granott, A. (1956), *Agrarian Reform and the Record of Israel*, London: Eyre and
    Spottiswoode.
Haasdijk, S. (1992), 'The Lack of Uniformity in the Terminology of the International
    Law of Remedies', *Leiden Journal of International Law* 5: 245–63.

Hadawi, S. (1970), *Village Statistics 1945: A Classification of Land and Area Ownership in Palestine*, Beirut: Palestine Liberation Organization Research Center.

Hadawi, S.(1988), *Palestinian Rights & Losses in 1948*, London: Saqi Books.

Hanieh, A. (2001), 'The Camp David Papers', *Journal of Palestine Studies* 30, no. 2: 75–97.

Hatamiya, L. T. (1999), 'Institutions and Interest Groups: Understanding the Passage of the Japanese American Redress Bill', in R. L. Brooks (ed.), *When Sorry Isn't Enough: The Controversy over Apologies and Reparations for Human Injustice*, New York: New York University Press.

Helmick, S. J. (2004), *Negotiating Outside the Law: Why Camp David Failed?*, London: Pluto Press.

Helton, A. C. (2005), 'End of Exile: Practical Solutions to the Palestinian Refugee Question', *Fordham International Law Journal* 28:1325–60.

Herzl, T. (1936), *The Jewish State: An Attempt at a Modern Solution of the Jewish Question (Der Judenstaat)*, 3rd edn, London: Central Office of the Zionist Organization.

Higgins, R. (1997), 'Time and the Law: International Perspectives on an Old Problem', *International & Comparative Law Quarterly* 46: 501–20.

Hochstein, R. (1996), 'Jewish Property Restitution in the Czech Republic', *Boston College International and Comparative Law Review* 19: 423–47.

Holtzmann, H. M. and Kristjansdottir, E. (2007), *International Mass Claims Processes: Legal and Practical Perspectives*, Oxford: Oxford University Press, pp. 17–18.

Housing and Property Restitution in the Context of the Return of Refugees and IDPs – Preliminary Report of the Special Rapporteur, Paulo Sergio Pinheiro, UN Doc. E/CN.4/Sub2/2003/11.

Howlett, S. (2001), 'Palestinian Private Property Rights in Israel and the Occupied Territories', *Vanderbilt Journal of Transnational Law* 34: 117–67.

Human Rights Watch, 'Human Rights Watch Policy on the Right to Return', Right to Return – Human Rights Watch Policy Page (hrw.org) (accessed 14 April 2024).

Human Rights Watch (2021), 'A Threshold Crossed: Israeli Authorities and the Crimes of Apartheid and Persecution' available at www.hrw.org (accessed 14 April 2024).

International Crisis Group, A Middle East Road Map to Where?, International Crisis Group (ICG), 2 May 2003, https://www.refworld.org/reference/countryrep/icg/2003/en/33205 (accessed 14 April 2024).

International Crisis Group, *'Palestinian Refugees and the Politics of Peacemaking', ICG Middle East Report No.22, 5 February 2004*, www.crisisgroup.org (accessed 14 April 2024).

In re Fiebig (Special Court of Cassation - Holland), 9 Dec. 1950, Annual Digest and Reports of Public International Law Cases, 1949, Vol. 16, 487.

In re Von Lewinski (called von Manstein), (British Military Court at Hamburg - Germany), 19 Dec. 1949, Annual Digest and Reports of Public International Law Cases, 1949, Vol. 16, 509.

In re Krauch and Others (I.G. Farben Trial), (United States Military Tribunal at Nuremberg), 29 July 1948, Annual Digest and Reports of Public International Law Cases, 1948, Vol. 15, 668.

Island of Palmas Case (United States v. the Netherlands), 1928, R.I.A.A., Vol. II, p. 829.

Israel Lands Administration Law, 5710–1960, 25 July 1960.

Jean-Baptiste Caire Case, (France and Mexico: Mixed Claims Commission), 7 June 1929, Annual Digest and Reports of Public International Law Cases, 1929–30, Vol. 5, 146.

Jessup Newton, N. (1999), 'Indian Claims for Reparations, Compensation, and Restitution in the United States Legal System' in R. L. Brooks (eds), *When Sorry Isn't Enough: The Controversy over Apologies and Reparations for Human Injustice*, New York: New York University Press.

Jiryis, S. (1973), 'The Legal Structure for the Expropriation and Absorption of Arab Lands in Israel', *Journal of Palestine Studies* 2, no.4: 82–104.

Joint Pilot Study by Badil, the Norwegian Refugee Council and the Internal Displacement Monitoring Centre, *Displaced by the Wall: Forced Displacement as a Result of the West Bank Wall and Its Associated Regime*, September 2006, available at www.badil.org (accessed 14 April 2024).

Joint Publication by OCHA/IDD, UN Habitat, UNHCR, FAO, OHCHR, the Norwegian Refugee Council (NRC) and the Internal Displacement Monitoring Centre (IDMC), *Handbook on Housing and Property Restitution for Refugees and Displaced Persons: Implementing the Pinheiro Principles*, March 2007, available at www.internal-displacement.org (accessed 14 April 2024).

Jones, L. (2003), 'Giving and Taking Away: The Difference Between Theory and Practice Regarding Property in Rwanda', in S. Leckie (ed.), *Returning Home: Housing and Property Restitution Rights of Refugees and Displaced Persons*, New York: Transnational.

Jones v. Ministry of the Interior of the Kingdom of Saudi Arabia (Secretary of State for Constitutional Affairs intervening) [2005] Q.B. 699.

Judicial Decisions: International Military Tribunal (Nuremberg), Judgment and Decisions (1947), *American Journal of International Law* 41: 172–333.

Kagan, M. (2005), 'Do Israeli Rights Conflict with the Palestinian Right of Return?', Working Paper No.10, BADIL Resource Center for Palestinian Residency & Refugee Rights, www.badil.org (accessed 14 April 2024).

Kagan, M. (2007a), 'Destructive Ambiguity: Enemy Nationals and the Legal Enabling of Ethnic Conflict in the Middle East', *Columbia Human Rights Law Review* 38: 263–319.

Kagan, M. (2007b), 'Restitution as a Remedy for Refugee Property Claims in the Israeli-Palestinian Conflict', *Florida Journal of International Law* 19: 421–90.

Karhilo, J. (1995), 'The Establishment of the International Tribunal for Rwanda', *Nordic Journal of International Law* 64: 681–711.

Karmi, G. (1999), 'The Question of Compensation and Reparations', in G. Karmi and E. Cotran (eds), *The Palestinian Exodus 1948–1998*, Reading: Ithaca Press.

Kattan, V. (2005), 'The Nationality of Denationalized Palestinians', *Nordic Journal of International Law* 74: 67–102.

Kedar, A. (2001), 'The Legal Transformation of Ethnic Geography: Israeli Law and the Palestinian Landholder 1948–1967', *NYU Journal of International Law and Politics* 33: 923–1000.

Khalidi, W. (1988), 'Plan Dalet: Master Plan for the Conquest of Palestine', *Journal of Palestine Studies* 18, no. 1: 4–33.

Khalidi, W. (1992), *All that Remains: The Palestinian Villages Occupied and Depopulated by Israel in 1948*, Washington, DC: Institute for Palestine Studies

Khasawneh, B. H. (2007), 'An appraisal of the right of return and compensation of Jordanian nationals of Palestinian refugee origin and Jordan's right, under International Law, to bring claims relating thereto, on their behalf to and against Israel and to seek compensation as a host state in light of the conclusion of the Jordan-Israel peace treaty of 1994', doctoral thesis, University of London, London School of Economics, London.

Klein, E. (1999), 'Individual Reparation Claims under the International Covenant on Civil and Political Rights: The Practice of the Human Rights Committee', in A. Randelzhofer and C. Tomuschat (eds), *State Responsibility and the Individual: Reparation in Instances of Grave Violations of Human Rights*, The Hague: Martinus Nijhoff.

Kretzmer, D. (2002), *The Occupation of Justice*, Albany: State University of New York Press.

Kubursi, A. (2001), 'Valuing Palestinian Losses in Today's Dollars', in N. Aruri (ed.), *Palestinian Refugees: The Right of Return*, 217–51, London: Pluto Press.

Ladas, S. (1932), *The Exchange of Minorities: Bulgaria, Greece and Turkey*, New York: Macmillan.

Land for All, *From Conflict to Reconciliation: a New Vision for Palestinian-Israeli Peace*, booklet-english.pdf (alandforall.org).

Lapidoth, R. (1986), 'The Right of Return in International Law, with Special Reference to the Palestinian Refugees', *Israel Yearbook on Human Rights* 16: 103–25.

Law on Cessation of the Application of the Law on Temporarily Abandoned Real Property Owned by Citizens, FBiH Official Gazette, No.11/98.

Law on the Cessation of the Application of the Law on Abandoned Apartments, FBiH Official Gazette, No.11/98.

Law on the Cessation of the Application of the Law on the Use of Abandoned Property, RS Official Gazette, No.38/98.

Law of Return, 5710–1950, 5 July 1950.

Lawand, K. (1996), 'The Right to Return of Palestinians under International Law',
    International Journal of Refugee Law 8: 532–68.

Leckie, S. (2003a), 'New Directions in Housing and Property Restitution', in S. Leckie
    (ed.), *Returning Home: Housing and Property Restitution Rights of Refugees and
    Displaced Persons*, New York: Transnational.

Leckie, S. (2003b), *Returning Home: Housing and Property Restitution Rights of Refugees
    and Displaced Persons*, New York: Transnational.

Leckie, S. (2007), *Housing, Land, and Property Restitution Rights of Refugees
    and Displaced Persons: Laws, Cases and Materials*, Cambridge: Cambridge
    University Press.

Lee, L. T. (1986), 'The Right to Compensation: Refugees and Countries of Asylum',
    American Journal of International Law 80: 532–67.

Lee, L. T. (1992), 'The Preventive Approach to the Refugee Problem', *Willamette Law
    Review* 28: 821–32.

Lee, R. S. (2001), *The International Criminal Court: Elements of Crimes and Rules of
    Procedure and Evidence*, Ardsley: Transnational.

*Legal Consequences for States of the Continued Presence of South Africa in Namibia
    (South West Africa) Notwithstanding Security Council Resolution 276 (1970)*, ICJ
    Advisory Opinion, 21 June 1971.

Legal Consequences of the Construction of a Wall in the Occupied Palestinian Territory,
    ICJ Advisory Opinion, 9 July 2004.

Lessing, H. and Azizi, F. (2006), 'Austria Confronts Her Past' in M. J. Bazyler and R.
    P. Alford (eds), *Holocaust Restitution: Perspectives on the Litigation*, New York,
    New York University Press.

Levitt, J. (1997), 'Black African Reparations: Making a Claim for Enslavement and
    Systematic De Jure Segregation and Racial Discrimination under American and
    International Law', *Southern University Law Review*: 1–42.

Loizidou v. *Turkey* (Merits) *(Application no. 15318/89)*, 18 December 1996.

Loizidou v. *Turkey* (Art. 50) (40/1993/435/514), 28 July 1998.

Lustick, I. S. (1980), *The Arabs in the Jewish State*, Austin: University of Texas Press.

Lynk, M. (2000–1), 'Compensation for Palestinian Refugees: An International Law
    Perspective', *Palestine Yearbook of International Law* 11: 155–83.

Macklem, P. (2005), 'Rybna 9, Praha 1: Restitution and Memory in International
    Human Rights Law', *European Journal of International Law* 16: 1–23.

Makdisi, S. (2008), *Palestine Inside Out: An Everyday Occupation*, New York: W.W.
    Norton.

Malanczuk, P. (1997), *Akehurst's Modern Introduction to International Law*, 7th edn,
    London: Routledge.

Marsden, P. (1999), 'Repatriation and Reconstruction: The Case of Afghanistan' in R.
    Black and K. Koser (eds), *The End of the Refugee Cycle?*, Oxford: Berghahn Books.

Masalha, N. (1992), *Expulsion of the Palestinians: The Concept of 'Transfer' in Zionist
    Political Thought, 1882–1948*, Washington, DC: Institute of Palestine Studies.

Masalha, N. (2003), *The Politics of Denial: Israel and the Palestinian Refugee Problem*, London: Pluto Press.

Masalha, N. (2023), 'The Concept of "Transfer" in Zionist Thinking and Practice: Historical Roorts and Contemporary Challenges', Institute for Palestine Studies, Policy Paper, Issue No. 007.

Massad, J. (2006), 'Return or permanent exile? Palestinian refugees and the ends of Oslo', in J. Massad (ed.), *The Persistence of the Palestinian Question: Essays on Zionism and the Palestinians*, Abingdon: Routledge.

Merrills, J. G. (1998), *International Dispute Settlement*, 3rd edn, Cambridge: Cambridge University Press.

Minami, D. (2004), 'Japanese-American Redress', *African-American Law & Policy Report* 6, no. 1: 27–34.

Mc Nair, L. and Watts, A. D. (1966), *The Legal Effects of War*, Cambridge: Cambridge University Press.

Medved, M. (2003), 'Palestinian Claims of 'Right of Return' Block All Possible Negotiations', *Nexus* 8: 17–30.

Middle East Eye (MEE), War on Gaza: Israel 'in talks with Rwanda and Chad' to exile Palestinians | Middle East Eye, 5 January 2024 (accessed 12 April 2024).

Moratinos Non-Paper, reprinted in a Special Document File on the Taba Negotiations (2002), *Journal of Palestine Studies* 31, no. 3: 79–89 at pp. 81–9.

Morris, B. (2001), 'Revisiting the Palestinian Exodus of 1948' in L. Rogan and A. Shlaim (eds), *The War for Palestine: Rewriting the History of 1948*, Cambridge: Cambridge University Press.

Morris, B. (2004), *The Birth of the Palestinian Refugee Problem Revisited*, Cambridge: Cambridge University Press.

Murphy, S. D. (2000), 'Contemporary Practice of the US relating to International Law', *American Journal of International Law* 94: 102–39.

Nabulsi, K. (2004), 'The Peace Process and the Palestinians: A Road Map to Mars', *International Affairs* 80: 221–31.

NationalityLaw, 5712–1952, 1 April 1952.

Neuborne, B. (2006), 'A Tale of Two Cities: Administering the Holocaust Settlements in Brooklyn and Berlin', in M. J. Bazyler and R. P. Alford (eds), *Holocaust Restitution: Perspectives on the Litigation*, New York: New York University Press.

Norwegian Refugee Council, 'Ensuring Durable Solutions for Rwanda's Displaced People: A Chapter Closed Too Early', 8 July 1995, at pp. 5–8 available at www.internal-displacement.org (accessed 14 April 2024).

Office of the High Commissioner for Human Rights (OHCHR), Israel working to expel civilian population of Gaza, UN expert warns | OHCHR, 22 December 2023 (accessed 12 April 2024).

Office of the High Commissioner for Human Rights (OHCHR), UN Expert Warns of New Instance of Mass Ethnic Cleansing of Palestinians, Calls for Immediate Ceasefire | OHCHR, 14 October 2023.

Official Records of the Second Session of the General Assembly, Supplement No.11,
 United Nations Special Committee on Palestine (UNSCOP), *Report to the General
 Assembly*, A/364, 3 September 1947.

One Democratic State Initiative (ODSI), https://odsi.co/en.

Ongley, F.(1892), *The Ottoman Land Code*, London: William Clowes and Sons, Ltd.

Oppenheim, L. (1912), *International Law: A Treatise*, Vol. I, London: Longmans, Green.

Oppenheim, L. (1912), *International Law: A Treatise*, Vol. II,
 London: Longmans, Green.

Oppenheim, L. (1935), *International Law: A Treatise*, Vol. II,
 London: Longmans, Green.

Palestine Land Society (2005), *Financing Racism and Apartheid: Jewish National Fund's
 Violation of International and Domestic Law*, London at p. 3.

Papamichalopoulos and Others v. Greece *(Application no. 14556/89)*, 31 October 1995.

Pappe, I. (2006), *The Ethnic Cleansing of Palestine*, Oxford: Oneworld Publications Ltd.

Philpott, C. (2005), 'Though the Dog Is Dead, the Pig must Be Killed: Finishing with
 Property Restitution to Bosnia-Herzegovina's IDPs and Refugees', *Journal of Refugee
 Studies* 18, no. 1: 1–24.

Philpott, C. (2006), 'From the Right to Return to the Return of Rights: Completing
 Post-War Property Restitution in Bosnia Herzegovina', *International Journal of
 Refugee Law* 18: 30–80.

Phosphates in Morocco, Preliminary Objections, 1938, P.C.I.J., Series A/B, No.74, 10.

Prettitore, P. (2003), 'The Right to Housing and Property Restitution in Bosnia and
 Herzegovina', BADIL Resource Center for Palestinian Residency & Refugee Rights,
 www.badil.org.

Progress Report of the United Nations Mediator on Palestine Submitted to the
 Secretary-General for Transmission to the Members of the United Nations, A/648,
 16 September 1948, Part V.

*Protocol of Agreement between the Government of the Republic of Rwanda and the
 Rwandese Patriotic Front on the Repatriation of Rwandese Refugees and the Settlement
 of Displaced Persons*, signed at Arusha, 9 June 1993.

Quigley, J. (1997), 'The Oslo Accords: More than Israel Deserves', *American Journal of
 International Law and Policy* 12: 285–98.

Quigley, J. (1998), 'Displaced Palestinians and a Right of Return', *Harvard International
 Law Journal* 39: 171–229.

Quigley, J. (1999), 'The Role of Law in a Palestinian-Israeli Accommodation', *Case
 Western Reserve Journal of International Law* 31: 351–81.

Quigley, J. (2005), *The Case for Palestine: An International Law Perspective*, Durham,
 NC: Duke University Press.

Qurie, A. (2006), *From Oslo to Jerusalem: The Palestinian Story of the Secret
 Negotiations*, London: I.B. Tauris.

R v Bow Street Metropolitan Stipendiary Magistrate ex parte Pinochet Ugarte (No.3)
 [2000] 1 AC 147 (HL).

Ratner, M. and Becker, C. (2006), 'The Legacy of Holocaust Class Action Suits: Have they Broken Ground for Other Cases of Historical Wrongs', in M. J. Bazyler and R. P. Alford (eds), *Holocaust Restitution: Perspectives on the Litigation*, New York: New York University Press.

Rempel, T. (1999), 'The Ottawa Process: Workshop on Compensation and Palestinian Refugees', *Journal of Palestine Studies* 29, no. 1: 36–49 at p. 45.

Rempell, T. (2003), 'Housing and Property Restitution: The Palestinian Refugee Case', in S. Leckie (ed.), *Returning Home: Housing and Property Restitution Rights of Refugees and Displaced Persons*, New York: Transnational.

Renzulli, J. J. (1992), 'Claims of U.S. Nationals under the Restitution of Laws of Czechoslovakia', *Boston College International and Comparative Law Review* 15: 165–88.

Report of the Committee on the Exercise of the Inalienable Rights of the Palestinian People, Official Records of the General Assembly, Thirty-first Session, Supplement No.35 (A/31/35), 21 July 1976.

Report on Immigration, Land Settlement and Development by Sir John Hope Simpson, C.I.E., Cmd 3686, October 1930, London, H.M. Stationery Office at Chapter V.

Report presented by the Secretary of State for the Colonies to Parliament by Command of His Majesty, Cmd 5479, July 1937, London, H.M. Stationery Office at chapter XII.

Report of Sub-Committee 2 of the Ad Hoc Committee on the Palestinian Question, General Assembly Official Records, UN Doc. A/AC.14/32, 11 November 1947.

Report of the Ad Hoc Committee on the Palestinian Question, General Assembly Official Records, UN Doc. A/516, 25 November 1947.

Report of the Committee on the Exercise of the Inalienable Rights of the Palestinian People, Official Records of the General Assembly, Thirty-first Session, Supplement No. 35 (A/31/35), 21 July 1976.

Request for Advisory Opinion on *Legal Consequences arising from the Policies and Practices of Israel in the Occupied Palestinian Territory, including East Jerusalem*, filing of written comments on 14 November 2023 (www.icj-cij.org).

Restitution of Land Rights Act 22 (South Africa), 25 November 1994.

Rita Saulle, M. (1999), 'The International Criminal Court', *UC Davis Journal of International Law and Policy* 5: 119–31.

Road Map, published in Special Documents: The Road Map (2003), *Journal of Palestine Studies* 32, no. 4: 83–99.

Robinson, N. (1962), *Spoliation and Remedial Action: the Material Damage Suffered by Jews under Persecution, Reparations, Restitution and Compensation*, New York: New York Institute of Jewish Affairs.

Robinson, R. (2001), *The Debt: What America Owes to Blacks*, New York: Plume.

Robinson, R. (2004), 'What America Owes to Blacks and What Blacks Owe to Each Other', *African-American Law & Policy Report* 6, no. 1: 1–13.

Rogan, L. and Shlaim, A. (2001), *The War for Palestine: Rewriting the History of 1948*, Cambridge: Cambridge University Press.

Roht-Arriaza, N. (2004a), 'Reparations Decisions and Dilemmas', *Hastings International and Comparative Law Review* 27: 157–219.

Roht-Arriaza, N. (2004b), 'Reparations in the Aftermath of Repression and Mass Violence' in E. Stover and H. M. Weinstein (eds), *My Neighbor, My Enemy: Justice and Community in the Aftermath of Mass Atrocity*, Cambridge: Cambridge University Press.

Roodt, M. J. (2003), 'Land Restitution in South Africa' in S. Leckie (ed.), *Returning Home: Housing and Property Restitution Rights of Refugees and Displaced Persons*, New York: Transnational.

Rosand, E. (1998), 'The Right to Return under International Law Following Mass Dislocation: the Bosnia Precedent?', *Mich. J. Int'l L.* 19: 1091–139.

Rosand, E. (2000), 'The Right to Compensation in Bosnia: An Unfulfilled Promise and a Challenge to International Law', *Cornell International Law Journal* 33: 113–58.

Rosenne, S. (1995), *The World Court: What It Is and How It Works*, 5th edn, London: Nijhoff.

Rosenne, S. and Ronen, Y. (2006), *The Law and Practice of the International Court of Justice: 1920–2005*, 4th edn, Leiden: Martinus Nijhoff.

Ross, D. (2004), *The Missing Peace: The Inside Story of the Fight for Middle East Peace*, New York: Farrar, Straus and Giroux.

Roy, S. (2006), *Failing Peace: Gaza and the Palestinian-Israeli Conflict*, London: Pluto Press.

Ryuichi Shimoda et Al. v. *The State, (District Court of Tokyo – Japan), 07 Dec. 1963*, International Law Reports, 1966, Vol. 32, 626.

Sabet, A. G. E. (1998), 'The Peace Process and the Politics of Conflict Resolution', *Journal of Palestine Studies* 26, no. 4: 5–19.

Said, E. W. (1996), *Peace and Its Discontents*, New York: Vintage Books.

Said, E. W. (2006), 'A Method for Thinking about Just Peace', in P. Allan and A. Keller (eds), *What Is a Just Peace?*, New York: Oxford University Press.

Samy, S. (2010), *Reparations to Palestinian Refugees: A Comparative Perspective*, London: Routledge.

Sands, P., Mackenzie, R. and Shany, Y. (1999), *Manual on International Courts and Tribunals*, London: Butterworths.

Senechal, T. J. and Hilal, L. (2013), 'The Value of 1948 Palestinian Refugee Material Damages: An Estimate Based on International Standards', in R. Brynen and R. El-Rifai (eds), *Compensation to Palestinian Refugees and the Search for Palestinian-Israeli Peace*, 132–58, London: Pluto Press.

Shehadeh, R. (1982), 'The Land Law of Palestine: An Analysis of the Definition of State Lands', *Journal of Palestine Studies* 11, no. 2: 82–99.

Shehadeh, R. (1993), *The Law of the Land*, Jerusalem, Palestinian Academic Society for the Study of International Affairs (PASSIA) available at www.passia.org (accessed 12 April 2024).

Shelton, D. (2005), *Remedies in International Human Rights Law*, 2nd edn, Oxford: Oxford University Press.

Sher, G. (2006), *The Israeli-Palestinian Peace Negotiations, 1999–2001: Within Reach*, London: Routledge.

Shiblak, A. (1996), 'Residency Status and Civil Rights of Palestinian Refugees in Arab Countries', *Journal of Palestine Studies* 25, no. 3: 36–45.

Shihadeh, R. (1993), 'Can the Declaration of Principles Bring About a 'Just and Lasting Peace'?', *Eur. J. Int'l L.* 4: 555–63.

Special Document File on the Madrid Peace Conference, *Journal of Palestine Studies* 21, no. 2 (1992): 117–49.

Special Dossier (2002), *The 'Sabra and Shatila' Case in Belgium, Palestine Yearbook of International Law* 12: 183–289.

South Africa Constitution No.108, 18 December 1996.

S.S.'Wimbledon', 1923, P.C.I.J., Series A, No.1.

Staible, P., Edison, K. and Rosenblum, L. (2004), 'Updates from the Regional Human Rights Systems', *Human Rights Brief 27* 11, no. 2: 27–30.

Statement of Policy presented by the Secretary for the Colonies to Parliament by Command of His Majesty, Cmd 6019, May 1939.

Stein, K. W., *The Land Question in Palestine, 1917–1939*, Chapel Hill: University of North Carolina Press, 1984.

Swisher, C. E. (2004), *The Truth About Camp David: The Untold Story About the Collapse of the Middle East Peace Process*, New York: Nation Books.

Swiss Banks Settlement: In re Holocaust Victim Assets Litigation: http://www.swissban kclaims.com (accessed 14 April 2024).

Taba Negotiations: The Moratinos Non-Paper, January 2001.

Takkenberg, L. (1998), *The Status of Palestinian Refugees in International Law*, Oxford: Oxford University Press.

Tamari, S. (1996), *Palestinian Refugee Negotiations: from Madrid to Oslo II*, Washington, DC: Institute for Palestine Studies, p. 38.

Tamari, S. (2005), 'Palestinian Refugee Property Claims: Compensation and Restitution', in A. M. Lesch and I. S. Lustick (eds), *Exile and Return: Predicaments of Palestinians and Jews*, Philadelphia: University of Pennsylvania Press.

The Factory at Chorzow (Jurisdiction), *1927*, P.C.I.J., *Series A*, No. 9 at p. 21.

The Factory at Chorzow (Merits), *1928*, P.C.I.J., *Series A*, No. 17 at p. 47.

The Law to Deny the Right of Return – 2001, Israel's Law to Deny the Right of Return – 2001, reprinted in *Palestine Yearbook of International Law* 11 (2000–1).

The Republic of South Africa institutes proceedings against the State of Israel and requests the Court to indicate provisional measures (icj-cij.org) (dated 29 December 2023).

Tomuschat, C. (1999), 'Individual Reparation Claims in Instances of Grave Human Rights Violations: The Position under General International Law', in A. Randelzhofer and C. Tomuschat (eds), *State Responsibility and the Individual: Reparation in Instances of Grave Violations of Human Rights*, The Hague: Martinus Nijhoff.

Tulin, A. (1947), *Book of documents submitted to the General Assembly of the United Nations relating to the establishment of the national home for the Jewish people: Balfour Declaration, Palestine Mandate, American-British Palestine Mandate Covenant, British white papers, observations of Permanent Mandates Commission, pronouncements of presidents and resolutions of Congress of the United States, Jewish Agency statements and other relevant documents 1917–1947*, New York: The Jewish Agency for Palestine.

Ulsamer, L. (2006), 'German Economy and the Foundation Initiative: An Act of Solidarity for Victims of National Socialism', in M. J. Bazyler and R. P. Alford (eds), *Holocaust Restitution: Perspectives on the Litigation*, New York: New York University Press.

United Nations Committee on the Exercise of the Inalienable Rights of the Palestinian People (CEIRPP), *The Right of Return of the Palestinian People*, ST/SG/SER.F/2, 1 November 1978.

UNCCP, *Stand taken by the Governments of the Arab States and the Government of Israel with regard to the task entrusted to the Conciliation Commission by the General Assembly*, W/1, 1 March 1949.

UNCCP, *Compensation to Refugees for Loss of or Damage to Property to be Made Good under Principles of International Law or in Equity*, W/30, 31 October 1949.

UNCCP, *Letter and Memorandum dated 22 November 1949, Concerning Compensation, received by the Chairman of the Conciliation Commission from Mr. Gordon Clapp, Chairman, United Nations Economic Survey Mission for the Middle East*, W/32, 19 January 1950.

UNCCP, *Returning Refugees and the Question of Compensation*, W/36, 7 February 1950.

UNCCP, *Analysis of paragraph 11 of the General Assembly's Resolution of 11 Dec. 1948*, W/45, 15 May 1950.

UN Division for Palestinian Rights, *The Need for Convening the International Peace Conference on the Middle East (in accordance with General Assembly resolution 38/58 C)*, 1 February 1989.

UNGA Res.181(II), *Future Government of Palestine*, 29 November 1947.

UNGA, *Application of Israel for admission to membership in the United Nations (A/818)*, A/AC.24/SR.45, 5 May 1949.

UNGA Res.273 (III), 11 May 1949.

UNGA Res.2452 (XXIII) (A-C), 19 December 1968.

UNGA Res.3210 (XXIX), 14 October 1974.

UNGA Res.36/120 C, 10 December 1981.

UNGA Res.3236 (XXIX), 22 November 1974.

UNGA Res.3237 (XXIX), 22 November 1974.

UNGA Res.35/207, 16 December 1980.

UNGA Res.36/146 C of 16 December 1981.

UNGA Res.36/226 A, 17 December 1981.

UNGA Res.38/58 C, 13 December 1983.

UNGA Res.39/49 D, 11 December 1984.

UNGA Res.40/96 D, 12 December 1985.

UNGA Res.41/43 D, 2 December 1986.

UNGA Res.42/66 D, 2 December 1987.

UNGA Res.43/176, 15 December 1988.

UNGA Res.44/42, 6 December 1989.

UNGA Res.45/83 A, 13 December 1990.

UNGA Res.46/75, 11 December 1991.

UNGA Res.51/129, 13 December 1996.

UNGA Res.55/128, 8 December 2000.

UNGA Res.56/83, 12 December 2001.

UNGA Res.59/35, 2 December 2004.

UNGA Res. 60/147, *UN Guidelines on Reparation*, 16 December 2005.

UNGA Res.61/407, 14 December 2006.

UNGA Res.62/61, 6 December 2007.

UNGA Res. 77/247, 30 December 2022.

UNGA Res. 78/75, 7 December 2023.

UNHCR EXCOM, *General Conclusions on International Protection*, No. 68 (XLIII), 9 October 1992. at para.(s).

UNHCR EXCOM, *Conclusion on Legal Safety Issues in the Context of Voluntary Repatriation of Refugees*, No.101 (LV), 8 October 2004.

UNHCR, Global Trends | UNHCR, June 2023 (accessed 14 April 2024).

UNHCR, Handbook on Procedures and Criteria for Determining Refugee Status under the 1951 Convention and the 1967 Protocol relating to the Status of Refugees, HCR/IP/4Eng/Rev.1, Reedited, Geneva, January 1992.

UNHCR, 'The Problem of Access to Land and Ownership in Repatriation Operations', Inspection and Evaluation Service, Eval/03/98, May 1998, www.unhcr.org (accessed 14 April 2024).

UNHCR Standing Committee., 'The Kosovo Refugee Crisis: An Independent Evaluation of UNHCR's Emergency Preparedness and Response', February 2000, EC/50/SC/CRP.12, www.unhcr.org. (accessed 14 April 2024).

United Nations Palestine Commission, *Legislative Power: the Question of the Continuity of Laws*, A/AC.21/W.27, 19 February 1948.

UNMIK Regulation 1999/10 on the *Repeal of Discriminatory Legislation Affecting Housing and Rights in Property*, 13 October 1999.

UNMIK Regulation 1999/23, 15 November 1999.

UNMIK Regulation No. 2000/60, 31 October 2000.

UN Press Release, Committee on the Exercise of the Inalienable Rights of the Palestinian People, Amid International Inaction, Israel's Systematic 'Demographic Engineering' Thwarting Palestinians' Ability to Pursue Justice, Speakers Tell International Conference | UN Press, GA/PAL/1439, 1 July 2021.

UNRWA, *Palestine Refugees*, www.unrwa.org.

UNSC Res., S/Res/46, 17 April 1948, S/723.

UNSC Res.237, 14 June 1967.

UNSC Res.242, 22 November 1967.

UNSC Res.338, 22 October 1973.

UNSC Res.687, 3 April 1991, Section E.

UNSC Res.1244, 10 June 1999.

UN Sub-Commission on the Promotion and Protection of Human Rights Resolution 1998/26, *Housing and Property Restitution in the Context of the Return of Rights for Refugees and Internally Displaced Persons*, 26 August 1998.

UN Sub-Commission on the Promotion and Protection of Human Rights Resolution 2002/7, *Housing and Property Restitution in the Context of Refugees and Other Displaced Persons*, 14 August 2002.

UN Sub-Commission on the Promotion and Protection of Human Rights, 'Principles on Housing and Property Restitution for Refugees and Displaced Persons', E/CN.4/Sub.2/2005/17, 11 August 2005.

U.S. Letter of Assurances to the Palestinians, 18 October 1001, reprinted in *Palestine Yearbook of International Law, Vol. VI* (1990–1), 281.

Van Der Auweraert, P. (2002), 'Holocaust Reparation Claims Fifty Years After: The Swiss Banks Litigation, *Nordic Journal of International Law* 71: 557–83.

Watson, G. R. (2003), *The Oslo Accords: International Law and the Israeli-Palestinian Peace Agreements*, Oxford: Oxford University Press.

Weiss, E. B. (2002), 'Invoking State Responsibility in the Twenty-First Century', *American Journal of International Law* 96: 798–816.

Weiss, M. I. (2006), 'A Litigator's Postscript to the Swiss Banks and Holocaust Litigation Settlements: How Justice Was Served' in M. J. Bazyler and R. P. Alford (eds), *Holocaust Restitution: Perspectives on the Litigation*, New York: New York University Press.

Weiss Fagen, P. (2006), 'UNHCR and Repatriation', in M. Dumper (ed.), *Palestinian Refugee Repatriation: Global Perspectives*, Abingdon: Routledge.

White, B., Israel's Ethnic Cleansing of Palestinians in the West Bank (arabcenterdc.org), Arab Center, 12 August 2022.

Wilde, R. (2019–20), 'Using the Master's Tools to Dismantle the Master's House: International Law and Palestinian Liberation', *Palestine Yearbook of International Law* 22: 3–74.

Witten, R. M. (2006), 'How Swiss Banks and German Companies Came to Terms with the Wrenching Legacies of the Holocaust and World War II: A Defense Perspective' in M. J. Bazyler and R. P. Alford (eds), *Holocaust Restitution: Perspectives on the Litigation*, New York: New York University Press.

Zirker, O. L. (2002), 'This Land Is My Land: The Evolution of Property Rights and Land Reform in South Africa', *Connecticut Journal of International Law* 18: 621–41.

Zittrain Eisenberg, L. and Caplan, N. (1998), *Negotiating Arab-Israeli Peace: Patterns, Problems, Possibilities*, Bloomington: Indiana University Press.

Zureik, E. (1994), 'Palestinian Refugees and Peace', *Journal of Palestine Studies* 24, no. 1: 5–17.

Zweig, R. W. (2001), *German Reparations and the Jewish World: A History of the Claims Conference*, 2nd edn, London: Frank Cass.

Index

www.ingramcontent.com/pod-product-compliance
Ingram Content Group UK Ltd.
Pitfield, Milton Keynes, MK11 3LW, UK
UKHW031126221224
452593UK00003B/40